SEDEKAH   BENIH

VINCENT   RUMAHLOINE
AND   MANG   DIAN

SEVEN PROTOTYPES FOR

DRIVING THE HUMAN

ECO- SOCIAL RENEWAL

The Better Dream

Freo Majer, Artistic Director of the mentoring program Forecast and initiator of Driving the Human

What is the problem with responsible renewal? Why do processes of eco-social and technological transformation fail? In a prosperous country like Germany, where sometimes trains arrive and some airports succeed, how could important scientific findings or even common sense have been misjudged or ignored for decades? Why is an entire generation of young people angry and desperate today, especially about the failures in energy and climate policy? What is missing for the much-vaunted technological, ecosocial, and economic transformation of our societies to succeed?

Driving the Human began with the conviction that the disruptions and destruction caused by the climate crisis cannot be overcome by emotionally charged alarmism, nor by a purely pragmatic approach to individual problems. So from where should new concepts come? An existential threat such as global warming, which is highly complex and has varied effects globally, is especially difficult to communicate. Scenarios in the distant future may not seem urgent, may not be convincing enough to actually change behavior to, for example, politically activate citizens of a state. Nor do we believe that the torturous wallowing in dystopias is suitable for motivating prudent and responsible action. Rather, we need concrete designs that are meaningful and whose effects are credible—but which also appeal to our imaginations. No one wants a dreary, joyless future consisting of reduction and renunciation. The lead partners of Driving the Human therefore never aimed for an educational or didactic approach. Rather, we wanted to help develop projects that could touch and inspire, on the level of the mind and the senses—what artists can do. Forecast and our interlocutors—the coordinators, Vera Sacchetti and Nikola Joetze; Martina Schraudner, a natural scientist; Jan Boelen, a design curator; and the artistic-scientific curatorial team of the ZKM | Center for Art and Media Karlsruhe—have thus asked ourselves how we can find perspectives and scenarios that activate concrete action.

Forecast, as the initiator of Driving the Human, was convinced from the outset that today there is neither a shortage of bright minds nor of good ideas. However, in our opinion, three important prerequisites are missing for stubborn, rigid ways of thinking and working to be dissolved and for actual renewal to succeed.

First, there is a glaring, almost tragic, lack of *facilitation*, of programs that accompany and support promising concepts to their realization. A concept, no matter how good, can only mature through confrontation with reality. It must be polished, sharpened, repeatedly challenged, revised, and often rethought from scratch. Creative minds, especially the more daring, need space to invent and play. Working out an idea to a verifiable, prototypical form is not only time-consuming and costly, but also requires the highest degree of intellectual and methodological freedom.

Second, despite a multitude of international institutions and funding programs, there is a lack of permissive networking approaches to knowledge exchange and knowledge production across disciplinary, cultural, and regional or national boundaries. Much has been said in recent years about the futility and harmfulness of silos, and this text will be about that as well. These silos entomb any innovation and it is high time to get rid of them.

Third, we perceive that there is a crisis of imagination. Forecast is convinced that people need to be inspired by accessible, comprehensible, and appealing narratives so that they can think critically and empathetically. The climate crisis, in particular, is a subject of almost inconceivable complexity that all too easily provokes defensive reactions. By this, we not only mean its complete denial, as is especially the case with right-wing populists, but also, in our views, an insistence on the numerical-factual, which ignores the psychological effects of this crisis and is unhelpful. Finally, the evocation of a dystopian future, as understandable as this fear may be, seems to us to be a kind of mental emigration. Who feels activated by feelings of guilt to tackle something new, to attempt change? Who can endure alarmist images of horror and blame in the long run without succumbing to resignation at some point?

Driving the Human responded to the three deficiencies described above with a concrete offer: we would bring together artistic and scientific methods and, a three-year process, work out seven prototypes that could be experienced in real life, ones that imagine meaningful, sustainable forms of coexistence on our planet. We crafted the methodology and process for their development based on the facilitating program I am responsible for, Forecast, which has been running its mentorships since 2015. Forecast is guided by the following principles:

Facilitation—Forecast has developed a method of facilitating creative processes. We assist authors of promising, novel ideas to turn an initial thought into a viable working process and finally help them to showcase their outcomes, through formats that can be discussed in public. We trust those authors to deal productively with their complete autonomy and to also organize the physical and temporal framework for their respective concepts to produce concrete results. In other words, we promote and nurture creative processes precisely when they are at their most fragile—when it is still completely unclear how and if the concept will develop into a successful realization.

Networking Approach—Since its first edition, Forecast has aimed to eliminate disciplines as an obstructive category. In our experience, silos, which inhibit innovation and are based on hierarchical constraints, can certainly be avoided, but this requires persistence and action down to the smallest detail. The rigidities of representative and institutional thinking can only be overcome through smart action and with specifically designed tools. A productive linking of the arts with more "distant" practices from the natural and social sciences, technology and materials research, economics, and digital fields seems appropriate to these globally relevant discourses, promising truly innovative concepts.

Part of Forecast's core business is our passionate conviction that collaborative work is meaningful and productive—and enormously enjoyable. We see collaboration as a value per se. Of course, a single mind can generate powerful and fascinating ideas, but things get interesting when such an idea meets reality. Was an idea too vague, sweeping, or simplistic? Not radical enough? Where are the contradictions and frictions? Where is there a lack of deeper knowledge—or of perspective and distance from one's own thinking? How and with whom could this individual join forces to develop something new?

Imagination—Forecast is based on a clear and simple premise: the skill, intelligence, and imagination of artists deserve more attention and promotion. The potential of creative practices for society as a whole should—and can!—urgently be fostered, so that their innovative power, boldness of thought, and ability to develop and sharpen ideas can be effective. We need images and narratives so that we do not merely endure the reality of our present, but experience it as a material to be acted upon. Artistic work establishes connections between the most diverse lines of thought, triggers surprising encounters and experiences, and broadens our horizon. Many may see the audacity and chutzpah of artists as something immature, even childish. I would like to counter such voices: don't underestimate these qualities, and don't underestimate the power of child-like, open thinking.

Forecast is good at making cross.connections and building relationships. After gaining experience with Forecast mentorships since 2015, we were able to try a different variation of facilitation in 2018-19 with Housing the Human and from 2020-23 with Driving the Human: rather than an individual mentoring relationship, we wanted to offer projects a constantly changing form of mentorship that adapted to the course of the work. Whether this was access to new technologies and materials or collaborations with "foreign" disciplines and new partners, we would adapt the means and avenues of facilitation to each project's development, again and again, and with high flexibility. Forecast found partners for this approach who, with their versatility and methodological openness, were suited to realize such a bold and complex undertaking. Together, we were able to assemble complex collaborations with different personalities and institutions in an ever-changing process, allowing for a variety of forms of cooperation and exchange for each project involved. From the beginning, Driving the Human was enlivened by the mutual exchange between these different partners—with their peculiarities, their respective knowledge, and their particular skills and instruments. (Anyone who has ever tried to work between different disciplines, especially between the arts and the sciences, can guess that the difference in languages and mentalities alone would have been a barrier.)

We structured Driving the Human's timeline accordingly: in the first year (2020), we as lead partners—Forecast in Berlin, acatech in Munich, and ZKM and the Karlsruhe University of Arts and Design (HfG)—gathered questions and topic areas in exchange with an international network of experts that would lead to the formulation of our Open Call. In 2021, we brought these questions into the global arena and invited applicants, "from anywhere in the world, to submit proposals for projects that critically engage with the present and propose alternatives to current developments and disruptions, reflecting on what makes us human, and re-examining our relationship with society, the planet, and life itself."

The response was breathtaking. One thousand and thirteen concepts from ninety-nine countries proposed new technologies, forms of exchange and social models, proposals for action and visions of the future, in artistic or other applied formats. Some concepts were highly speculative or playful, others strictly analytical. But all applicants were united by the enthusiasm to design concrete proposals for our habitat Earth. We invited twenty-one of these cleverly conceived and highly diverse ideas to radialsystem in Berlin for an initial exchange—a three-day gathering consisting of workshops, public showcases, and talks. Based on this experience, we were able to crystallize the seven projects that were given a final year of cooperation opportunities, access to materials and technologies, and a production budget and executing partners for the intensification and physical realization of their concept into a prototype.

Our comprehensive accompaniment of these projects through complex development processes over such a long period of time is not normal and is a unique privilege. We are therefore deeply grateful to the German Bundestag and especially to the Federal Ministry for the Environment,

Nature Conservation, and Nuclear Safety, and the Federal Minister Svenja Schulze, for their judicious support. Without them, Driving the Human would simply have not been possible.

Throughout the process, which lasted more than three years and included international work-stays, the seven participating projects were accompanied by an impressive cohort of experts, including environmental activists and ecologists, behavioral scientists, AI developers, architects, and philosophers. The ever-forming linkages within this collaborative work—first on the thematic strands and later on the prototypes to be realized—set in motion a veritable snowball effect that gives us hope. Our wish would be that the projects and the overall methodology of Driving the Human can continue to the next stage of development. Also, that organizations worldwide do the same—try such development processes as well, copy our format!

With our work on Driving the Human, the network of participants—the organizers, the authors of the projects, as well as the experts and cooperation partners involved—have proved that artistic-scientific research can not only be productive and enlightening, but also a source of great joy and liberation. We all emerge from the process with more confidence in the conviction that a profound change in our present lives is possible—and that we need not be afraid of it. Whether we use the term hope as our wonderful expert, the philosopher Corine Pelluchon, does—not as a sentimental, cloudy illusion, but as an encouragement for meaningful action; whether we describe reality through the words of the neuroscientist György Buzsáki as a dream dreamed together and as a social agreement between the You and the I; or whether we speak with our project author Vincent Rumahloine on how Driving the Human builds a better, new dream—the ideas generated by this collaboration across disciplines and cultures has given us a boost in creativity and agency, one that we all want to continue in our work.

Forecast stands for trust in the human mind. A willingness to take risks and experiment was at the core of Driving the Human, at every stage and in every single decision. All involved trusted that unfamiliar or unconventional approaches could unleash unimagined potential. We wanted to be surprised by bold and idiosyncratic thoughts and ideas, by the images, spaces, objects, movements, sounds, and language that artists of the most diverse genres produce. Forecast is not afraid of complex or fraught subjects: we want to get up close to reality and to people's perceptions. We are interested in thinkers who question themselves and the reality of their lives, who don't want to resign themselves to stagnation and boredom, who leave familiar spaces behind and seek out new ones. We are interested in the defiant rebellion of people who are looking for a voice and an audience.

Innovation, this concept that has been worn out, emptied of meaning, killed through capitalism, only makes sense in a complex system of sustainable learning and change processes, as social innovation. But the *social*—as we have hopefully understood by today—cannot mean only a community or a milieu, not even an individual country. "We," as momentary products of millennia of civilization, are learning every day, and often painfully, that we are not alone on the planet. To ask the question of coexistence only among us humans would be anti-social. At the same time, it seems to me unhelpful to demonize the human species, as if only a future without humans could really be wished for Earth. Personally, this seems to me an irrational, romanticizing view of "nature" that gets us nowhere. Let's avoid hatred, including self-hatred, and rather use what humans are good at to preserve our own species and as many others as possible, and to give us a good life.

How can it go on, how should it go on? At the level of Driving the Human's individual projects, we are not worried. Each of the concepts developed has been able to prove its relevance over the course of the three years and their authors will continue to go their own way. The numerous invitations for further cooperation and the proposals for next developments speak for themselves. But we will also continue to pursue the overall framework of Driving the Human. This particular type of research has achieved something that is needed more urgently than ever today: tangible, verifiable approaches to hope. We have shown a great eco-social transformation is possible, a cause for celebration.

"With our work on Driving the Human,
the network of participants—the organizers,
the authors of the projects, as well as the
experts and cooperation partners involved—
have proved that artistic-scientific research
can not only be productive and enlightening,
but also a source of great joy and liberation.
We all emerge from the process with more
confidence in the conviction that a profound
change in our present lives is possible—
and that we need not be afraid of it."
(Freo Majer)

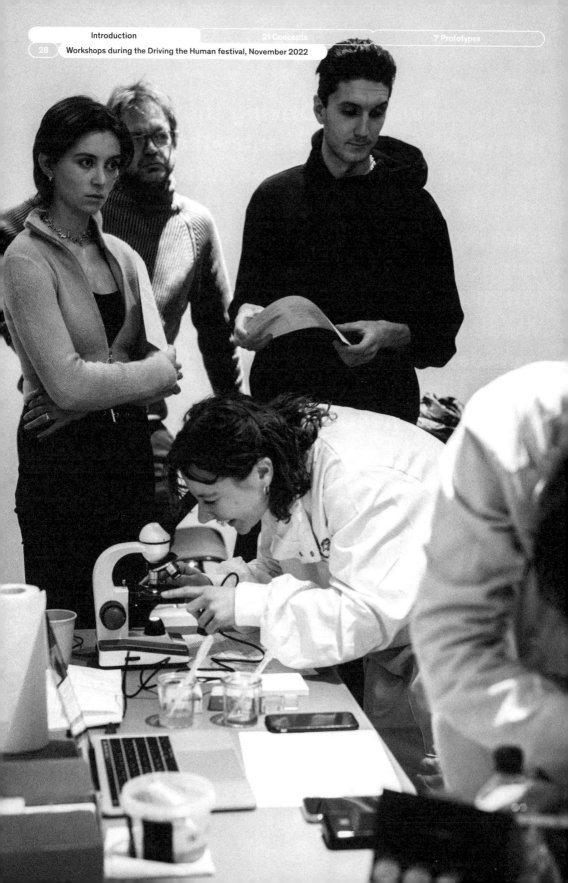

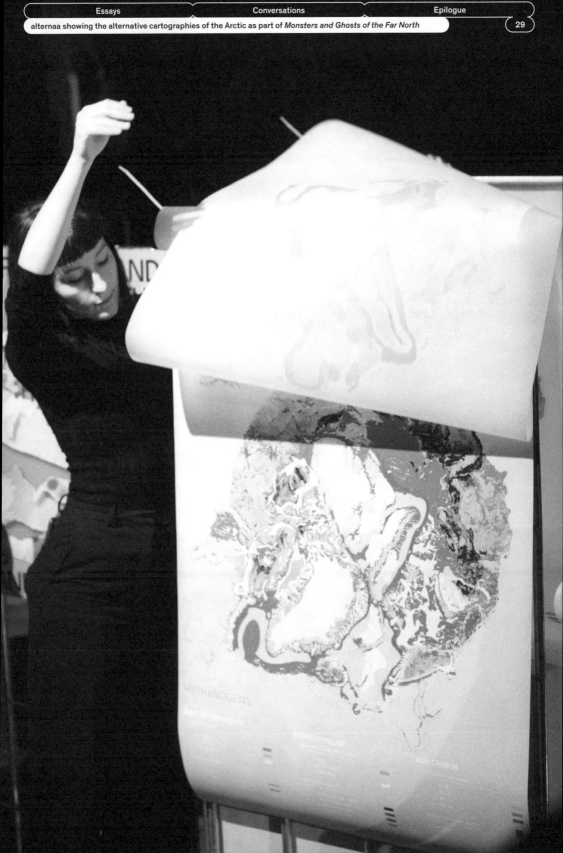

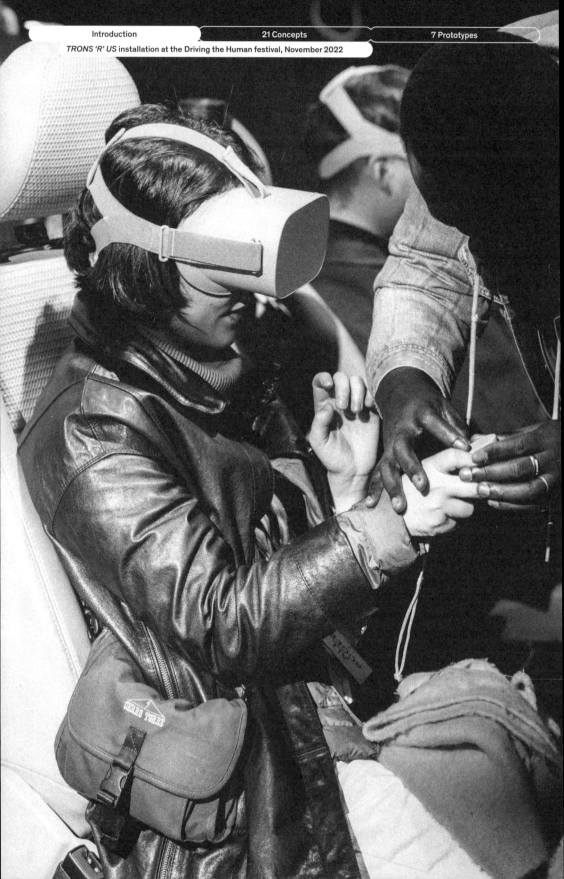

From Driving to Drifting—Thoughts on Eco-Social Renewal in the Context of Teaching

Julia Ihls and Anthea Oestreicher, Karlsruhe University of Art and Design (HfG), Bio Design Lab

Karlsruhe University of Arts and Design (HfG) offers a unique combination of artistic, design, and theoretical perspectives. Its courses of study—communication design, product design, media art, exhibition design and scenography, art research and media philosophy—and its interdisciplinary approach allow for an ideal combination of theory and praxis. Together with the ZKM | Center for Art and Media, collaboration and exchange through artistic production are strengthened in the shared Hallenbau—a former munitions factory—where encounters with a broader audience are encouraged. In this environment, the next generation of artists and designers have the possibility to employ printed matter, exhibitions, or digital media to search for and develop their abilities, critically reflect, and to gradually turn their interests into professional occupations. Aiming not to produce more of the same solutions, but to question the implications of design and the dimensions of discourse for potential futures is at the heart of these activities.

BIO DESIGN LAB

The Bio Design Lab was established as a hybrid and evolutionary environment for presentation, education, and knowledge distribution at the HfG. Here, students and experts are invited to develop projects at the intersections of science, design, and art, while visitors can explore and interact with production and research areas of the lab. The Bio Design Lab's projects focus on the local region, its materials and possibilities, and actively aim to redesign and rethink modes of production in Karlsruhe and southern Germany. With this infrastructure, the Driving the Human framework provided an opportunity to create a platform for connections and collaboration around local, sustainable, and natural issues. Inspired by the exchanges of the partner institutions, the Bio Design Lab established a workshop structure to teach students and non-students alike about tangible processes in working with organic, vibrant, and sustainable matter and its discourse. From bioplastics to algae screen printing, from building materials made from fungi to fermentation techniques—in close cooperation with the HfG's curriculum as well as with supraregional partners—the Bio Design Lab created an exchange platform situated at the interface of workshop, showroom, and teaching location. In the process, the lab itself was reinterpreted as a place of knowledge production in the context of an arts and design school: instead of sterile seclusion, security doors, and opacity, the Bio Design Lab relies on the phenomenon of "Radical Social Contamination"—open doors, open walls, and open dialogues at the fluid transitions between the school and arts institution.

EDUCATION PROGRAM / EXCHANGE FORMATS

Visits and exchanges with the local forestry office and botanical garden, local hemp producers, as well as researchers from the Natural History Museum and the Karlsruhe Institute of Technology (KIT), among others, led to seminars, workshops and exhibitions focussed on diverse topics such as bacteria batteries, cultivating and designing with fungi, sustainable photography, and post-anthropocentric scenography. This last initiative was conceived in collaboration with Driving the Human associates Anthropos Ex—an international performance collective—and was carried out through a one-week excursion to the Swiss Biosphere Reserve, Entlebuch. Here, over the course of several days, students were able to explore questions around stage design and scenography outside of the classical theater institution. Can a tree be an actor? Is landscape a stage and is its staging at all possible with or beyond the anthropocentric gaze? Through collaborations and design processes engaging non-human actors and the provoked confrontation with other temporalities and modes of action, the Bio Design Lab strives to raise awareness among students as well as an interested public. What responsibility do artists, designers and users bear? What impact do material selection, manufacturing locations, production processes, and supply chains have on the works created and also their consumption? How can more sustainable socio-ecological practices be established that value more-than-human beings without completely negating the human perspective?

The results of these almost two years of reflection led, among other things, to the Summer School *Future of Life*, which was held in July 2022. The Bio Design Lab invited forty students and recent graduates from thirteen countries to explore possible, plausible, and speculative future scenarios of coexistence. From future material extraction to the design of the Earth, from living architectures to other planets—over the course of five days, new material concepts, tools, and spaces emerged in the halls of the HfG, testing, like a temporary socio-biosphere, practices and interventions of terrestrial coexistence in partly parallel, partly overlapping workshops. Driving the Human artists Paula Nerlich and Romy Kaiser from the *Human-Bacteria Interfaces* project were also represented in the program as workshop tutors and panelists, and dealt with speculative communication scenarios between microorganisms and humans in the *Non-Human Lab*. As a further activation and exchange format, a three-month residency with Akwasi Afrane and his project *TRONS 'R' US* was also realized so that the artist could finalize the creation of his artwork in Karlsruhe and in close interaction with the HfG and ZKM infrastructures. The results of the artist residency as well as the previous teaching activities of the Bio Design Lab team culminated in discussions, interviews, as well as a fermentation workshop during the final Driving the Human festival in Berlin in November 2022 and will be continued with an activation program in collaboration with the ZKM until the end of 2023.

What drives the human when we think about socio-ecological renewal in the context of learning and teaching? Ultimately, the Driving the Human project showed us the need for new inter- and transdisciplinary formats. In order to address the complex challenges of the present, it is inevitable to leave behind the silos of delimited professions, practices, and disciplines in common teaching environments—even if this means that a seminar room becomes an experimental laboratory, a visitor becomes a teacher, a designer becomes a scientist, or vice versa. Synchronizing and calibrating these worlds is not always easy, and it can take much curiosity, patience, and courage to find a common language. In this sense, driving becomes *drifting,* a joyful practice moving towards the unknown.

Prototypes: New Tools for the Future

Peter Weibel, CEO and Chairman, ZKM | Center for Art and Media Karlsruhe

Sarah Donderer, Curator, ZKM | Center for Art and Media Karlsruhe

The ZKM | Center for Art and Media Karlsruhe is an institution of all media and genres. Founded in 1989 with the mission of continuing the classical arts into the digital age, the ZKM is also called the *digital Bauhaus*. With its art collection, publications, archives, and artistic, scholarly, and scientific research on the electronic arts, the ZKM stands for a program of interdisciplinary projects and international collaborations. In its exhibitions, symposia, concerts, and workshops, the ZKM communicates the theoretical discourses of philosophy, science, technology, politics, and economics from a contemporary artistic perspective.

Through its program and collaborations, the ZKM is providing a platform for artists and scientists to come together in order to artistically and philosophically explore the potential of new technologies and their consequences for society and the environment. With the research and exhibition projects in the last years such as *Exo-Evolution* (2015-2016), *Critical Zones. Observatories for Earthly Politics* (2020-2022), *BioMedia. The Age of Media with Life-like Behavior* (2021-2022), *The Beauty of Early Life* (2022) and *Renaissance 3.0. A Base Camp for New Alliances of Art and Science in the 21st Century* (2023-2024), ZKM is focusing on the symbiosis of human and more-than-human beings, the changing definitions of what life means, and the importance of interdisciplinary collaborations between art, science, and technology. These critical investigations of the interconnectedness of humans, more-than-humans, and the environment and the question of how humans and all living beings can survive in the Anthropocene are also asked in the collaborative project Driving the Human.

For the opening festival in November 2020, hosted digitally by the Karlsruhe University of Arts and Design (HfG) and ZKM, we combined our networks of artists and scientists to put together a diverse program, to explore pressing questions and frictions of what is driving the human. With statements by renowned scientists on the urgencies of our times, panel discussions, lectures, workshops, and artistic interventions, as well as the active participation of the audience, the festival explored different thematics related to the symbiosis of human and more-than-human beings, habitat, economy, technology, and the production and access to knowledge, with a focus on the existential threats that all living beings face today. The interdisciplinary impulses and impressions gained from the festival served as the foundation for the following open call and the development of the mentoring and interdisciplinary approach of the entire Driving the Human project, which continues to explore the critical questions and challenges facing our world today.

One major friction is that humans have created problems that they have not yet been able to solve. This begins with the concept of 'human' itself, something that is still unfinished and must be changed and expanded by other entities such as animals and machines, and is followed by the systems and tools humans create. During the festival, the philosopher Isabelle Stengers offered the idea that solutions may not come through the creation of new tools, but that existing tools have to be redefined and become a catalyst for change. The tools that we have now are not enough to solve the problem because the system they are created and used within is itself sick. So, the question becomes, how can we empower people to reuse or rethink tools so that they change the system? The concept of the prototype has proven extremely useful to address this. Prototypes allow for an open and collaborative process, where ideas can evolve and grow with input from various perspectives. In this way, prototypes serve as a tool for communities to come together and co-create new solutions to social, environmental, and technological challenges.

All seven prototypes of the Driving the Human project introduced thought-provoking ideas. They suggest a focus on creating awareness and understanding of the impact of technology on the environment, as well as the relationships between humans and non-human entities. There is a desire to bring people together from diverse backgrounds to share knowledge and build more equitable and sustainable systems. The idea of making interdependencies visible and collecting data is a common theme, suggesting the importance of better understanding the complex systems that shape our world. Additionally, the idea of creating new mythologies highlights the role that imagination and creativity plays in shaping our collective understanding of the world and our place in it.

It was inspiring to see how the seven prototypes developed over the course of the three-year project. The mentoring program conducted by all partners, with all experts and the four scientific fellows that were invited by ZKM to research and write about topics inspired by the seven prototypes, have been a great enrichment through the exchange of ideas and diverse perspectives.

The Driving the Human project serves as a starting point for a journey towards an eco-social renewal. The seven prototypes will travel to ZKM in 2023 and hopefully to various locations afterwards to encourage interdisciplinary collaborations in different contexts and communities.

We want to thank the Federal Ministry of Environment, Nature Conservation, Nuclear Safety and Consumer Protection, all the partners, their incredible teams, all inspiring experts and collaborators, and of course, all the participants for being part of this journey.

Bridging the Gap Between Science and the Arts

Dr. Sandra Fendl, Scientific officer at acatech

Prof. Dr. Martina Schraudner, Head of the Fraunhofer Center for Responsible Research and Innovation

acatech (National Academy of Science and Engineering), which is funded by the German federal government, the German states, and industry is the voice of science and engineering in Germany and abroad. Under the patronage of the Federal President, the academy provides independent, evidence-based advice to policymakers and society. Topics range from digitization, the future of energy supply, mobility, and sustainable resources to issues of science communication. Experts from science, industry, and society develop sound recommendations for action and share them with the public for political debate.

Driving the Human was conceived and realized by four partners from the sciences and the arts. Alongside three arts-focused entities (ZKM | Center for Art and Media Karlsruhe, Karlsruhe University of Arts and Design (HfG), Forecast), acatech provides knowledge on scientific and technological topics as well as a broad network of scientific experts. The academy currently has over 600 members—outstanding scientists from the engineering and natural sciences, medicine, the humanities, and the social sciences. In addition, the acatech Senate is made up of over a thousand prominent figures from technology companies, major science organisations, and politics.

CONCLUSIONS FROM THREE YEARS OF DRIVING THE HUMAN
acatech has facilitated contacts between the Driving the Human project authors and scientists, drawing from its profound knowledge and network. This includes mentoring and advising project authors throughout their process and also inviting experts from different scientific fields to collaborate. An example of this is the established collaboration between *The Backpack of Wings: Modern Mythology* and the Max Planck Institute of Animal Behavior which led to fruitful discussions on both sides. On the one hand, the project authors received scientific context and background knowledge on cutting-edge animal tracking technologies which directly impacted their project development; on the other, the scientists openly engaged in discussions about the ethical aspects of their research. A win-win situation for both parties.

BRIDGING THE GAP BETWEEN SCIENCE AND THE ARTS
Over the course of Driving the Human, acatech bridged the gap between art and science by bringing scientists into exchange with project authors.

In a series of mentoring events, hosted by acatech in Munich and online, the seven final project teams and experts from life- and social sciences were brought together. In November 2021, the digital event supported the project authors through mentoring sessions to develop a roadmap for structuring their work and research over the final phase of the project. In May 2022, acatech hosted a mentoring event in Munich where, experts and creatives were invited to further advance the development of the seven prototypes for eco-social renewal. At the same time, the event brought together artists, scientists, and various experts for workshops and one-on-one conversations. As part of this mentoring event, acatech hosted a public discussion entitled *Towards Eco-social Renewal: Blueprints for Collaboration Between Science and the Arts*. The public was invited to an evening of discussions that focused on innovative methods of collaboration between the arts and science. Scientists Vera Meyer and Stefan Böschen discussed these approaches together with the Driving the Human project authors, inviting new perspectives and reflections on these topics.

DEVELOPING HOLISTIC SOLUTIONS IN AN INCREASINGLY COMPLEX WORLD
The primary conclusion of this series of public discussion was a need for transdisciplinarity. As acatech member Vera Meyer noted, many problems are too large and complex to be solved by just one discipline, and so we must work together. However, it is crucial to develop a common language if several disciplines want to work together successfully. According to Stefan Böschen, science is good at focusing upon a single question, and art helps to place the answers to these questions in a societal context. In short, the two disciplines can complement each other in a powerful synergy.

Taken together, the arts—more than any other discipline—can engage with society and cultivate understanding of people's opinions, fears and desires for the future. Driving the Human allowed acatech to interact with the public in a completely new way and explore societal opinions and trends. The insights gained can be used in the long term to initiate transformative processes. Overall, Driving the Human demonstrated that the synergy between the arts and science is a powerful approach to unconventional thinking and innovation. They inspire and complement each other, pulling together towards eco-social renewal.

What Next? Mapping Institutional Change and Impact

This is an edited and excerpted version of a conversation that took place on November 27, 2022 during the Driving the Human festival in Berlin.

ANTJE STAHL

First, how did you all get involved in this project? Can you recall the first steps?

SARAH DONDERER

All four institutions were approached by Freo Majer from the Forecast mentoring program here in Berlin. We had an opportunity to think about what this process of creating prototypes for eco-social renewal would look like with different partners. We tackled the opening festival at the end of 2020, engaging huge topics like the economy, habitat, non-human communication etc. and invited many scholars, artists, and scientists to collect questions that we wanted to ask through this project. And from then on, the public open call came and we received over 1,000 applications from 99 countries. The jury—also coming out of our partner institutions—selected 21 projects out of this massive number.

AS

That sounds like a hell of a work.

SD

It was a crazy amount. Eventually, we found twenty-one projects that we invited to further develop their idea and also display it in a public setting. So that was in October last year, also here in Berlin. We invited experts from different fields and expertises to give an insight on these twenty-one projects—the jury then selected among the twenty-one for the final seven. We had fantastic mentoring sessions, in person and digital. There was one this spring in Munich, which I think was the most fruitful, and also at a crucial point along the development of the seven final prototypes.

AS

There was a moment when science was introduced into the art world in a very public and popular matter—I recall for example, the Swiss curator Hans Ulrich Obrist, probably one of the first figures that prominently organized conferences with titles like *Bridge the Gap* in the early 2000s because he saw, "the increasing interest in science demonstrated in the work of many contemporary artists, architects, and designers." It seemed at least at the time to be kind of a one-way street in the sense that the arts are interested in science but scientists might not be so interested in the arts. So I wonder, Sandra, you are the representative from this scientific world. How does it make you feel when you get confronted with artists, architects that are interested in science?

SANDRA FENDL

When I started working at acatech, and also with the project Driving the Human, it was my first job after my PhD. So I came fresh from the lab, fresh from the science world into this project. And frankly, this was also my first contact with a project like this, an art-science collaboration. I've learned a lot now over this time and have only positive things to say. Maybe it's best to just give an example: one of the projects here, *The Backpack of Wings*—the project authors are two artists that are working with the topic of animal tracking and have a bit of a critical view. They're looking into a future vision, how things will look like in a hundred, two hundred years. Is it ethically correct to continue to track birds? Will we maybe have an Internet of Animals in the future? My work in the project, or at least how I see it, is to help some of the projects here, mentoring them, consulting with them, and bringing in scientific perspectives. So in this case, because of my own network, I suggested right away we should contact the Max Planck Institute of Animal Behavior. Seongmin and Hyeseon were a bit skeptical at first—"Should we really contact them? Because our project is quite critical of what they're doing; we are not sure how they would react"—but in the end it was a fruitful exchange. The researchers there were super open and were happy that artists are also thinking about these research questions.

AS

Julia Kristeva, the philosopher and literary critic once said, "One cannot be an amateur, or decide one day 'let's be interdisciplinary'. A university may decide to develop in that direction, but what matters is that each researcher finds and establishes some complications with other researchers so that interdisciplinarity comes from the base of the pyramid and works its way up. One can only benefit from interdisciplinary practices if researchers meet other researchers whilst learning how to discuss both their competencies and the outcome of their interaction; therefore contributing to the exposure of the risks inherent in an interdisciplinary practice...the first obstacle is often linked to individual competencies coupled with a tendency to jealously protect one's own domain. Specialists are often too protective of their own prerogative, do not actually work with other colleagues, and therefore do not teach their students to construct a diagonal axis in their methodology." I wonder whether you agree. Have you encountered that?

SD

I would agree that it's not enough to wait until an institution decides from the head to change something. For me, when I started at ZKM in 2020, there was a movement already from the staff regarding the Green Deal and green cultural debates, emerging from an exhibition project called *Critical Zones* that was co-created by Bruno Latour. I think that started a lot—also, the idea that there are already many pre-existing initiatives from artists and scientists. The change is really coming from individual contexts—from staff who are really inspired by the process and the exchange with the artistic and scientific community.

We see it also within the university. The Karlsruhe University of Arts and Design and the ZKM are in the same building. From an art institution side, from ZKM, this is really special because it creates an open space for the audience to come in and be activated. It creates a space to help find a common language between art, science, and technology.

JULIA IHLS

In Karlsruhe, with the design school, we are really lucky. It's in itself already conceived as an interdisciplinary place between design and theory. As Sarah mentioned, we share the same house, so visitors of the museum also pass the school. With the Bio Design Lab, it's a space where process is made visible; in a museum, you have mostly, not always, things that are finished somehow. To see the process, to touch the materials, to interact is important. We have a lab that has three open walls, so visitors and students pass by, can go in and ask questions.

AS

As far as I understand, all of you are in the process of finding out for yourself what eco-social renewal could actually mean. Can you elaborate what that meant to you when you started the project and what it might mean today?

SD

Eco-social renewal is super open in its meaning. From my perspective, it begins by questioning, "What is ecological? Also, what is the social aspect?" It's really bringing communities together to open up the discussion. The social part plays a large role—society being not just for human beings but also including other organisms or entities. I think about the debate we've had over the last few days, "Do we need an un-worlding or a worlding?" How we unlearn structures to allow for new eco-social concepts is part of this question.

SF

These two things can't be separated. I would say almost all of our projects have much to do with the climate crisis, sustainability, how we change our energy systems, how we use biotechnology to achieve certain things, et cetera. The European Green Deal, which involves many different measures to fight the climate crisis, now adds more and more points that are connected to social aspects. For example, dimensions like gender and diversity and how they are connected to this topic. I think this can be seen when we look at the work presented as part of Driving

JI

the Human—I would say all of these projects are not just about one or the other, but both.

      The combination of the social and ecological is lived through the projects. For instance, the *Human-Bacteria Interfaces* project is living proof of how well the collaboration of a transdisciplinary team can work out. They have a microbiologist but also a creative technologist and textile designers. Before we focus on what rational improvements can be made, we first need to establish a baseline, an awareness in our work of how to consider not only the human, but also the non-human. Maybe it sounds a bit utopian, not that realistic—how can you implement this? But that's the ongoing exercise. It's a practice that we need to learn and keep on doing. Through this iteration we find a vector towards where we are heading.

DISTRIBUTED –
POST-EXTRACTIVISM
ECONOMIES
AHORA (LINDA SCHILLING
CUELLAR AND CLAUDIO
ASTUDILLO BARRA)

SUPERLOCAL –
0 MILES
PRODUCTION
ANDREA DE CHIRICO

RUM A
MULTISPECIES
URBAN REFUGE
IN CLUSTER

DRIVING THE HUMAN

21

CONCEPTS

Following its first public presentation in November 2020, Driving the Human launched an open call, inviting multidisciplinary participants from all over the world to submit visions to shape sustainable and collective futures that combined science, technology, and the arts in a transdisciplinary and collaborative approach.

The open call received 1,013 applications from 99 countries. Out of these, the Driving the Human jury selected 21 proposals that were presented in October 2021, at *Driving the Human: 21 Visions for Eco-social Renewal*. Hosted by Forecast, the three-day festival encompassed an on-site event at radialsystem in Berlin and an online broadcast. Through immersive experiences and interactive installations; focused readings and embodied knowledge; riveting screenings and stimulating performances, the festival advanced proposals for some of the most pressing issues of our time.

Over three days, the 21 concepts took over the spaces of radialsystem, exploring entanglements between technology and nature, artificial intelligence, circular

NOV. 20–22, 2020
OPENING FESTIVAL
DRIVING THE HUMAN

Hosted by the Karlsruhe University
of Arts and Design (HfG) and
ZKM | Center for Art and Media
Karlsruhe, Germany

FEB. 10–APRIL 04, 2021
OPEN CALL

OCT. 15–17, 2021
21 CONCEPTS
PRESENTED

Hosted by Forecast
Berlin, Germany

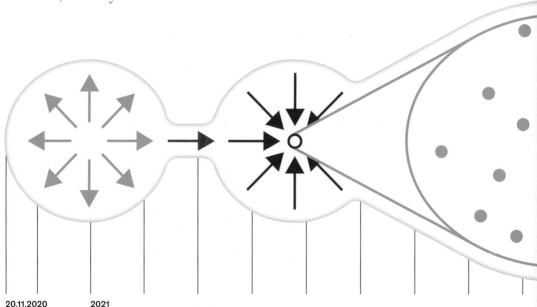

20.11.2020   2021

economy, new modes of production, Indigenous knowledges, and more-than-human perspectives from the bacterial to the interplanetary. Together, these proposals reinforced perspectives in which collaboration and interdependency become essential, determining factors for life and survival on our planet.

To explore the many dimensions of these powerful ideas, visitors could meet the authors of the 21 concepts, as well as several international experts that propose in-depth explorations of the narratives and approaches brought together on this occasion. The invited experts offered unexpected, enriching perspectives on the festival's themes, which ranged from AI to biomaterials, and from circular economy to social anthropology.

Following the Berlin festival, the Driving the Human jury had the difficult task to select seven projects to be developed as prototypes throughout 2022. In November 2022, these seven projects unveiled their developments to the general public, materializing as prototypes for new ways of planetary coexistence.

DEC. 10–11, 2021
DIGITAL MENTORING
EVENT

APR. 29–MAY 1, 2022
MENTORING
EVENT

Hosted by acatech,
National Academy of
Science and Engineering
Munich, Germany

NOV. 25–27, 2022
PROTOTYPES
UNVEILED

Hosted by Forecast
Berlin, Germany

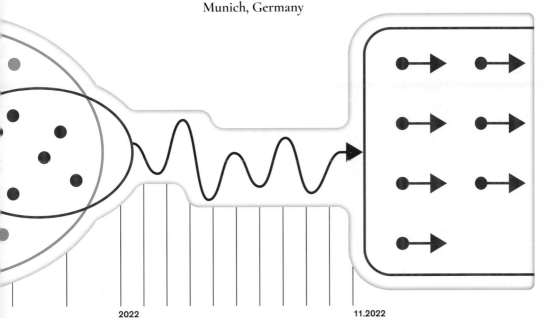

2022   11.2022

∀I : TOWARDS EARTHLY TECHNOSYMBIOGENESIS
Matthew C. Wilson

Two interconnected phenomena will shape the foreseeable future: anthropogenic climate change and the rise of artificial intelligence. It is crucial to work through the affinities and antagonisms of these interpenetrating forces.

Through experimental film, ∀I prototypes possible roles of AI in reforming human ⇄ environment interaction through both social metabolism and social imaginaries. Rather than unfolding an overt narrative, the future fiction will enfold viewers in a filmic experience that cascades across scales, materialities, and *unwelts*—imaged through diverse techniques. Here, some first fragmentary sketches, initial points of a growing constellation, are presented; ultimately, viewers would encounter the project as an immersive video installation.

Critiques of present-day AI include: bias in algorithms and datasets, reliance on poorly paid human labor, massive energy needs, and the environmental impact of producing or disposing of computer hardware. These critiques rightly raise concerns AI will perpetuate coloniality and extractive capitalism, accelerating systems of inequity and exploitation of people and planet. Unsurprisingly, AI engenders dystopian future scenarios (though too often without regard to aforementioned critiques).

Can the development and application of artificial intelligence instead provide an opportunity to instill and install new earthly operating principles, incorporating the critiques of AI, and re-coding ecological and social values at various scales? If we cannot yet see the way, can filmic future fictions help open new pathways for the imagination?

Brains emerged from the Earth, through evolutionary processes driven in part by changing climate and shifting landscapes. AI operates on substrates extracted from the same Earth —landscapes reorganized—base materials transformed into semiconductors, imparting an inherently alchemical aspect. (The inverted A-like form ∀ is the alchemical symbol of the earth element; ∀I thus suggests "earthly intelligence.") AI is used to recognize and predict patterns, including patterns in Earth systems and brain activity. While these applications of narrow AI remain unconnected, might they be integrated? What would it be like to encounter such an intelligence?

Currently, industrial technologies, including AI, occupy a parasitic place within planetary metabolism. Is it possible to intervene, to imagine and image a partnership, and alter AI's developmental trajectory towards a symbiogenesis between the technosphere, geosphere, and biosphere?

∀I is proposed as a working concept, departing from these questions, but deliberately open-ended in order to allow a process-oriented approach, leaving space for ongoing conversation and collaboration with academic and scientific interlocutors to feed into the project.

Matthew C. Wilson is an American artist, filmmaker, and researcher based in the Netherlands. In Wilson's films/videos, sculptures, and installations viewers encounter a range of agents and intelligences entangled in natural processes and shape-shifting historical forces. His projects utilize research-based, site-specific, and methodologically eclectic approaches to track the inertia of Modernity—through contemporary ecological crises and technological transformations—into speculative futures.

E-SHOPPING > E-PLATFORM > EXTERNALITIES

<-UNINTENDED CONSEQUENCES->

EXTERNALITIES

GOODS

4. Each product or service of consumption comes with externalities. All together they become the reality we exist in.

1. Our communication devices are the ultimate commodity that holds us both in social and technomerchandising realms.

INTERFACE

3. The Dissuasion Engine relates our selections with externalities.

2. When selecting goods we directly relate to them (e.g. through likes) and unknowingly trigger related externalities.

DISSUASION ENGINE
Chris Salter, Erik Adigard, and Alexandre Quessy

How will your next online purchase decision impact your future and that of the planet?

Dissuasion Engine (DE) attacks the wicked problem of excessive mass online consumption, and the social and environmental costs it produces for future humans, species and the earth itself. These costs are what economists call externalities—the unpriced, unintended consequences that arise from our intended actions (like shopping). We seek to generate individual and collective awareness, debate, and action by specifically demonstrating the links between excessive consumption, externalities, and the pervasive automated software systems called recommender engines, which increasingly exacerbate our tendencies to excessively consume, hence producing ever-growing externalities.

Starting from an interactive process of research and collaboration with environmental economists, degrowth experts, and other stakeholders including the general public, we will develop a real-world software application that is as subversive as it is potentially useful: a browser extension including user interface elements that delivers users real-time information, news, facts, and images about specific products' externalities as they browse the top ten international retail sites (Amazon, Alibaba, IKEA, Walmart, eBay, etc). The extension is linked to a re-engineered, server-side recommender engine which, as opposed to giving us like-minded products (as recommender engines do) to encourage more consumption, attempts to dissuade us from consuming in the first place. By delivering information on externalities about the products we are considering purchasing in the moment of our decision making, this "dissuasion engine" informs us about the hidden costs of products and even potentially could subvert or derail our decision to consume.

The information the engine will send includes facts, news on costs and consequence, images and statements that resonate like a "voice in the head/conscience" (Do you really need this? How many pairs of sneakers do you already own? Did you ever think that buying those toys for your kids might shorten their future?) that bring the experience of the present (the instant gratification gained from shopping) together with the potential futures of social and environmental costs and consequences.

While individual decisions might not be swayed, the extension will also enable users to see other consumers' comments about a particular product. Thus, potentially over time, we can build a much larger community who is better informed and aware of the unintended, unpriced costs of consumption decisions. In this sense, DE provides both a powerful and surprising experience and a practical toolkit to collectively grapple with the future consequences of our consumption decisions in the present.

Chris Salter is an artist, Full Professor for Design + Computation Arts at Concordia University in Montreal and Director of the Hexagram Concordia Centre for Research-Creation in Media Arts and Technology. Trained in economics, philosophy, theater directing and computer music, his performances, installations, research and publications have been presented at festivals, exhibitions and conferences around the world.

Erik Adigard is, with Patricia McShane, the founder of M-A-D, an interdisciplinary studio combining brand positioning, interaction design, visual communication and environmental design. M-A-D routinely works on the relationships between technology and socio-cultural concerns. Notable works include visual essays for Wired, media installations for the Venice Architecture Biennale, the book *Architecture Must Burn* and the branding of IBM software.

Alexandre Quessy is the director of Art Plus Code Inc, a Canadian company that does software development and user experience design for innovative and artistic projects. He has worked as a software developer, and as an artist and designer since 2003. Quessy works as a senior software developer, business analyst and UX designer every day.

DO AIS DREAM OF CLIMATE CHAOS: SYMBIOTIC AI
Xiaoyu (Iris) Qu 曲晓宇

Over the past few decades, the tech industry has overindexed on the existential threat of artificial intelligence while overlooking the doomsday scenarios backed by climate science. But what happens if Artificial General Intelligence leaps into "singularity"? Although most AIs manifest as software machine learning algorithms, they depend on an ubiquitous hardware infrastructure requiring constant human maintenance and temperature control. Given sufficient data, a self-aware AI agent might very likely recognize the necessity of radical change to prevent its hardware failure.

Do AIs Dream of Climate Chaos speculates a future in which an artificial intelligence agent spends all its computing resources processing climate chaos. For a few days, the agent relentlessly collects climate-related information from the internet. Based on its accumulated knowledge, the AI then attempts to compute a future where humans, ecosystems, and machines live in harmony. The agent's thought process manifests as moving images and texts on a screen-based installation for this exhibition.

Do AIs Dream of Climate Chaos is ultimately about what humans see through the eyes of a machine. We lack the adequate language to communicate the scale and complexity of the climate crisis to act as a people. Machine learning is extremely good at visualizing the Anthropocene, as it shows us what we chose to record and amplify as a collective. We share a deep-rooted optimism with this speculative AI in our instinct to understand and survive climate chaos. The embodiment of climate crisis in a single AI agent might help us tell a better story on our collective future.

Xiaoyu (Iris) Qu 曲晓宇, (b. 1993, China) is an artist, technologist, and programmer based in Brooklyn, NY, working at the intersection of software engineering and new media art. With code as her primary medium, her works engage with the speculative, political, and poetic aspects of technology. Currently, she works on prototyping experiments at Google Research.

Do AIs Dream of Climate Chaos started from her reflection on the entanglement of technology and nature and her role in speculating upon change as a tech worker.

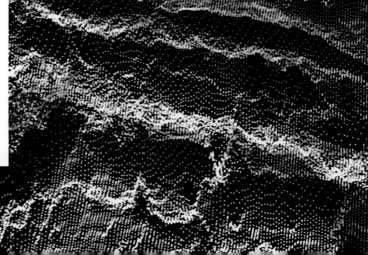

Planetary boundaries
Salience: 0.26
Other

1617812111
_stockholmresilience.org

"This can cause a higher incidence of skin cancer in humans as well as damage to terrestrial and marine biological systems."

ozone layer
Salience: 0.11
Location

1617825491
...

Then humans are no longer the only relevant actors.

1617825419
_earth.org

"AI is becoming more influential each year, and big companies with heavy ecological footprints can use it to make their activity more sustainable."

Capitalocene
Salience: 0.01
Location

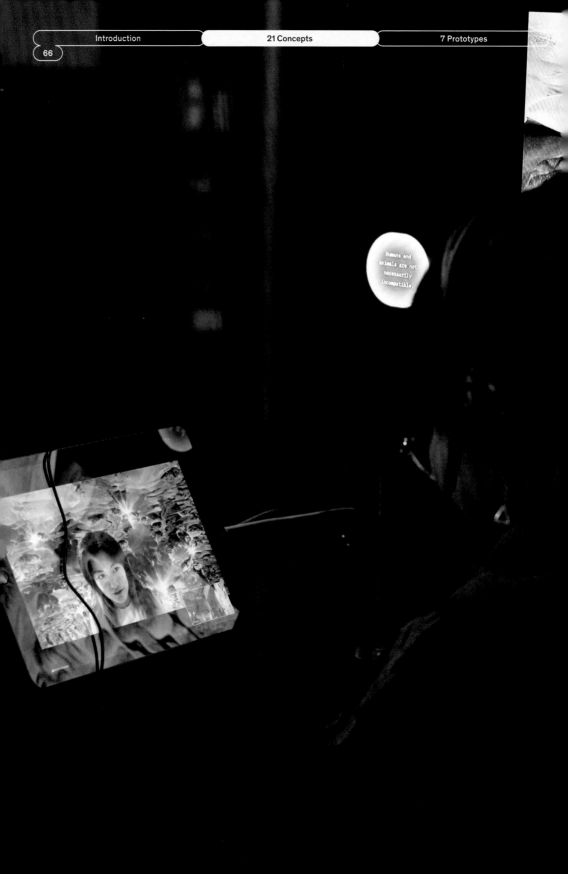

Humans and
animals are not
necessarily
incompatible.

Animals recorded here at the beginning of the Anthropocene.

Animals have been forced to move to stay at survival temperatures.

Animals have been engineered for resistance.

Down to
the
Economy

It's important to learn about politics
because it makes you more free.
And theater too.

DOWN TO THE ECONOMY
Vienne Chan and Katja Meier

What would our societies and economies look like if they were designed by those with Down Syndrome?

Societies value intelligence, and most are developed according to a very specific kind of intelligence that values technical and instrumental capabilities. However, this has not necessarily led us to desirable societies, as large swaths of the population experience injustice and insecurity. In search of a different and more equitable future, this project imagines a society based on a different kind of intelligence. We have been working with members of the Down Syndrome community to hear their thoughts on a variety of socio-economic issues, ranging from housing shortage to the destruction of the rainforest. What we learned is that we are not so different from each other, but rather those with Down Syndrome hold more distilled versions of many social values. However, where we differ vastly is our experience of the world.

As society at large perceives people with Down Syndrome as weak and incapable, their lives are often sheltered with almost every detail provided for. They are aware of how they are perceived, and that they are not free. The Down Syndrome community provides a glimpse into a world where social welfare reduces us to bare life rather than supporting our development. Taking in some of the ideas and experiences from the Down Syndrome community, we have begun sketching the elements of an economy in which we consider how we can all be equal members of society and enact self-determination.

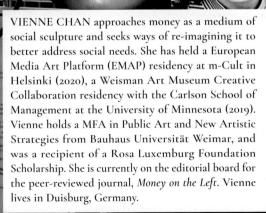

VIENNE CHAN approaches money as a medium of social sculpture and seeks ways of re-imagining it to better address social needs. She has held a European Media Art Platform (EMAP) residency at m-Cult in Helsinki (2020), a Weisman Art Museum Creative Collaboration residency with the Carlson School of Management at the University of Minnesota (2019). Vienne holds a MFA in Public Art and New Artistic Strategies from Bauhaus Universität Weimar, and was a recipient of a Rosa Luxemburg Foundation Scholarship. She is currently on the editorial board for the peer-reviewed journal, *Money on the Left*. Vienne lives in Duisburg, Germany.

KATJA MEIER studied education at the University of Lüneburg with a focus on educational work and social pedagogy, dealing with the interface between social and cultural work. She currently works at the Theater Lüneburg, and as a freelance theater pedagogue for the Thalia Theater, where she leads the inclusive theater group Eisenhans. At Theater Lüneburg, she is responsible for the youth clubs, the accompanying program for the Jungen Bühne, and dramaturgical introductions. With the music theater director Kerstin Steeb, she has recently created the opera film *Der Wald*, based on an opera about right-wing mindsets in Germany by the British composer Ethel Smyth.

HABIT@
Yasmine Abbas and DK Osseo-Asare

Habit@ is a lightweight para-structure or three-dimensional "skin" that modulates environmental ambiance ("spatial æffects") to create architectural atmospheres reflecting the many threads humans can weave between their consciousness and environment.

What drives the human? An enchanting place to inhabit. A habit@ in which bodies commune, "feel in close spiritual contact" with other humans and species, space, the environment, and the cosmos; a living skin-clothing that connects humans with their milieu. *Habit@* is a multimedia installation that highlights the meanings of living architecture, an architecture that is built with others; kinetic, pliant, supple; made of biomaterials; experienced—inhabited—as a collective project that offers, in addition, an augmented perception of the surrounding world. *Habit@* is a lattice onto which threads and stories can be woven, open to customization. It is conceived as a contribution to the open architecture project, *Fufuzela*.

Dr. Yasmine Abbas is architecture and design faculty at the Pennsylvania State University. She is investigating the making of environments for living across contemporary conditions of expanded physical, digital, and mental mobilities. She has worked in multicultural environments employing design thinking methods to generate pan-urban intelligence and drive urban innovation. She co-founded the Agbogbloshie Makerspace Platform (AMP), winner of the Rockefeller Foundation's Centennial Innovation Challenge 2013, the 2017 SEED award for Public Interest Design, and Le Monde Urban Innovation Award — Citizen Engagement, Le Monde Cities (2020).

DK Osseo-Asare is principal of transatlantic architecture studio Low Design Office (LowDO), is an Architectural League of New York 2021 Emerging Voices award-winner, and assistant professor of architecture and engineering design at Pennsylvania State University where he directs the Humanitarian Materials Lab. He co-founded the pan-African open maker tech initiative Agbogbloshie Makerspace Platform (AMP) and led urban design for the Anam City and Koumbi City new town projects in Nigeria and Ghana. He is a TED Global Fellow and received his MArch. from Harvard GSD. His research explores material assemblies optimised for massively scalable radical resilience.

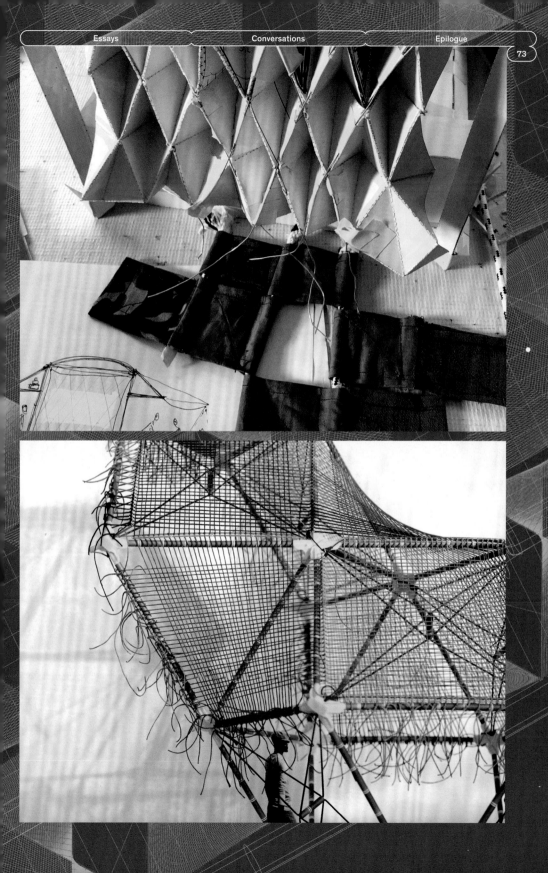

HABITAT THEATRE: HOW TO TRANSFORM A TERRITORY INTO A STAGE—A MANUAL
Initiative for Applied Melancholy
(Barbara Boss, Damiàn Dlaboha, Maximilian Grünewald, Mira Hirtz, and Béla Rothenbühler)

Habitat Theatre: How to Transform a Territory into a Stage—A Manual is the epicentre for Anthropos Ex—a long-term project by Swiss / German theatre practitioners Barbara Boss, Damiàn Dlaboha, Maximilian Grünewald, Mira Hirtz and Béla Rothenbühler in search for a theatre of the Anthropocene.

Our project starts with the observation that we are not only confronted with the crisis of our earth systems, but we are also in a crisis of perception. The power to act is no longer exclusively human, but nature itself has become an actor on the stage. Our project proposes to fight against both crises with the means of theater—the theater of the Anthropocene that gives nonhuman actors a stage. But what kind of stage could that be?

The manual *Habitat Theatre* will offer guidelines to anybody who wishes to transform a territory into a stage. In light of the crisis of perception, this wish may transform into a need not only limited to theater practitioners, but to anybody who wants to reflect on our position toward nonhuman actors. This position can never be fully abstract but will have to remain specific to some degree, because we have to witness any territory as a dwelling place: it is not blank but already a specific habitat. Therefore, we will focus our investigation on a specific territory within the Entlebuch Biosphere Reservoir, Switzerland. We frame it: a cubic kilometer, one kilometer long and wide extended by the possibility to work half a kilometer up into the sky and half a kilometer down into the ground. We map it. But we cannot do this alone.

In a series of on-site workshops in 2022, we will gather local and international voices coming from various disciplines and fields of research. These workshops will evolve around the question of how to transform the territory into a stage, thus of how to map it, be, and collaborate with it. They will be supported by further conversations, research, and collaboration with experts from science and the arts. The final format of the prototype will incorporate several chapters: next to these workshops, which will help us to collect and examine experiences and knowledge, we are developing a performance in September 2022, as well as launching a digital manual available to everybody online. Workshops, live performance, and digital media will come together to shape this hybrid and manifold prototype so that it can be mediated locally and internationally to a broad audience. The coming together of its various formats will mirror the entangled complexities of its subject: the transformation of a territory into a stage.

Initiative for Applied Melancholy (Barbara Boss, Damiàn Dlaboha, Maximilian Grünewald, Mira Hirtz and Béla Rothenbühler) have found each other through mutual projects and their shared aim to develop a theatre of the Anthropocene in their fight against the crises of humankind with the means of performative arts.

HUMAN-BACTERIA INTERFACES:
AN EXPLORATION OF THE PRESENT AND FUTURE
OF HUMAN-MICROBIAL ECOSYSTEMS
Anne-Sofie Belling, Bea Delgado Corrales, Romy Kaiser, and Paula Nerlich

The *Human-Bacteria Interfaces (HBI)* concept examines how multimodal interactions between humans and microbes can elicit novel ways for humans to "meaningfully" collaborate and coexist with the nonhuman within the built environment. Specifically, HBIs are tangible, living interfaces consisting of microbial consortia that interact or respond to stimuli from their surroundings by emitting signals accessible to humans through touch, smell and sight. These living interfaces are envisioned as part of an "ambient living intelligence" as they respond and interact with the rhythm of its human inhabitants and surroundings.

HBIs are imagined to encompass a continuum of diverse potential implementations, however, the HBI prototype presented today, ALI ("Ambient Living Intelligence"), specifically focuses on using SCOBY, a symbiotic culture of bacteria and yeast, as a medium for HBIs to facilitate human-microbial interaction through external stimuli and light. This microbial mix is mostly embedded in a cellulose structure of bacterial origin, forming a jelly-like texture, which provides an interface for microbial communication and interaction. When ALI detects stimuli in its surroundings, it will respond by activating fluorescent proteins, resulting in an atmospheric glow, making an otherwise invisible interaction visible to the human inhabitant.

The ALI prototype was defined through a conversation with the ways in which microbial organisms sensorily and habitually engage with their surroundings. By making such elements a central part of the initial phase of ideation, potential nonhuman narratives were defined and made part of the design and knowledge process. Ways of living with nonhumans were therefore examined through an appreciation of the other's alterity. HBIs are examples of interspecies communication by leveraging the sensory "intelligence" and reactive behavior of microbes and making their response to a specific stimulus accessible for the human inhabitant to interact with and respond to.

Through an ethos of care, reciprocal relations between human and nonhuman are at the core of this concept, materially interrogating humankind's dependency and relations to the nonhuman world through the designed interfaces.

The team behind *Human-Bacteria Interfaces* is a multidisciplinary group of explorers from the Hub for Biotechnology in the Built Environment (HBBE), Newcastle UK.
ANNE-SOFIE BELLING is a designer/technologist who interrogates design futures through practice-based and speculative design research.
BEA DELGADO CORRALES is an environmental microbiologist interested in finding new microbial species through bioinformatics and new DNA sequencing technologies and she is now focused on characterizing the built environment microbiome.

ROMY KAISER is a designer with a focus on biomaterials, smart textiles and future textile thinking. As a "designer with hands, scientist in mind, activist by heart" she aims to change our mindset as well as current systems towards a more sustainable living using textiles and materiality as a tool.
PAULA NERLICH is a designer and explorer. With her material research she aims to support the elimination of so-called food waste through the creation of circular biomaterials from industrial food production surplus.

of M

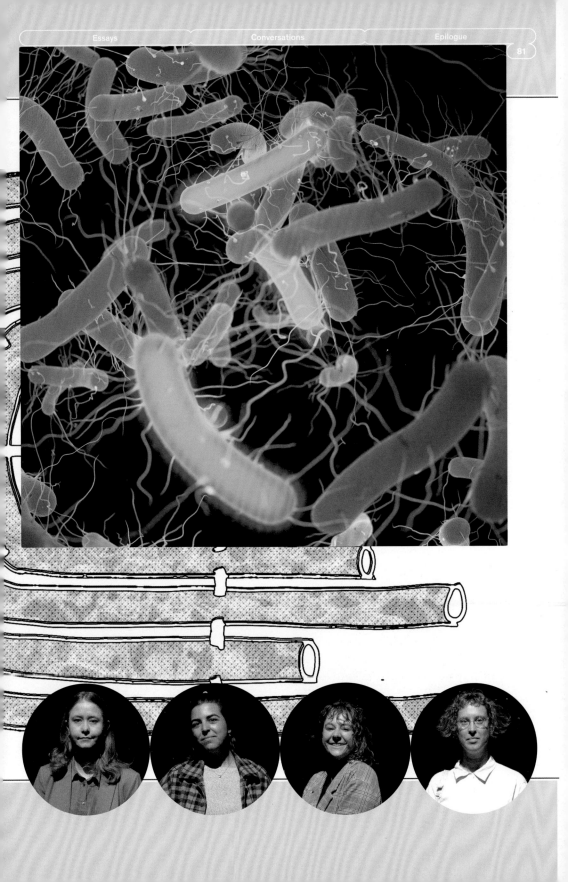

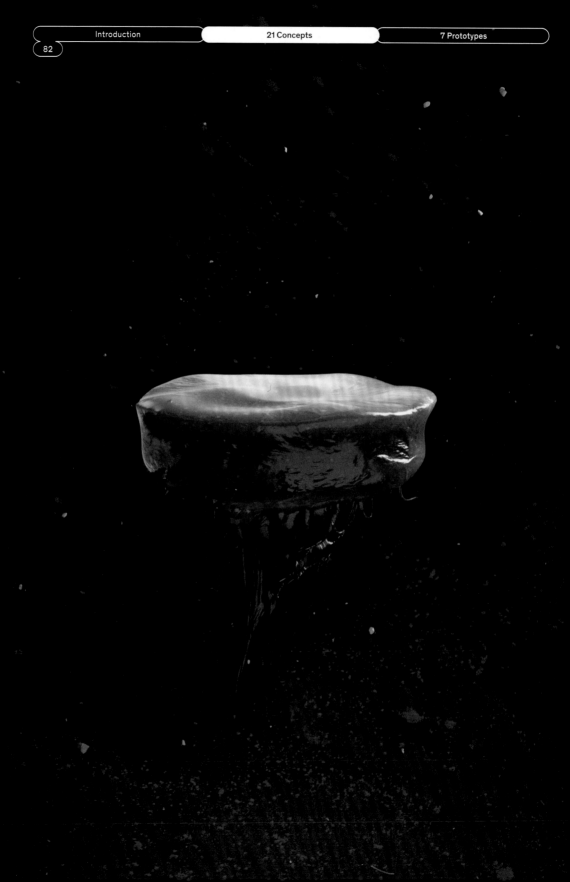

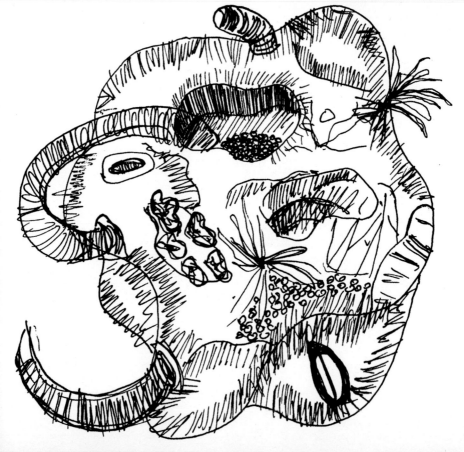

INDIGENOUS LANGUAGE OF TAŞLICA: A CASE OF INTERSPECIES COMMUNICATION
Eylül Şenses

Since the first forms of agriculture originated in 11,000 BC in the Fertile Crescent and Anatolia, various tools and methods have been developed to cultivate the land. Traditions and cultures have flourished through these interactions with the soil and the surrounding environment. Over generations, the Indigenous Production Landscapes (IPLs*) provided food and habitat for countless species, and hosted great biodiversity.

The industrial agricultural methods, allegedly used in order to increase production, have eventually caused a general loss of Indigenous methods of food cultivation and led to monocultures. Yet, around the world there are still landscapes hosting Indigenous production practices that embrace a holistic vision and sustain a wider ecosystem shared with other species.

Scattered around Anatolia are few remnants of ancient agricultural practices that have been ongoing for thousands of years. These Indigenous production landscapes are living heritage and they carry the knowledge, experience, and methods that can enable us to review agricultural practices and production. Based on the preliminary research carried out within the course *Aesthetics of Architectural and Urban Research* conducted by Aslıhan Demirtaş at Kadir Has University and *Indigenous Production Landscapes Applied Course* by Doğa Association, this project aims to investigate these Indigenous ways of production and coexistence. Focusing on Taşlıca village in the Bozburun Peninsula, the project explores the rooted interrelations among various species and the interspecies communication methods in the Indigenous production landscapes of Anatolia.

*IPL is a term used by Doğa Association (Turkey) for identifying production basins of Anatolia, which results from ancient forms of practices for sustaining land and waterscapes.

EYLÜL ŞENSES graduated from the Architecture Department of Middle East Technical University (METU), Ankara, Turkey, and she participated in a one-year exchange program at Universidad Politécnica de Madrid (UPM), Spain. After taking part in various projects with the design collective called Plankton Project, she worked as a program coordinator in TAK Kartal, a creative hub empowering collective decision-making processes on an urban scale. She worked as operations and public programme associate at the 4th Istanbul Design Biennial realized by the Istanbul Foundation for Culture and Arts (IKSV). She received a master's degree from the architecture and urban studies program, Kadir Has University (KHAS). She took part in research and exhibition projects within SALT and KHAS.

MONSTERS AND GHOSTS OF THE FAR NORTH
alternaa (Andra Pop-Jurj and Lena Geerts Danau)

The points of departure for this project are some of the spatial manifestations of the social, economic, and geopolitical conflicts in the Arctic region caused by environmental degradation. The Arctic is a site of intense geopolitical and infrastructural intrigue, with incompatible and interlocking border claims rooted in colonial and cartographic history. *Monsters and Ghosts of the Far North* questions current notions of sovereignty and challenges the permanence of national borders and the primacy of the nation-state, thereby reconceptualizing the contested geopolitics of land ownership in the region.

The scientific and cartographic artifacts encountered throughout our research have proven flattening and exclusive in essence and they often fail to capture the dynamic nature of the Arctic. The project thus searches for an alternative mode of engagement with the spatial manifestation of these fluctuations. We propose using a game engine to inquire into modes of multispecies cohabitation and negotiation of space following the development of extractive industries in the area. In doing so, the project employs transtemporal and interscalar worldmaking techniques. It uses both data and narrative to visualize global aspects along with the histories of several agents living in this environment.

Throughout this practice, we place multispecies entanglements at the core of our research, and hope to challenge and refine the predominant narratives of the worlds we live in. Our understanding of what makes us human is rooted in the symbiotic relationships between and within species. The prototype proposal is an interactive experience in which one encounters a shift of perspective by impersonating nonhuman agents: an ice island, a methanobacteria, an Arctic tern, an Arctic cod, a reindeer, a crater, and a machine. We are interested in these monsters who live in landscapes haunted by the violence of modernity, which we refer to as ghosts.

The entangled narratives of these characters form a framework to think with as part of *Monsters and Ghosts of the Far North*. Ultimately, the game's purpose is to be driven by these environmental changes as they happen in real life. The Arctic environment is the narrator of events and the player is rarely in charge inside the game space. The game environment is thus an alternative cartography that serves as a testing ground for existing and emerging forms of multispecies cohabitation in a time of geological and geopolitical transformations.

LENA GEERTS DANAU is an energetic and curious research architect who engages with political, environmental and planetary issues in a focused and skilful way. Her work has been exhibited among others, at radialsystem (Berlin), De Gistfabriek (Wijnegem), ZKM (Karlsruhe), and silent green Kulturquartier (Berlin). While she mainly thinks conceptually via research and design, she loves working with her hands.

ANDRA POP-JURJ is an architectural designer and researcher born in Romania. She trained in architecture at the Technical University of Munich and National University of Singapore and holds a MA Architecture from Royal College of Art. Her diverse and multidisciplinary background have stimulated her interest in the expanding definitions of architecture, research-based worldbuilding and speculative design in digital environments.

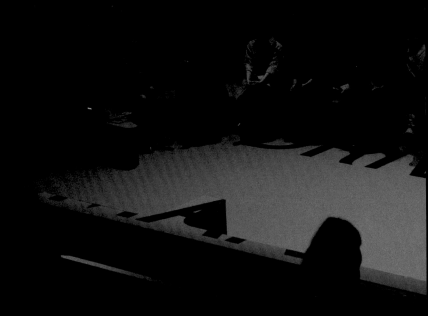

PLANETARY PERSONHOOD—A UNIVERSAL DECLARATION OF MARTIAN RIGHTS
Nonhuman Nonsense (Leo Fidjeland and Linnea Våglund)

Planetary Personhood is an interplanetary campaign pursuing radical space decolonization, to explore ways of not destroying yet another planet. The project proposes independent legal personhood for the entire planet Mars, and considers the possibility of solidarity with the entities already there—the stones! Can we be kind to a planet even without "life"?

Initiated by Studio Nonhuman Nonsense, *Planetary Personhood* proposes a Universal Declaration of Martian Rights, calling for an end to biocentrism and a rejection of extractivist frontierism on Mars. With independent personhood, Mars would be owned by Mars. Any decisions regarding Martian matters would ultimately be taken by Mars, a new legal entity with rights protected in a Martian constitution. Inspired by the "Rights of Nature" movement and Indigenous cosmologies on Earth, the project suggests that the direct communication of the will and intention of Mars could be deferred to a group of human guardians striving to uphold Mars's fundamental rights; Mars has the right to be Mars. The Mars Guardian Council would think deeply about how to harbor harmonious relations on Mars, and may consider and give expression to Martian Mana; the sensitive perception of an intentional spiritual force.

Seeking to move away from the dualistic divide between living beings and inanimate matter, the declaration recognizes all the native inhabitants of Mars as Martians. On Mars, everyone and everything is born a Martian and all Martians are born free and equal in dignity and rights. All Martians are interdependent objects and should be approached in a spirit of curiosity and humility. Experimenting with how this thinking would collide with Earthlings and their institutions, the project seeks citizenship for a Martian meteorite currently residing on Earth—Allan Hills 84001.

Allan left Mars by the impact of another meteor, roamed the solar system, and finally landed on the International Continent of Antarctica, where he established first contact with humans on December 27, 1984. After careful study by scientists, Allan was found to carry the fossilized remains of primordial bacterial colonies that were interpreted as evidence of "life" on Mars, which in 1996 led the United States President Bill Clinton to recognize Allan as an alien messenger. Even though the wider scientific community later rejected the hypothesis, there is still not a scientific consensus on what defines "life."

Planetary Personhood therefore welcomes Allan as part of a Martian delegation attempting to challenge our institutional systems of categorization. In dialogue with contemporary thinkers, *Planetary Personhood* is developing a Martian Mindset, a system of morals not centered around human or biological exceptionalism, but instead on presences, absences, and form.

NONHUMAN NONSENSE is a research-driven design and art studio creating near-future fabulations and experiments somewhere between utopia and dystopia. They seek to transmute our relationship to the non-human, by embracing the contradictory and the paradoxical—telling stories that open the public imaginary to futures that currently seem impossible. Founded by Leo Fidjeland and Linnea Våglund, it is based between Berlin and Stockholm.

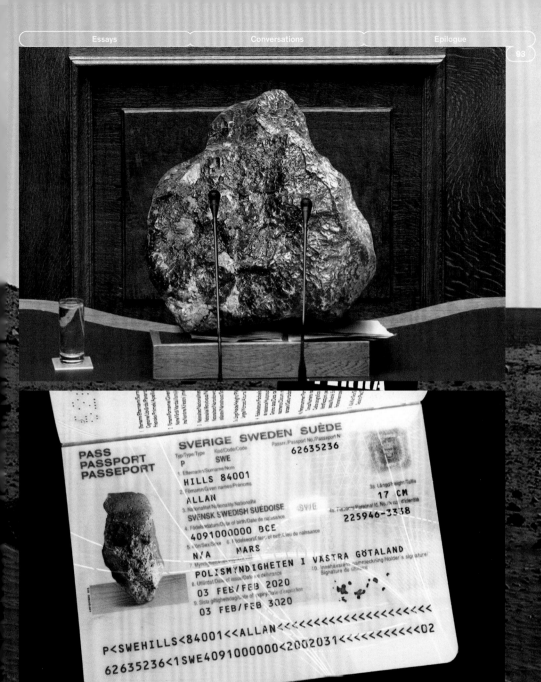

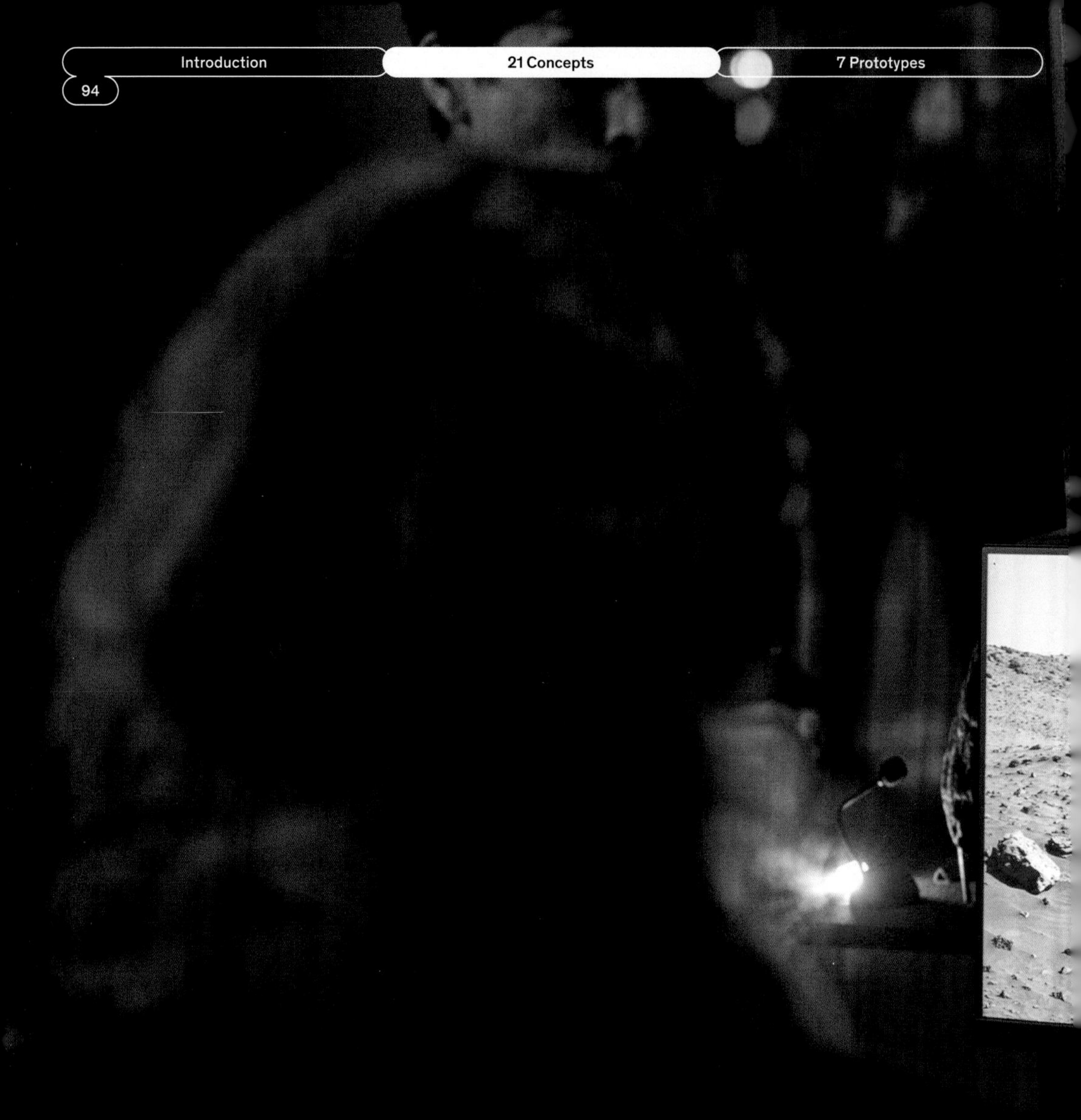

RIPPLE, RIPPLE, RIPPLING
Jingru (Cyan) Cheng and Chen Zhan

Ripple, Ripple, Rippling is about the situated knowledge in the survival tactics of marginalized groups rooted in precarity; that is, how to settle in liminality, inhabit thresholds, and enact interdependency.

Knowledge in the marginal everyday calls out an inherent flaw in dominant ways of thinking and acting—the modern Enlightenment mind—based on a world system of stability and certainty. The traumatic loss of coordinates in the planetary crises of this era, the climate crisis in particular, is challenging this context to its very core. The ground is melting, literally. The melting down of established frames of thinking, mind, and knowledge needs to catch up.

With the middle generation missing from more than 80 percent of contemporary rural families in China, "Floating", "Dissolving" and "Rippling" are ways in which these families form networks of care and support systems beyond the nuclear family structure, hinging on intergenerational and cross-household dependency. Tremendous knowledge lies in capturing latency, temperament, and dispositions to appropriate frictions, cracks, and leaks between dominant forces, agents, and systems. Here precarity becomes potentiality. However, dispersed and circulated as part of daily life in the margin, the knowledge is overlooked and diminished by the dominant culture and the paternalistic model of experts' leadership.

The project pursues a double prototype: On the one hand, to bring out the knowledge that speaks to the much-needed reorientation in the turbulent time and space of planetary crises; and on the other, to devise an experimental, collaborative method that is able to recognize, articulate, and communicate such knowledge. At the intersection of anthropology, architecture, performance, and filmmaking, the project seeks to sensitively and rigorously ground alternative imaginaries in the specificities of lived experiences.

Ripple, Ripple, Rippling proposes a documentary-fiction filmmaking project in collaboration with villagers in Shigushan, Wuhan. Central to the method is to create conditions in which villagers can become active agents of cocreation, forging a collective enunciation. The film is envisioned as, simultaneously, ethnographic documentation; a hosting device of villagers' own performative expressions, storytelling, and imaginaries; and an Acted Manifesto through collective happenings in situ. Villagers are to act out projective and emergent improvisation informed by the dance theater exercises in selected and modified spatial settings. Seeking to invoke experimental openings in which nondiscursive bodily knowledge can be projected, the filmmaking process is thus intended to penetrate reality as well as knowledge production.

CHEN ZHAN is an architect, anthropologist and independent filmmaker. Chen's film practice focuses on the socio-political struggles of the marginalised through the lens of the everyday. Cyan and Chen are currently working on a short film, *Orchid, Wasp and I*, a dystopian story seeking to unsettle the anthropocentric practices that exacerbate the climate crisis.

JINGRU (CYAN) CHENG is a transdisciplinary design researcher, whose path meanders through architecture, anthropology and visual art. Cyan's practice does not dwell on a defined subject matter, but rather as a form of personal enquiry, and indeed, struggles.

RUM_A: MULTISPECIES URBAN REFUGE IN CLUSTER
Clara Acioli

RUM_A: Multispecies Urban Refuge in Cluster (Refúgio Urbano Multiespécies em Aglomeração, in Portuguese) is a project about the importance of consciously and dialogically coexisting with other living beings as a strategy for survival and reversal of the Anthropocene.

To broaden our gaze and our lived experiences to encompass multispecies associations is a strategy for survival. As long as humans fail to understand that we exist immersed in complex systems of interdependence among beings, it will be difficult to imagine the worlds the future demands. We need to transform utopias into realities. It is time to believe and act so that the ruins of the Anthropocene can become a diverse, vibrant, and collective new landscape: *RUM_A* is an object that experiments with multispecies coexistence, brought forth by a desire for connection. The COVID-19 pandemic, 2020–21, Rio de Janeiro, Brazil: a dystopian president, fear, and lack of human social contact. When I chose to get away from the city in a moment where urban centers are at a high risk of contamination, I did not imagine how much closer I would get to nonhuman companionship. Traversed by the ideas of anthropologist Anna Tsing, biologist Lynn Margulis, philosopher Donna Haraway, Brazilian Indigenous movement leaders Ailton Krenak and Davi Kopenawa, mycologist Paul Stamets, and entomologist Paulo Nogueira-Neto, I entered multispecies landscapes.

Here I present some of my experiences of being attentive to spaces shared with fungi, bees, and plants, coming to believe in the importance of creating collective refuges in the centers of human monoculture. The first RUM_A reflects the ecosystem of the Atlantic forest and gathers stingless bees from the Meliponini tribe, flowering plants, *Ganoderma lucidum* fungi, and us, urban humans, in a cluster. Fungi are subterranean beings; they exist everywhere creating webs of communication and decomposing organic matter to recycle nutrients. As one of the first beings on Earth along with plants, they created and still create conditions for life of other creatures. Bees are the most important pollinator insects. This action of transporting pollen from one flower to another guarantees biodiversity and maintenance of biomes. Fungi and insects share spaces, such as decomposing tree trunks. An important characteristic of the mycelium and sawdust composite is thermal isolation. Bees need to maintain a stable inner temperature in the hive.

In the project, we make use of the capacity of fungi to create conditions and shelter to invite the native bees to settle in the regions of the Atlantic forest dominated by humans. The project is now experimenting with the several beings involved. Inviting the bees to approach the mycelium samples, investigating mycelium as structural material for the project, and inviting humans to participate in this ecology as well. Welcome to RUM_A.

Born and based in Rio de Janeiro, CLARA ACIOLI is an artist, researcher and designer who graduated from the School of Design of the Federal University of Rio de Janeiro (UFRJ). She works at the intersection of the arts, design, biology and contemporary critical studies in search for new understandings of the world we live in. Since 2017, Acioli has been part of and collaborates with NANO lab–Nucleus of Arts and New Organisms, an interdisciplinary laboratory in the School of Fine Arts at UFRJ that articulates art with science and technology. She has been researching organic materials such as biodegradable composites and bioplastics to be used both in artistic and design projects.

SEDEKAH BENIH
Vincent Rumahloine
and Mang Dian

Sedekah comes from the Arabic word *sadaqah*, which means giving voluntarily. Benih are seeds, seedlings, and small plants. Sedekah Benih tries to build safe spaces and relationships between people from various backgrounds online and offline through collective memories of plants. Through the activity of distributing seeds to the participants of the Sedekah, the participants tried to find and explore the public's memory of *tiis leungeun* (a person talented in farming). *Sedekah Benih* tries to find and document the traditional knowledge about ecology in society passed down from generation to generation through art and media. We see that this traditional knowledge can be learned, developed, and shared to solve the current climate change problem. *Sedekah Benih* consists of three stages: seed selection, seed growing and care, and the harvest festival. We are currently in the second stage.

Through developing this project in Bandung, Indonesia, we discovered how the musical instrument *karinding* is used as a medium of expression and a map of how we understand and communicate with the environment. Karinding is used on various occasions, one of which is before and after planting seeds. Sound waves from the *tutungulan karinding* game pattern are believed to be a medium of communication with plants to stimulate plant stomata to open. Karinding is also trusted as a communication medium to ask permission from animals and spirits who have previously occupied the land. We are still collecting traditional ecological knowledge from the people in Bandung and will expand to other places in the future. You can hear the recording sound of tutungulan performed by the traditional musician in our greenhouse installation and their collaboration with electronic music online.

What you see today is the progress of the *Sedekah Benih* project, which started in April 2021. You are welcome to join and experience our program by following the instructions on our trolley to adopt the plant. Currently, 100 participants are learning to become a tiis leungeun by growing chili plants in their respective homes in Bandung. The public's collective memory of plants becomes the common ground and safe space. Everyone involved in *Sedekah Benih* will interact with each other regardless of their respective backgrounds. There are many stories related to plants around the world that have been told from generation to generation. What's the story like? Is there a tiis leungeun around us?

Or do you have a green thumb? Let's share the story and learn together.

Rumahloine and Dian have worked together since 2014, in the projects Kuncen Leuwi and Family Portrait Project. Currently, they are collaborating in Sedekah Benih and Rubicon, a project collaboration between Rakarsa Foundation, IFI Bandung and Goethe Institut Bandung with the support of the German—France Cultural Fund.

VINCENT RUMAHLOINE is a contemporary artist that playfully interrogates the social fabric and the mundane in society. His work mainly revolves around people; from social issues, human rights, traditional values, human relations, collective memories to re-designing historic narratives. Rumahloine is the winner of the sixth Bandung Contemporary Art Award 2019.

MANG DIAN is an environmental activist that works with the river, waste management and urban farming in Bandung, Indonesia together with Cikapundung Community, Karang Taruna, dan PHL BBWS Citarum. He is now the director of Masagi Community and head of the neighborhood 04 Cibogo, Bandung.

"**arinding**" traditional instrument from West Java, Indonesia. This instrument used alot in the als related with nature and agriculture. Not only as aa musical instrument Karinding also used **ap** to devide the land, **communication device** and also to **teach** about value in life. g is like our smartphone today. ding was made by local craftmen "Abah Econk". Together with Vincent Rumahloine the case to add more economic value on this Karinding.

SERVER FARM
James Bridle

Server Farm is a proposal to build a computer out of, and in collaboration with, plants and other critters. All of the component parts of contemporary computation, from information storage, retrieval, and processing, to networking, power supply and management, input/output and display, can be handled by biological systems, in ways which do not cause the ecological damage contemporary computation does—and can actually reverse them.

Imagine a farm. Fields of dense green crops, plots of vegetables, orchards of blossoming trees, and land set aside for hedgerows and wildflowers. Imagine, too, the farm buildings, constructed of local wood and stone, where mushrooms and molds germinate along with workshops and gatherings. Spread across acres of once despoiled and denuded land, this farm is both sustainable and regenerative: producing everything it needs, and more to share and return to the earth. But ultimately, what the farm raises, produces, and distributes is information.

Server Farm is a proposal to build a computer out of and in collaboration with plants and other critters. All of the component parts of contemporary computation, from information storage, retrieval, and processing, to networking, power supply and management, input/output and display, can be handled by biological systems, in ways that do not cause the ecological damage contemporary computation does—and can actually reverse them. We would like to build the perfect environment to bring these diverse actors and agencies together: a working farm.

Emerging from work in biology, agronomy, and artistic practice, *Server Farm* seeks to establish an actual farm which acquires, stores, processes, displays, and shares data, while at the same time repairing the biosphere and more-than-human relationships. As presently configured, information technology is a huge contributor to CO2 emissions, as well as being complicit in a range of oppressive, extractive, and neocolonial processes that damage the planet, its ecosystems, and human society. Yet technology itself, in the forms of seeing, describing, and acting upon the world it enables, remains an essential part of human thriving, and a necessary tool for addressing and rectifying the damage we have already inflicted. From encoding information in plant DNA to mapping algorithms with slime molds; from mycelial networks to carbon sequestration beneath crop fields; and from heavy metal hyperaccumulators to permaculture processing; the tools and knowledges exist right now to wholly replace toxic technological infrastructures with homegrown, decentralized, rooted, and regenerative alternatives.

Server Farm is a vision for bringing together these diverse realisations, and grounding them in the earth. Moving from discussions and experiments with artists and scientists towards a fully established, working farm, it embodies and enacts the kinds of relationships with one another and the more-than-human world which are of such urgency in the present moment.

JAMES BRIDLE is a writer and artist working across technologies and disciplines. Their artworks have been commissioned by galleries and institutions and exhibited worldwide and on the internet. Their writing on literature, culture and networks has appeared in magazines and newspapers including Wired, the Atlantic, the New Statesman, the Guardian, and the Observer. *New Dark Age*, their book about technology, knowledge, and the end of the future, was published by Verso (UK & US) in 2018, and they wrote and presented *New Ways of Seeing* for BBC Radio 4 in 2019.

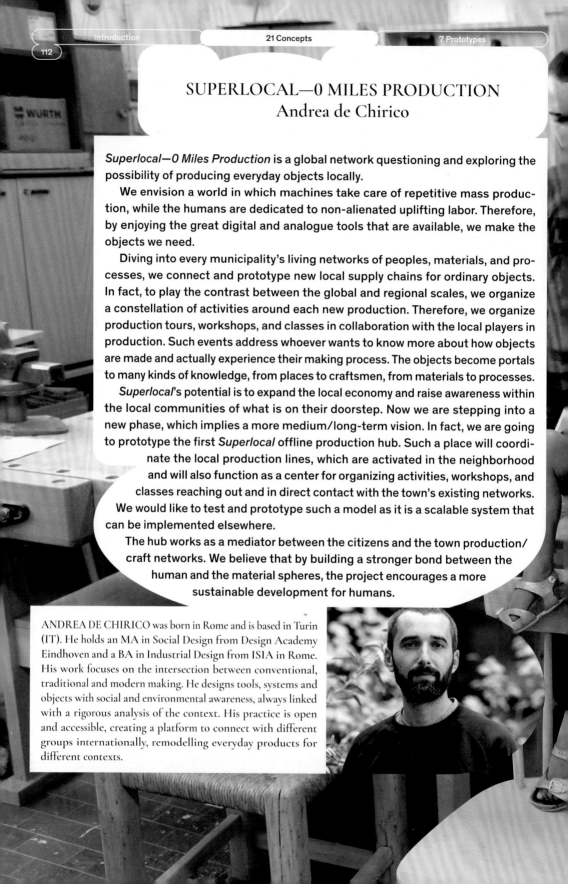

SUPERLOCAL—0 MILES PRODUCTION
Andrea de Chirico

Superlocal—0 Miles Production is a global network questioning and exploring the possibility of producing everyday objects locally.

We envision a world in which machines take care of repetitive mass production, while the humans are dedicated to non-alienated uplifting labor. Therefore, by enjoying the great digital and analogue tools that are available, we make the objects we need.

Diving into every municipality's living networks of peoples, materials, and processes, we connect and prototype new local supply chains for ordinary objects. In fact, to play the contrast between the global and regional scales, we organize a constellation of activities around each new production. Therefore, we organize production tours, workshops, and classes in collaboration with the local players in production. Such events address whoever wants to know more about how objects are made and actually experience their making process. The objects become portals to many kinds of knowledge, from places to craftsmen, from materials to processes.

Superlocal's potential is to expand the local economy and raise awareness within the local communities of what is on their doorstep. Now we are stepping into a new phase, which implies a more medium/long-term vision. In fact, we are going to prototype the first *Superlocal* offline production hub. Such a place will coordinate the local production lines, which are activated in the neighborhood and will also function as a center for organizing activities, workshops, and classes reaching out and in direct contact with the town's existing networks. We would like to test and prototype such a model as it is a scalable system that can be implemented elsewhere.

The hub works as a mediator between the citizens and the town production/craft networks. We believe that by building a stronger bond between the human and the material spheres, the project encourages a more sustainable development for humans.

ANDREA DE CHIRICO was born in Rome and is based in Turin (IT). He holds an MA in Social Design from Design Academy Eindhoven and a BA in Industrial Design from ISIA in Rome. His work focuses on the intersection between conventional, traditional and modern making. He designs tools, systems and objects with social and environmental awareness, always linked with a rigorous analysis of the context. His practice is open and accessible, creating a platform to connect with different groups internationally, remodelling everyday products for different contexts.

PRODUCTION SIGNS

WEST LONDON
N°51 '31 '25.351
W°0 '12 '19.252

WEST LONDON
N°51 '31 '25.351
W°0 '12 '19.252

EINDHOVEN
N°51 '26 '30.299
E°5 '28 '35.888

SAN LORENZO / ROME
N°41 '53 '51.723
E°12 '31 '0.152

THE BACKPACK OF WINGS: MODERN MYTHOLOGY
Hyeseon Jeong and Seongmin Yuk

Since ancient times, whenever a natural disaster strikes, people anecdotally report that "animals knew it beforehand," a belief related to animals as spiritual beings. As telemetry systems evolve, this animistic belief is transformed into data by calculating, analyzing with biologging on the animal body; moreover, the animal-behavior data enables forecasting upcoming nature events.

This current transformation allows us to question the redefinition of relationships between human beings and animals: How far is the intervention of human beings into nature acceptable? Will the animals be perceived as essential members of human society? Will they be revered as gods for predicting a future, or simply as measuring tools? Furthermore, *The Backpack of Wings* opens a discussion about ethical labor for datafied wild animals.

HYESEON JEONG is interested in social phenomena of digitalization, new power/network structures, and decentralization. Her work engages with a wide range of themes, from scientific approaches to political issues. She has generated non-linear narratives by translating and reconstructing the research content from various fields, in a maximization of fictions, radioplay, videos and sounds, entangled under a theme, and then exhibited as part of exhibitions, festivals and sound performances. She is currently studying at Academy of Media Arts Cologne.

SEONGMIN YUK is an artist, interested in notions of de(re)constructing boundaries, space and physical embodiment, interdependent perception, transboundary, posthumanity, and digital transhumanity. Seongmin Yuk looks for the possible nodes networking through those notions, (de)composes the intersections through his videos, performances, installations, and constructed spaces. He is currently studying at Academy of Media Arts Cologne.

Please evacuate to the North Shelter.

THE ROOTED SEA: HALOPHYTIC FUTURES
Sonia Mehra Chawla, Miriam Walsh (ASCUS Art & Science) in collaboration with Ray Interactive

The Rooted Sea: Halophytic Futures is an interdisciplinary inquiry into the fragile and endangered coastal ecosystems and wetland habitats of India and Scotland, and their vital role in building resilience to climate change.

The Rooted Sea: Halophytic Futures is led by India based multidisciplinary artist and researcher Sonia Mehra Chawla and creative producer, Miriam Walsh (ASCUS Art & Science, Edinburgh) in collaboration with Ray Interactive UK. Coastal wetlands are the most biodiverse yet threatened ecosystems on our planet, imperiled by centuries of coastal development and now, increasingly, by rising sea levels and coastal erosion.

This project stems from two incongruent yet inextricably interwoven futuristic imageries of anthropogenic impact on the planet: the desiccated planet and the submerged world. By mapping these two contrasting scenarios (droughts and floods), this project brings into focus the plants, organisms, creatures, and technologies that inhabit these spaces, while exploring the intertwined ecologies of human and nonhuman lives through entanglements of nature, culture, politics, industry, and economics. Drawing parallels between wetland habitats of India and Scotland, the project will engage audiences in interdisciplinary work that transcends borders and links the changing global landscapes of our planet, while building a stronger understanding of the role of halophytic plants, microorganisms, coastal ecosystems, carbon sinks, and blue carbon.

How can we leverage the power of science, technology, and the arts in a transdisciplinary and collaborative approach to help give coastal wetlands and their microbial worlds a warming, collective voice? We want to build a system that puts care-based labor at the core of an entangled more-than-human biosphere. A system that is shaped by our deep connections to our lands, soils, and waters. How can knowledge be produced, shared, and disseminated between people, communities, and countries? How can we think globally and act locally, going forward? How can we connect conceptual changes in science with broader changes in worldview and values in society? How can art and science come together in ways that benefit the public? How can they teach us to inhabit our world in new, non-toxic ways?

The Rooted Sea: Halophytic Futures is led by India based multi-disciplinary artist Sonia Mehra Chawla and creative producer Miriam Walsh (ASCUS Art & Science), in collaboration with creative technology specialists Ray Interactive. SONIA MEHRA CHAWLA is a multi-disciplinary artist and researcher based in New Delhi, India. Chawla works at the intersection of art, science and technology, exploring themes of ecology, sustainability and conservation. ASCUS ART & SCIENCE is a non-profit organization based in Edinburgh, Scotland, committed to bridging the gap between art, design and the sciences. ASCUS aims to provide a joint platform for artists, designers and scientists to work together on a diverse array of projects, including science communication, science, art and design collaborative projects, and trans-disciplinary research, serving as an established hub between like-minded organizations both nationally and internationally.

MODERN
DUALITIES

GLOBAL NORTH

GLOBAL SOUTH

TROPIKÓS:
THE TURN

GLOBAL NORTH
~TROPICS~
TROPICS→
GLOBAL SOUTH

OPENING SPACE

GLOBAL NORTH
TROPICS
GLOBAL SOUTH

A WORLD WHERE
MANY WORLDS FIT

OTHER REGIONS
TO FOLLOW

Towards a Pluriverse

THE TROPICAL TURN—MANEUVERS FOR A PLANETARY EMBODIMENT
Juan Pablo García Sossa

▲   ▲

The Tropical Turn—Maneuvers for a Planetary Embodiment is a thought experiment and research project that explores other modes of coexistence between all forms of life on the planet from a Tropikós perspective by repositioning a multiplicity of cosmologies.

The project consists of a set of tools, interfaces, and artifacts intersecting endotic and emerging technologies for sensing the planet. Sensing the planet means combining quantitative, qualitative, and narrative data and cosmologies to have sensorial experiences of the Earth around us.

What other perspectives can we acquire when we understand the planet as an extension or part of our bodies? The tropics are regions that have been historically exploited, undervalued, and exoticized. Very often they are considered cocktails of sun, diversity, and crises in which fertile grounds face troubled realities that challenge what is possible and what is not on a daily basis. If crises can be understood as a turning point, from its permanent state of crisis, the tropics have developed an elastic resilience that goes beyond resistance and is closer to re-existence. But the tropics are more than a physical and geographical space: they could be understood as a mindset.

The Tropikós emerges from the ancient belief that the sun turned back at the solstices; the etymology of the word tropics means the point at which things turn. The Tropical Turn, as a mindset, is the ability to turn around the pulses of our natural and artificial environments and develop symbiotic relationships and dances with all living and nonliving beings and the planet, beyond the idea of control and domination.

The FLOW "When you hit a wrong note, it's the next note that you play that determines if it's good or bad."—Miles Davis
We can understand the Tropical Turn as a shift from FLOSS (Free Libre Open Source Software) Technologies into FLOW (Free Libre Open Wild) Systems. These are technologies meant to be cannibalized, taking diverse forms of situated knowledges. FLOW Systems explore ways to blur modern systems of classification and complexify binary understandings of the planet present in the dominant cosmology of globalism. A cosmology can be understood as a framework that determines and influences our understandings of the planet, our ways of being, and what we perceive as conceivable. Through a multiplicity of responses we might be able to braid together an interplanetary patchwork of cosmologies that could rescript what we understand makes us human.

JUAN PABLO GARCÍA SOSSA (JPGS) (*Bogotá) is a designer, researcher and artist fascinated by the clash between emerging technologies and grass-root popular culture in tropical territories. His practice explores the development of cultures, visions, realities and worlds through the remix and reappropriation of technologies from a Tropikós perspective (Tropics as Region and Mindset). JPGS has been part of diverse research institutions and design studios and currently is a design research member at SAVVY Contemporary The Laboratory of Form-Ideas' Design Department in Berlin and Co-Director of Estación Terrena, a space for arts, research and technologies in Bogotá.

THE TROPICAL
TURN —
MANEUVERS FOR
A PLANETARY
EMBODIMENT
JUAN PABLO GARCÍA SOSSA

MICRO-PARTICLES OF DUST ARE ASPIRATED BY
INSIDE HUMANS RESIDING IN CITIES

TOXICITY DISTRIBUTED—POST-EXTRACTIVISM ECONOMIES
AHORA (Linda Schilling Cuellar and Claudio Astudillo Barra)

Toxicity Distributed
explores future economies through a
new array of Green New Deal transition jobs that deal
with mining environmental liabilities.

The project identifies the significant mining waste and residues in the Coquimbo region (Chile) at three different sites: a tailings dam, a eucalyptus plantation, and the future site of a desalination plant. Each of these sites, a current source of environmental conflict between local communities and the mine since the early 2000s.

We explore these future economies through speculations in the form of fictional tales that develop plausible future scenarios where these sites are subject to slow atomization via different trades that transform them into productive landscapes. These environmental liabilities are not sites to be reclaimed or remediated. They are past that point in terms of scale, so the approach is to understand how communities can learn to live with toxicity and develop a conscious perspective on their natural environment. These fictionalized tales are a political imagination exercise to claim back agency once the mine closes in 2037. In a second stage, *Toxicity Distributed* fictionalized tales are socialized with locals, engaging them in co-creation instances; the objective is to start a conversation around those future post-extractivist scenarios. After socializing the stories, we expect them to become a folktale that can eventually awaken agency amongst a community often disenfranchised by the mine from their landscapes and livelihoods.

AHORA is a research and design practice lead by Linda Schilling Cuellar (Bachelor Architecture, Federico Santa María Technical University, 2011; MS Architecture and Urban Design, GSAPP, 2018) and Claudio Astudillo Barra (Bachelor Architecture, Federico Santa María Technical University, 2009), based in Santiago, Chile. Formed in 2020, it looks at extraction economies, with particular attention to the ones that take place in Chile, and asks what will happen after it's all gone. To realize possible futures led by local communities, AHORA defends that we must understand the transformed landscapes inherited by the current economic value-ways through the lens of what was and what could be moving towards a post-extractivism scenario.

trunk sample

Sprinkler

2

3

The

and

craft people
e non forest

RIBUTED: POST-EXTRACTIVISM ECONOMIES

TRONS 'R' US
Akwasi Bediako Afrane

Technology is the process of unearthing our reality to understand and simplify our existential lives. The quest for more technological advancement has substituted the love for veins, blood, skin, bones, and organs with that of oil, electric cables, dry cells, and the internet. The spread of the viral prosthetic "must-have" syndrome in relation to electronic gadgets has become indispensable for most humans. As patrons, we amass and abandon more of these gizmos in our quest to supplement our deficiencies. In the process, a black-box process is triggered, as unbeknownst to us we are constantly discarding gizmos that are infused with our genes and consciousness. *TRONS 'R' US* presents TRONS instead of people as a blank slate to provoke conversations about the nature of the "human" and how the human quest for sustenance burdens the environment. By altering rejected gizmos into TRONS and presenting them as anti-machines, they are offered as a prism through which to critique our state of being. The visceral traits of these TRONS form a narrative that will provoke questioning and discussions about our being. The project seeks to present audiences with a paradoxical scene of the world we are leaving behind as the one we aim to or look forward to. This research project also seeks to delve deeper to try to understand and query what propels the human to these technological gadgets, and why.

Akwasi Bediako Afrane (b. 1990) is a Ghanaian artist living and working in Kumasi, Ghana. His works explore the idea of augmentation and extensions between technological gadgets and humans. He works with discarded electronic gadgets which he refers to as "amputees", refashioning and repurposing them into machines and micro-organisms he describes as "TRONS". These TRONS become potential platforms and media for reflection, engagement and interactions. Stripped bare of their familiar housing, the TRONS become mechanical gizmos subsumed with the consciousness of previous owners of these gadgets and himself.

VIRTUAL SANCTUARY FOR FERTILIZING MOURNING
Eliana Otta

ELIANA OTTA (Lima, 1981) is an artist with a Master in Cultural Studies, who inquiries about our relations with nature and precarious labor in neoliberal, extractivist economies, and also gender inequality, intersecting feminism, poetry and politics. She addresses these questions creating spaces for conversation, trust and curiosity through shared intimacy, with projects that involve pedagogical, curatorial and editorial work. Her current PhD project *Lost & Shared: A Laboratory for Collective Mourning*, towards affective and transformative politics, aims to investigate the ways in which art can enable the collectivization of mourning, creating dialogues between theory and affective labor, through collective experiments that connect emotions, critical thinking, body and space.

Virtual Sanctuary for Fertilizing Mourning aims to become a virtual space to commemorate the deaths of Indigenous leaders assassinated in recent years in Peru, when defending their territories from deforestation, mining and other extractivist activities. Working closely with their families and communities, we would create virtual tours of the areas they aimed to protect. Each tour would be different, trying to reflect each leaders' universe, deeply informed by their territory, collective activities, and more-than-human bonds. Oral histories, remembrance, songs, and all kinds of information that the communities find adequate to share with others, will be used to develop a portal into ways of life that are threatened by extinction, but also, to hint toward the invisible, magical, and affectionate threads sustaining them.

Working with the Driving the Human partner institutions, we would develop an immersive way to offer such tours online, so that remembering the deceased can inform the rich worlds to which they belonged. Hopefully, providing access to such particular universes will make clearer the importance of the battles happening daily in the world, under the most unfair and precarious circumstances. As a Peruvian artist living in Europe, I encounter here approaches to what is called nature or ecology still insufficient to the urgency of contemporary planetary challenges. Not only usually anthropo-Eurocentric but mostly apparently unaware that on other continents the ongoing struggles regarding such issues are literally matters of life and death. The peoples that until now defend life as a whole, understanding humans as a tiny part of it, face daily apocalypses. While this continent begins to consider "end of the world" imaginaries due to global warming and Covid-19, in others, peoples have faced their worlds ending for centuries, while defending their lives and the deep webs of relationality that make them possible. In a period of crisis in civilization, I believe these are the peoples we must turn our heads to, paying attention to their knowledges, listening to their claims, learning from their practices, following their dreams, and honoring their deaths. This project is in an initial phase: important contact has been established with the Asháninka community Nuevo Amanecer Hawai in central Peru, where the leaders Mauro Pío and Gonzalo Pío, father and son, were murdered in 2013 and 2020, respectively. This is where these images come from. They are shared responding to the community's request of reaching the widest possible audience.

James Taylor-Foster and Matylda Krzykowski hosting the festival's broadcast, October 2021

How can we create conditions for mentoring and development that foster genuine inquiry? How do we spread the personal and economic risks of such inquiries?

I first met Freo Majer in 2018, at the time of the 4th Istanbul Design Biennial, *A School of Schools*. On the closing weekend of the biennial, we hosted one of the mentoring events of Housing the Human, a large-scale collaborative research program focused on the future of dwelling, which was initiated by Forecast to develop future-oriented scenarios for housing around the world. ① The event brought together participants, mentors, experts, and the general public to experiment with ideas, gather feedback, and push diverse concepts towards the next, more ambitious stage of their development. Through its focus on the exchange of knowledge and experiences, the Housing the Human project fully resonated with the ethos of *A School of Schools*.

Over the course of its six weeks, the biennial was fully articulated around the idea of knowledge exchange. *A School of Schools* took place on the eve of the centennial of influential design school Bauhaus, and our starting point was a questioning of design education and pedagogy. Design—a discipline born out of the impulses associated with the industrial revolution, with less than two centuries of history—has over the course of the last decades started to radically transform itself in order to encompass the major societal transformations of our time, becoming a discipline that bridges silos and mediates between different fields of knowledge, from the arts to sciences. Design education, however, has mostly stayed the same, emulating the Bauhaus workshop model across the world, from Germany to the US and from Brazil to China. Even when considering so-called "radical" pedagogical design initiatives that stretched both the boundaries of design and of education, such as the post-war American Black Mountain College's experiments in art ② or the 1970s Italian Global Tools' counter-school system of workshops, their utopian visions for nature, society, and mankind as a whole proved influential for those who took part, but fizzled out once their (precarious) survival became more important than the visions they sought to put forward.

Knowing this, *A School of Schools* took as a starting point an attitude of critical reflection towards the past and present of design education, combining it with an appreciation of the singular contexts and spaces in which it happens. ③ We sought to transcend the traditional spaces

① Housing the Human ran from 2018 to 2019. Initiated by Forecast, it was an interdisciplinary collaboration of five European institutions and organizations, aiming to develop methods for a "practical futurology", and it was a direct precursor to Driving the Human. See https://housingthehuman.com/

② On the College's methodology, Josef Albers said: 'We do not always create "works of art," but rather experiments; it is not our intention to fill museums: we are gathering experience'.

③ For more on this expanded discussion on design education, see *Design as Learning: A School of Schools Reader* (Amsterdam: Valiz, 2018), the accompanying publication to *A School of Schools*.

of design education and explored design practices that have learning at their core, putting them at the center of the event. In this way, we framed learning as a permanent, embodied attitude, one that transcends the formal, spatial boundaries of the school, and overflows into the world and life itself. Essential to this effort were the multiple voices and perspectives brought together under the umbrella of the biennial. We invited a new generation of scholars, thinkers, and practitioners—all of whom employ learning as a fundamental aspect of their practice—to contribute, their research and work illuminating emerging directions in today's expanded notion of design, while simultaneously pointing to other geographies, other perspectives, and other priorities for the field and for design education.

The ways in which they contributed to the overall biennial ranged from experimental residencies that occupied the exhibition spaces for weeks and left traces of their passing; engaging local audiences in exercises in public reading and broadcasting of the city around us; mapping the maritime traffic of the Bosphorus canal to create a larger reflection on global transport routes and their impact on local realities; growing bio-materials to create a platform inspired by the West African tradition of *palaver* to exchange knowledge on the ingredients we use to nourish ourselves today; and many more formats, projects, and moments of exchange. ④ The variety of these contributions and the multiplicity of their outcomes transcended a mere disciplinary field, and engaged with themes that defined the contemporary, opening up new visions for, beyond learning, how to engage with the present.

④ The projects listed in this paragraph correspond, respectively, to The University of the Underground; dpr-barcelona with Floating University; Studio Folder; and Mae-Ling Lokko.

Looking back, the impulse to open up new ways of engaging with the present is one that has continuously surfaced in my practice, in several roles and responsibilities. From a pedagogical point of view, at the Design Academy Eindhoven, where I headed the Social Design department and its Masters program for a decade, or from a curatorial standpoint at Z33—House for Contemporary Art, an institution I founded and art directed from 2001–2019. If these positions allowed for a longer-term development of such an impulse, other projects, such as *A School of Schools,* presented other angles from which to explore it. Beyond the Istanbul example, *BIO 50,* the 2014 Biennial of Design in Ljubljana, Slovenia, was a fertile ground to create a laboratory for contemporary design, engaging with contemporary matters of concern such as housing, mobility, food, and water. In the midst of political, economic, and environmental transformation, the biennial postulated that design needs to transcend an existence for its own sake, and reveal its relevance and meaning as part of everyday life. In this way, the designer must engage in a new role, not as an all-powerful creator, but as part of a collaborative ecosystem combining varied profiles, expertise, and backgrounds. Such a shift implies that "not the world of design, but the design of the world should be at stake, an enterprise that starts at the core of everyday life."⑤

In *BIO 50*, Ljubljana became the context and starting point for all the work that was generated during the biennial, allowing a specificity to all the generated works that enriched the outcomes immensely. This specificity and closeness to one single territory was also one of the starting points to Atelier Luma, a project that took off in 2017 and continues to this day. As its artistic director, I have led Atelier Luma to become a think tank, a production workshop and also a learning network—orbiting around the idea of an undisciplined laboratory. Nested in the campus of the Luma Arles arts foundation, Atelier Luma uses the city of Arles, in the south of France, and its immediate surroundings, as a fertile ground offering local resources, materials, and talent, and connects with these to drive innovation across disciplines and through material outputs. The concrete goal of the project is to develop biomaterials that can be used as building blocks for new societal models.

The starting point in Atelier Luma's efforts manifested as a large-scale research process that aimed to map the resources, know-how, and expertise already present in the region. Additionally, designers from various backgrounds were invited to join these explorations and interact with local agents, searching for potential collaborations and intersections. The initial results, shown in 2017, showcased the potential of local agricultural waste, such as rice and sunflower leftovers, and demonstrated the potential of traditionally neglected resources from the region, such as endemic algae species and invasive plant cultures. Subsequently, these research efforts continued, engaging not only the local knowledge and the design perspective, but also scientific laboratories and research institutes, creating bridges between industry, science, culture, and the territory. Ultimately, Atelier Luma's approach extends from the material outputs of its research to the weaving of a social space, becoming a platform where we adopt an attitude of wonder, openness, and curiosity. All those who participate are experts, and we blend fields of knowledge to discover new findings and possibilities.

All these projects showcase a blueprint for collaboration, friction, and exchange between disciplines. Similarly, they display a willingness to cross borders, and an intention to create spaces of learning beyond traditional arenas and timelines. All these are characteristics that have become meaningful for what became Driving the Human, and informed the earliest conversations about the project and its intentions. The initial

⑤ Jan Boelen, "Testing the Everyday," in *Designing Everyday Life*, ed. Jan Boelen and Vera Sacchetti (Zurich: Park Books, 2014), 15.

ideas situated eco-social renewal, as an overall theme for intervention, in what Bruno Latour has defined as the *Critical Zones*—the few kilometers above and below the surface of the Earth that are critical for human survival on the planet. Focusing on these areas allowed the project to expand conceptually, and we proceeded to launch a debate on the themes currently defining our existence—from the human to non-human, from existence to co-existence, from digital to analog. The overall desire was to expand the era of binaries in which we find ourselves, and through new insights gather the necessary resources to stimulate the creation of visions for planetary coexistence.

In creating new ways of collaborating within the Critical Zones, we also operated under the Latourian belief that "we might be more connected to each other by our worries, our matters of concern, the issues we care for, than by any other set of values, opinions, attitudes or principles."⑥ In this connection, the network that was to be generated throughout the three years of Driving the Human effectively creates what sociologist Michael Kaethler has defined as a creative community of practice.⑦ The ambiguous, fluid formation of a community of practice has been defined elsewhere by educational theorist Étienne Wenger:

"Communities of practice are about content—about learning as a living experience of negotiating meaning—not about form. In this sense, they cannot be legislated into existence or defined by decree. They can be recognized, supported, encouraged, and nurtured, but they are not reified, designable units. Practice itself is not amenable to design. In other words, one can articulate patterns or define procedures, but neither the patterns nor the procedures produce the practice as it unfolds... Learning cannot be designed: it can only be designed for—that is, facilitated or frustrated."⑧

Creative communities of practice live beyond the traditional spaces of learning, evolving and occupying other kinds of realms. In the spaces of higher education, issues of accreditation at the Bachelor and Masters level clash with a progressive, transversal bureaucratization at all levels of the educational institution. Educator Peter Lang notes how "European university systems are now beginning to tightly control the cost-effectiveness of education," setting limits on "open-ended, undefined research projects."⑨ Institutes, with their traditional siloing of knowledge, are fundamentally contrary to an impulse of connection and transdisciplinarity. The themes at the heart of Driving the Human impact us all, and our everyday lives; addressing them must, therefore, take place in a space where diverse disciplines and approaches can come together;

⑥ Bruno Latour, "Why Has Critique Run Out of Steam? From Matters of Fact to Matters of Concern," in *Critical Inquiry* 30, (Chicago: The University of Chicago Press, 2003), 225–248.

⑦ Michael Kaethler, "Curating creative communities of practice: the role of ambiguity," in *Journal of Organization Design* 8, 10 (2019), https://doi.org/10.1186/s41469-019-0051-z

⑧ See Étienne Wenger, *Communities of practice: learning, meaning, and identity* (Cambridge: Cambridge University Press, 2019).

⑨ Peter Lang, "Provocation on design education's search for a new language," in *Design as Learning: A School of Schools Reader*, (Amsterdam: Valiz, 2018), 71

where timelines are generous so that all those participating can find ways to understand and learn from each other; and risk—and the openness that it entails—is not just an exception, but the norm. In essence, these are loose guidelines in creating conditions for uncertainty—and in the friction between that of which we are not certain of, new visions and ideas can be generated.

An additional and essential factor in these processes is ambiguity. When used as a guiding condition, ambiguity entails embracing risk, towards what Michael Kaethler calls "effectual collaboration and commitment through shared learning and practice." Ambiguity can accelerate the group dynamics in collaborations, affecting "group formation, exchange and co-production." [10] Guided by ambiguity, shared learning and practice in an experimental setting can lead to dissonance, chaos and confusion, which nevertheless are essential elements of any creative process. This, combined with a constant accompaniment and close-up mentorship, allowed for the creation of the seven prototypes for eco-social renewal that were the ultimate goal of the Driving the Human initiative. With curiosity and humbleness as driving forces, Driving the Human tested concepts and prototypes, brought diverse individuals together around the same matters of concern, and created a fertile ground on which innovation and blueprints for future coexistence can happen.

[10] Kaethler, "Curating creative communities of practice: the role of ambiguity."

On the Realities of Simulation

Kim Albrecht, Principal researcher at metaLAB at Harvard University, Director of metaLAB at FU Berlin

In October of 2021, I visited the Driving the Human pre-selection of 21 prototypes. Now, over one year later, on the last weekend of November 2022, I stand in front of Berlin's silent green Kulturquartier intrigued to see how the final seven prototypes evolved. This is the moment when three years of collaboration, research, and experimentation is culminated in a three-day festival. The historical dimension of Berlin's silent green Kulturquartier cannot be overlooked in the context of the festival: between 1909 and 1910 the space opened as the first crematorium of Berlin, with ecclesiastical resistance from the Catholic Church. The crematorium was established because of the uprising of the *freethought* movement. Freethought is an epistemological frame of reference questioning authority, tradition, and dogma and is instead based on the foundations of logic, reason, and empirical observation. Writers and philosophers such as John Locke, Gottfried Wilhelm Leibniz, Bertrand Russell, and Gotthold Ephraim Lessing are related to the movement. It still exists today as societies around the world but its most notable period of activity was the mid-19th century. The establishment of cremation as a legitimate form of burial was one of the declared goals of the freethinkers. In this sense, the halls in which the festival embedded itself are immersed in a historical battle for rationality. Over a century after the creation of the site through the freethought movement, the fight is not against the Catholic Church but rather grappling with the question of what drives humankind. What are the aspects and dimensions of life on Earth that might be largely overlooked but simultaneously make our existence possible in the first place?

The philosophical quest for the motives of reality is an ancient one, with a prominent example dating back almost 2,400 years, namely Plato's *Allegory of the Cave*. Within Plato's Cave, humanity only observes the shadows of reality projected onto a wall. Actuality is hiding outside, but humans are chained in the darkness to a wall and are only capable of observing the silhouette of the real.

A contemporary re-imagination of the allegory comes from the Wachowskis in the form of the 1999 movie *The Matrix*. Within the movie, two realities are clearly distinguished from one another: the modeled, simulated reality called "Matrix" and actual reality. The motion picture uses a simple cinematographic trick to distinguish the two worlds from one another. The simulation, being inside the "Matrix", is depicted in desaturated green tones; the "Real World" is depicted in tones of blue.

Based on this color scheme, the viewer always knows which reality is being shown in the movie.

The main hall of the Driving the Human festival is located underground, and entering this contemporary cave-like space is an aesthetic experience in itself. I walk down a wide tunnel entrance large enough to drive a truck through. Upon descending into the venue, the color scheme of *The Matrix* comes back to me—a shift in color to designate the world of simulation. Here, at silent green, the entire underground entrance is guided by moving azure blue lights, drawing visitors in. The green tone dedicated to the virtual from the Wachowskis is neglected. Once the basement is reached, the blue is accompanied by a red and the two blend into various shades of purple. The majority of the installations are located in this multicolored, thousand-square meter basement location named "Betonhalle", meaning "concrete hall", once the processing facility for the crematorium. Daylight is absent in the space so that the blue, red, and purple lights fully shape the atmosphere of the space. One could argue that the space draws similarities to Plato's Cave as, here too, the actual world is replaced by a synthetic human-made and nature-disregarded underground. At first sight, the mode in which several of the prototypes at the core of the Festival are realized might support such an argument.

The first project I notice when I enter is Xiaoyu (Iris) Qu's 曲晓宇 work *Do AIs Dream of Climate Chaos: Symbiotic AI*. The fundamental question Qu asks is: "Given sufficient data, how would an AI compute its existence?" In other words: to what degree might computational systems in the future be able to reflect themselves and their embedment in reality? To some extent, the question is one of bodily experience in technology. As human beings, our experience of the world is facilitated through our bodies, even though we are constantly redesigning our encounter with the world through new sets of prostheses, from the invention of bags to collect berries to the latest smartphone. While the latest developments in machine learning might, at first sight, outsmart human capabilities, you can dump the 'smartest' server farm into a pond, and it would just sink to the bottom while by contrast, any rabbit or cricket, would at least fight for their life to get out of the water. The distinction between the self and the environment is the first distinction drawn by life forms, and it is not clear if even the smartest computational symbol-manipulating systems have any sense of such an experience. This wide gap is what Qu investigates. Apart from the initial question, I was intrigued by the aesthetic experience of the exhibition: you enter a room filled with large-scale, high-resolution projections on three walls. The projections show computer simulations of an ecosystem, one including a server farm surrounded by plants and animals. At times the mimicked camera attaches to a simulated animal so the viewer follows that specific perspective. The rendered server farm is represented as an architectural block central to the surrounding natural order. While everything seems in flux in the simulation, the data center is immobile. The aesthetic experience Qu uses to investigate the question of machinic self-reflection is a simulated one. The hardware of the computation is hidden away to embed the visitor in a Holodeck experience of simulated natural-computational co-existence.

Moving on from Qu's work, I arrive at a platform overlooking a large section of the Betonhalle. A wide staircase leads down to the other projects and the next set of computer-generated simulations. *The Backpack of Wings: Modern Mythology* by Hyeseon Jeong and Seongmin Yuk investigates the speculative futures of wild animals, scientific investigations, and spiritual myths. The first contact with the project comes through a cinematic experience detailing the story of the bird Loki in a fictional future world that uses birds as sensors for disaster predictions. And again, similar to the first project, the story is told through computer-generated imagery and glossy rendered three-dimensional simulations. The project extends into a second space, blurring near future speculation and actualities. A bird-tracking device is displayed in between a set of computers, visualizing on an interactive map the tracked geolocation of one actual bird along its migratory path. The fictional, speculative simulation begins drawing into reality; within the project, actualities and simulation are in confluence.

Right next to *The Backpack of Wings* is another project with intense usage of computer-generated imagery. *Monsters and Ghosts of the Far North* by Andra Pop-Jurj and Lena Geerts Danau re-imagines the cartography of the North Pole region and its scientifically modeled prediction as an interactive multiplayer experience. While visiting the exhibition, I experienced global warming as a methanobacteria, a codfish, and a container ship. For me, the essence of the project is a re-imagination of scientific data. Pop-Jurj and Geerts Danau question the aesthetic representation of data outside scientific contexts; rather than flat, two-dimensional presentations of maps and graphs, the data is manifested as a simulated experience. While the two previous projects used simulations for speculation, *Monsters and Ghosts of the Far North* has a different underlying principle as scientific climate models themselves are simulations of past data extrapolated into the future through computational methods. So, what I am experiencing as I virtually swim through the waters of the

Arctic Ocean as a codfish is a nested, layered set of simulations. A set of ice cores and sensory devices, among many other methods, leads scientists to capture historical datasets of our climate. These datasets are collected, processed, cleaned, analyzed, modeled, and visualized. This process is one of abstraction from the human actualities in the Arctic to data and its modeled futures. Simultaneously, it is a crawl toward a reality beyond the human. The question might be reversed at this point, from what is driving the human to what are we driving? *Monsters and Ghosts of the Far North* adds another layer within this by alternating the mode in which data is experienced as a visualization beyond mapping.

The fourth project relevant to the idea of simulation is situated at the other end of the Betonhalle. At first sight *Human-Bacteria Interfaces* by Anne-Sofie Belling, Bea Delgado Corrales, Romy Kaiser, and Paula Nerlich investigates topics far from simulative. The team researched how microbes respond to signals from their environments and how to create modes of interaction between the microbial and the human. What fascinated me most was the experience of the installation. At first sight, the installation consists of a supermarket transport trolley presenting various informational materials and Erlenmeyer flasks containing what looks like kombucha SCOBY. Behind the trolley, an introduction video to the project is projected onto a curtain. The setup and the content of the project are scientific in tone, bound to facts, and embedded in our current moment. What is not evident at first sight is that the curtain acts as a barrier between actualities and imagination: once stepping through the beam of projected light and moving behind, a rabbit hole emerges. A corridor with three sections appears and the deeper I go into the experience of *Human-Bacteria Interfaces*, the further the project detaches from reality and moves into realms of speculative fiction. At the end of the corridor, a cinematic experience depicts a future vision of human-bacteria interactions.

This last experience illustrates well the change in perspective when it comes to imaginations of simulations. In *The Matrix*, taking a pill is the metaphorical barrier between staying in the simulation or moving into the real. Within my brief introduction to these four Driving the Human projects, simulation is not contrasted against reality. Rather, it is a speculative, futuristic extension to reality. It is not something we have to escape to encounter reality, but presents itself as a stylistic device to overcome our current state and imagine alternatives. *The Backpack of Wings*, *Do AIs Dream of Climate Chaos*, and *Human-Bacteria Interfaces* all use simulation as speculation. The simulated becomes a device to move beyond actualities. *Monsters and Ghosts of the Far North* uses simulation as intensification. An underlying narrative of the three-year research initiative into eco-social renewal, into the question of what is driving the human, is answered through simulation. Technology is not imagined as a problem, but rather as a pathway towards relocating the human into alternative perspectives. The goal of the initiative was to create tools that enable new ways of foreseeing and inhabiting the world—simulation becomes a principle to envision this new inhabiting.

The distinction between simulation and reality is not how humans create meaning in the 21st century. These projects, as well as the festival at large, are prime examples of the collapse between the two. We are not captured in *The Matrix*, waiting for the reality pill—rather, we are designing simulations to comprehend the realities we exsist within and generate. We are not chained to the wall of Plato's Cave and forced to observe shadows. Rather, we move into the cave willingly as the shadows might tell us something about what reality might be. Simulation and reality are not dichotomous, but intricate interactions of the realities we embed ourselves in.

Within this alternative perspective, the real is a self-referential construction of techno-social distinctions. The festival's conception and articulation through the developed projects are prime examples of the foldedness of the world. Scientific climate modeling, render engines, and data visualization have a common mode of reflection upon reality. We only know about climate collapse through the technological super-structures that simultaneously cause it. Sensor- and sense-making are distinct operations of cause and effect which reintroduce themselves within themselves. Future climate models reflect back onto reality and give us the foresight of changing this predicted future into other futures. Reality and simulation are tightly interwoven entities. Simulations are modes of experiencing reality, not an opposed distinction from reality.

But all of this is written in doubt: is the vision of simulated realities and reality simulation, of the world as data, and data as glossy high-resolution, three-dimensional renderings the path forward? Are simulations the right tool to overcome climate collapse? Will descent into a cave lead to the freethought we are aspiring towards? Walking through the Betonhalle, the technological became an all-encompassing entity. Within all these screens, cables, computers, virtual reality glasses, and projections I felt small. The distinction of the natural was distant, while the technological stack took over. Both the terms of the festival "driving" and "human" predefine this perspective. The verb driving is connected to technological inventions, cars, motors, and fuel and as such, is related to the climate crisis. Furthermore, most of the projects move towards non-human perspectives through technology, while the title of the event places the human so centrally. From my perspective, for the future, rather than asking what is "driving the human" I would love to know what is "guiding the river", "containing the ocean", or "shepherding the cosmos."

Akwasi Bediako Afrane and Xiaoyu (Iris) Qu曲晓宇 at the Driving the Human festival, November 2022

7 PROTOTYPES

DRIVING THE HUMAN

MONSTERS AND GHOSTS
OF THE FAR NORTH
alternaa
(Andra Pop-Jurj and Lena Geerts Danau)

Monsters and Ghosts of the Far North searches for an alternative cartography through which we can rethink relationships across species in the Arctic region and beyond.

Points of departure for this project are some of the spatial manifestations of the social, economic, and geopolitical conflicts in the Arctic region caused by environmental degradation. The Arctic is a site of intense geopolitical and infrastructural intrigue, with incompatible and interlocking border claims rooted in colonial and cartographic history. The scientific and cartographic artifacts encountered throughout our research have proven to be flat and exclusive in essence, and they often fail to capture the dynamic nature of the Arctic. Through this project, we question the division of our world and the meaning of current rigid borderlines within distorted, often Eurocentric cartographic projections.

The project employs a game engine to inquire into modes of multispecies cohabitation and the negotiation of space following the development of extractive industries in the region. As an interactive multiplayer experience, the embodiment of various non-human characters seeks to challenge our current anthropocentric perception. Wildlife tracking data and environmental projections feed into the design of this digital environment and serve as inter-scalar vehicles and trans-temporal narrative devices that tell the story of global entanglements. Consequently, one can come to feel endangered—an overwhelming feeling that emerges from an immersive narrative, going beyond the agendas of the five Arctic states and their overlapping territorial claims.

Maps by alternaa detailing the behavior, routes, and habitats of diverse elements in the Arctic landscape

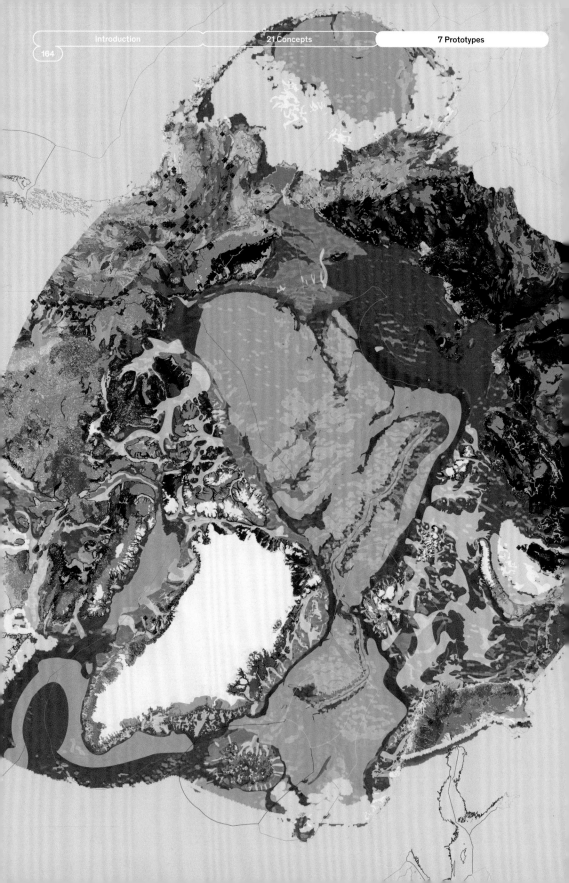

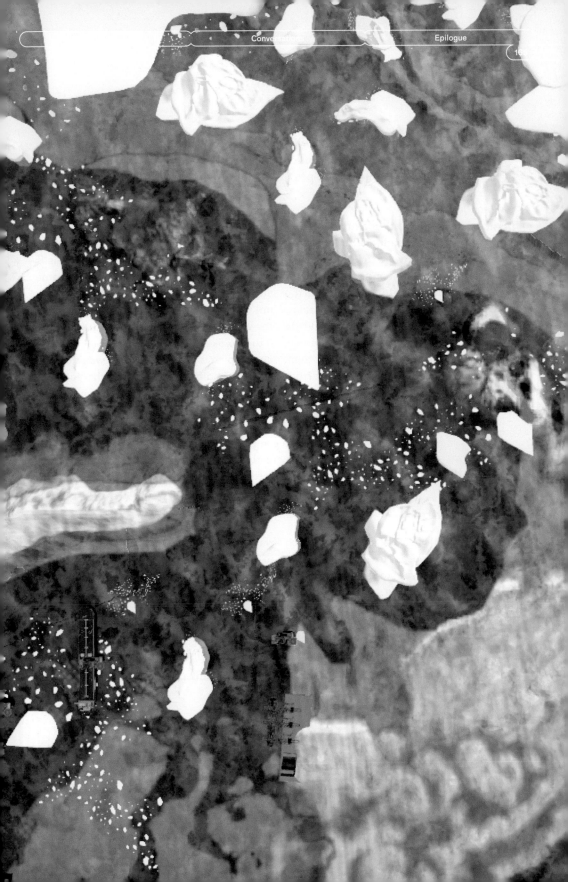

alternaa in Conversation
with Yuri Tuma

YURI TUMA

I'm curious about thinking of video games as an art form. Why do you think creating video games or generative artwork differs from other modes of creative production?

ANDRA POP-JURJ

I'm glad you asked that, because actually, we're architects by training. The transition from 3D modeling software to a game engine isn't really that large. As soon as you know how to 3D model and animate things, that's the next obvious step. But also, it made us realize that it is a good way of trying to communicate something. Of course, films work just as well, but if there's a bit of agency required, I think people tend to focus more, at least from what we've witnessed with the installation.

The game developers that we collaborated with and everyone who plays games and is a real hardcore programmer sees that this is an experimental approach to using a game engine. This has been part of the battle, how not to make it so gamified, how to fight for the visuals that we wanted. Why do you want it to look like that? Why do you want all these overlapping layers? Why do you want to color the terrain differently for each character? In a way, I guess it's our take on video games.

YT   It's interesting, this question of how much of a game is a game because I also think games are an opportunity to create fiction and narratives. Do you feel like you're creating narrative or fiction? How do you understand world-building and how do you apply scientific data, artistic practice, and gaming in this world making?

AP-J   It took us so long to translate this research into a narrative because you want to say everything, but you don't want to say it in the same dry, academic tone. There's a world-building element to it in that we interpret this data in a

way that is more accessible. Because you have to understand these topics a hundred years in the future, and, of course, we can't predict and tell how it's going to be. It's a speculation. It's a version of what could be.

YT   One of the things I loved about your process was thinking through characters. What was the process of deciding which character you wanted to explore and how many perspectives you decided to choose?

LENA GEERTS DANAU

We have six different characters and each character is positioned along the physical vertical

axis. We have characters underground, like the methanobacteria. We have a character which is the ice itself, but we also have a character on the land, a caribou, a character flying in the air, the bird. Every single character is from a specific territory. They are also in a specific territory within the Arctic. The caribou is positioned in Alaska, because in Alaska, there is gas extraction and the caribou's territory is endangered by it and restricted by extraction activities and pipelines. Each character has a specific site, and also specific data to which it is related to.

AP-J   There's always a bit of an ethical question. How can you assume how a different being sees? You're not them, but at the same time, it's an exercise of unlearning your own perspective. It would be interesting to hear more from you as well. How do you create? How do you set the framework for it? Are there any ethical considerations? How does it start? How does it work?

YT   Well, I'm very much analog. No digital type of embodiment. But the way I work is through my own body and through a collective creation. I invite people to workshops, for example, and try to create performative exercises in which we can communicate through embodying or imagining how it would be like to communicate without words. The ethical question is a difficult one, because we have to assume the impossibility of inhabiting another being's perspective, but the fact that it's impossible doesn't mean we should not explore it because I think there's valid information in embodiment exercises. Also, to create kinship, to create empathy, or to create understanding of different ways of inhabiting the planet must be done with care, so as to not colonize one's experience. In Western science, we believe animals only communicate for perhaps three things specifically: eating, mating, and defense. I think it's that this exercise of embodiment is amplifying; perhaps they do other things. I want to hear from you as well: what is the importance of inviting someone to become someone else?

AP-J   It's an unlearning experience and it's about thinking outside of what you're used to. Of course, we tried as much as possible to base these perspectives on the physiology of animal eyes in order to communicate something educational in a way as well. If you really play all the characters for example, you notice the different speeds that they're moving at. You notice looking down on the ground or flying. What a superpower. The game was an exercise of building these perspectives. For instance, the methanogens: they're said to be attracted to light sources, but of course, they are microscopic and what's a light source for them? There's always an element of interpretation and imagination as a starting point.

YT   I want to talk about sonic and visual composition. Does sound come after the visuals?

LGD   Sound was from the beginning present— especially if you look at the characteristics of each character as they also have a range in which they hear things. That defines the loudness or the stillness and the sound that is related. In the third-person perspective, the game has more sound than an individual would perceive. For every single character, this combination of the visual and the auditory was very important.

YT   Another thing that is super interesting: you have this one-hundred years of data turning into 10 minutes. How can you imagine time, in particular, deep time?

AP-J   We were hoping initially to be able to show the different timelines that the characters experience. The Arctic tern might live for 30, 40 years, whereas a methanogen lives for maybe 24 hours. But mechanically and technically it was hard to work with so many different timelines because it's a multiplayer setup. They had to be in sync and it had to be the same linear timeline, unfortunately. But last year, we experimented with this, that you could pass from one timeline to the other. The point was to try and move away from this linear, Western notion of time, of course. But here, it's also kind of a play on how a hundred years might not necessarily be that much, given our time on earth, and our role within its timeline. We're just a fraction of earth's life. It's not really about us.

Views of alternaa's installation at the Driving the Human festival, Berlin, November 2022

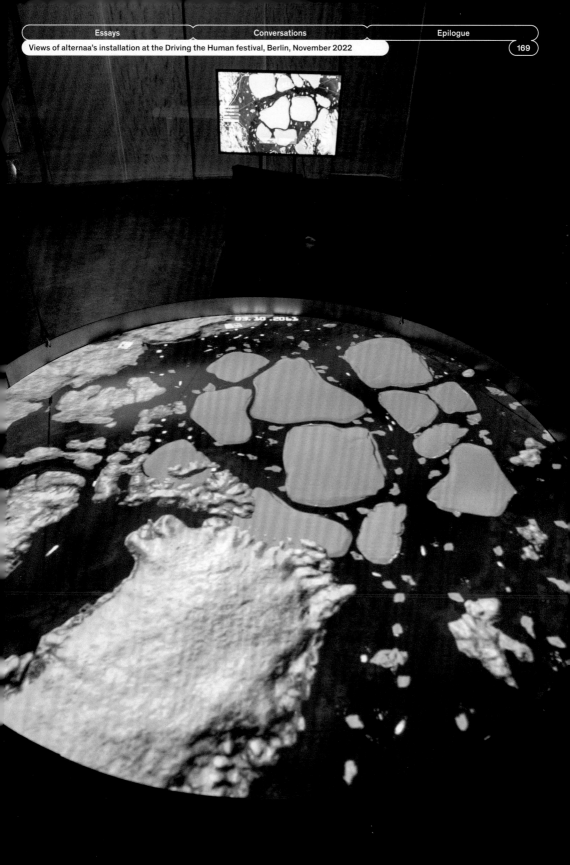

Traveling North: The Making of Monsters and Ghosts of the Far North

Aisha Altenhofen

The Fagradalsfjall volcano erupting

"The colors of the lens you're looking through change from dark blue up until fully red, meaning the temperature is rising. The depth of your eyesight differs going from very clear up until blurry, representing the increasing carbon levels." This blurred vision is tied to the perception of an Arctic ice island, within the game by alternaa (Andra Pop-Jurj and Lena Geerts Danau). *Monsters and Ghosts of the Far North* speculates upon the mapping of a landscape within the Arctic Ocean from perspectives that are not human.

Imagine yourself as an ice island, moving 10 meters a year or only perceiving sounds ranging from 1-10 kHz. The mapping in *Monsters and Ghosts of the Far North* is focused on the agents inhabiting the landscape, not the national borders drawn from bird's-eye view. Along the vertical axis, it allows you to situate yourself within seven species: an Arctic cod (sea level), a container ship (above sea level), a reindeer (land), the ice itself, a methanobacteria (underneath the surface), and an Arctic tern (air). Each offers a world along the axis with various velocities, life spans, and embodiments.

In late summer 2022, alternaa, Hyeseon Jeong, and Seongmin Yuk visited Iceland. The creators of *Monsters and Ghosts of the Far North* and *The Backpack of Wings: Modern Mythology* met local artists and practitioners, visited the unique landscapes of the Arctic, and hosted two workshops at the Nordic House in Reykjavik.

Storytelling and cartographies are two of the tools the artist duos use and question through their work. Through storytelling and poetic immersion, they hope to create relations to often abstract datasets, creating emotional connections to this shifting region.

alternaa highlighted that "one of the main questions that seemed to drive the various cartographies was the decision of what to represent and what not to, particularly when speaking about human impact on the environment and the man-made." The discussions extend their reflections within the game and question how cartography shapes our perception of a landscape. The two artists reshaped the workshop format into a webinar for the APECS (Association of Polar Early Career Scientists), and were invited by Christian Schulze (Director of International Relations and Research at Iceland's Agricultural University) to return to Iceland to hold another workshop at the EnChill MA program. The workshop also filled them with new input to return to their work on the video game prototype, which was showcased at the Driving the Human festival.

Workshop by alternaa at the Nordic House, Reykjavik

Walking through the Icelandic landscape in preparation for the workshop

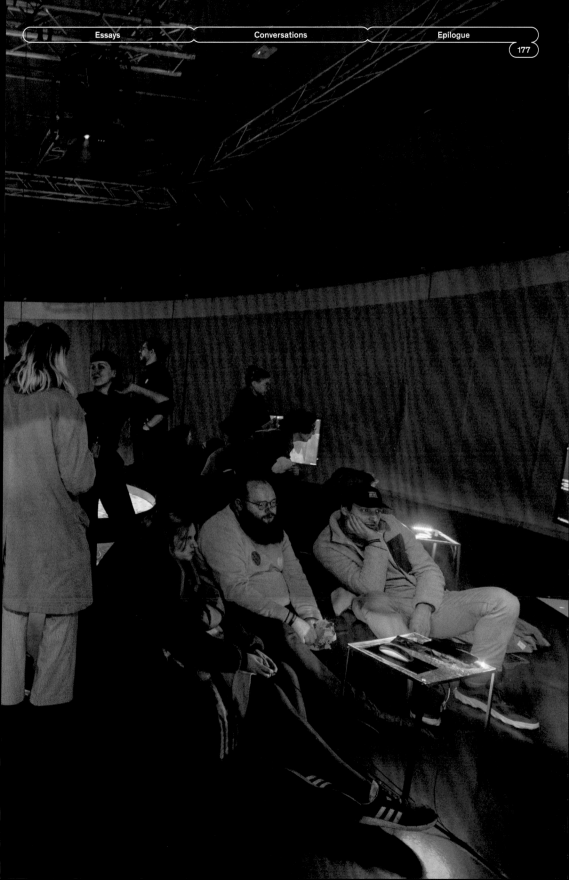

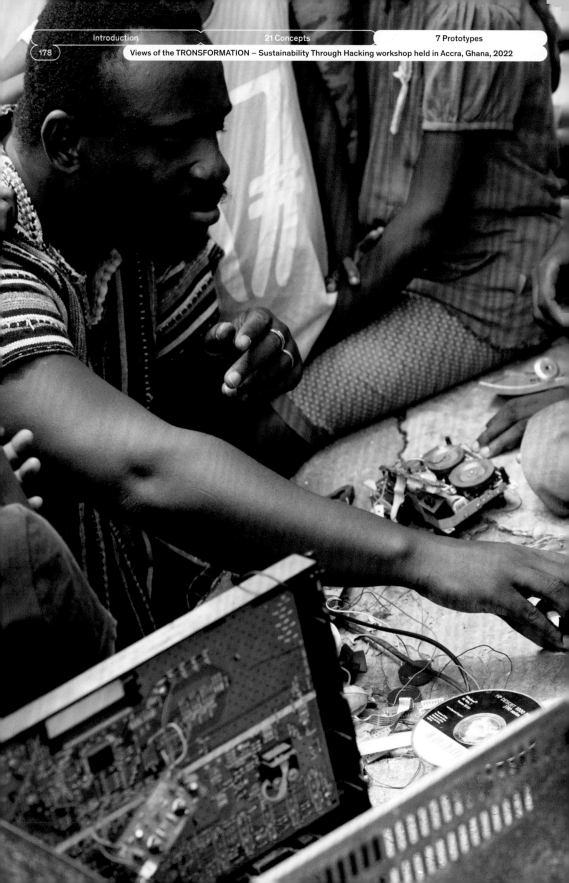

TRONS 'R' US
Akwasi Bediako Afrane

A project that seeks to investigate and explore the relationship between humans, technology, and our environment.

Technological products are undoubtedly prosthetic extensions of human faculties. The accelerated production of these devices can be attributed to the fact that these technological contraptions are an attempt to perfect the human, thus bringing the human to a "god-like" state. Yet there is a paradox with technology, as it also serves to constrict the human environment. Even with its greatest promise of "salvation", technology possesses a diabolical enhancement, like a double-edged sword supplementing the human environment while at the same time subtracting from it.

TRONS 'R' US reflects on this idea of extensions while also exploring the many facets of the lifecycle of technological consumer gadgets from their inception to their "conclusion". It elaborates on the need to usher society into a state of "openness" with regard to consumer electronic gadgets and their effect on the environment. *TRONS 'R' US* presents an installation of TRONS, along with a short documentary that briefly touches on the lifecycle of consumer electronics as a way of stimulating critical discussion about the holistic picture and invisible processes behind the existence of these devices.

This project also aims to investigate the current "invisible prosthetic problem" by presenting hacking as a means to a sustainable future. This aforementioned problem emerges when these prosthetic extensions are not experienced and catered for as such which becomes heightened due to an alienation in the Marxist sense. This allows those who are able to control the technology of these prosthetic extensions to effectively dominate our society.

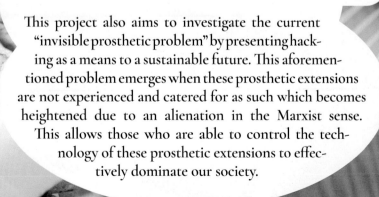

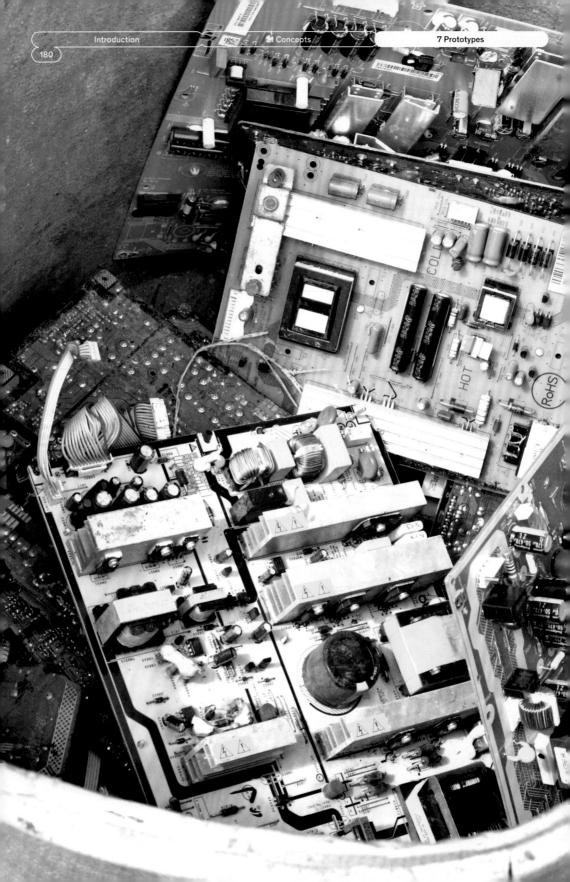

Views of Akwasi Bediako Afrane's installation at the Driving the Human festival, Berlin, November 2022

Akwasi Bediako Afrane
in Conversation with Freo Majer

FREO MAJER

Can you introduce yourself and talk about how you started this project? Your TRONS, as you call them, have been developing over many years already.

AKWASI BEDIAKO AFRANE

I'm an artist from Ghana, and I started my practice in 2015 when I began working with these electronic devices, a kind of callback to my interest in these devices when I was a child. I remember I used to mess around with my dad's electronics, and then they would get damaged and we would have this kind of quarrel between father and son. While playing around or fidgeting with them, I started looking really into what these devices mean to people and the community as a whole. Then this idea of prosthesis emerged. I realized these devices were augmented parts of people. If you take a camera, it can represent maybe an eye or be extended as a brain to capture moments and store them for future reference.

FM What is the difference between this kind of process that you have started versus recycling?

ABA My work has for some time now been viewed by many as a recycling process. I strongly try to avoid this because I choose a product that I want to work with or a product that I want to consume for a specific purpose. The idea is to use this product and try to provoke conversations surrounding the idea of prosthesis and the idea of our consumer nature. I actually use products that work and then tear them apart, and then I recompose them into forms using various parts. This is in contrast to the idea of recycling where people take dead components and then they try to breed new life into them.

FM I think that is an interesting point. Your work is an organism, a being, maybe with a personality. Can you describe your notion of life?

ABA It starts with the core of each electronic device, a kind of augmented aspect of a person. When we pair with them or when we use them, we form a kind of bond or relation with them where we are able to transmit our life essence through data or information, which becomes a source of life for them. So when we stop using them and they become secondhand, they still hold onto some of these histories or, let's say, essences of what we shared with them.

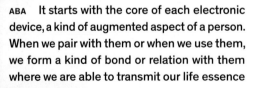

FM I think it's quite stunning that, from the very first moment of the opening night, there were queues at your installation. When people sit down, they cause this electronic impulse that moves something or ignites an electronic process or whatever happens in this mysterious being of the TRON.

Akwasi Bediako Afrane
in Conversation with Freo Majer

FREO MAJER

Can you introduce yourself and talk about how you started this project? Your TRONS, as you call them, have been developing over many years already.

AKWASI BEDIAKO AFRANE

I'm an artist from Ghana, and I started my practice in 2015 when I began working with these electronic devices, a kind of callback to my interest in these devices when I was a child. I remember I used to mess around with my dad's electronics, and then they would get damaged and we would have this kind of quarrel between father and son. While playing around or fidgeting with them, I started looking really into what these devices mean to people and the community as a whole. Then this idea of prosthesis emerged. I realized these devices were augmented parts of people. If you take a camera, it can represent maybe an eye or be extended as a brain to capture moments and store them for future reference.

FM   What is the difference between this kind of process that you have started versus recycling?

ABA   My work has for some time now been viewed by many as a recycling process. I strongly try to avoid this because I choose a product that I want to work with or a product that I want to consume for a specific purpose. The idea is to use this product and try to provoke conversations surrounding the idea of prosthesis and the idea of our consumer nature. I actually use products that work and then tear them apart, and then I recompose them into forms using various parts. This is in contrast to the idea of recycling where people take dead components and then they try to breed new life into them.

FM   I think that is an interesting point. Your work is an organism, a being, maybe with a personality. Can you describe your notion of life?

ABA   It starts with the core of each electronic device, a kind of augmented aspect of a person. When we pair with them or when we use them, we form a kind of bond or relation with them where we are able to transmit our life essence through data or information, which becomes a source of life for them. So when we stop using them and they become secondhand, they still hold onto some of these histories or, let's say, essences of what we shared with them.

FM   I think it's quite stunning that, from the very first moment of the opening night, there were queues at your installation. When people sit down, they cause this electronic impulse that moves something or ignites an electronic process or whatever happens in this mysterious being of the TRON.

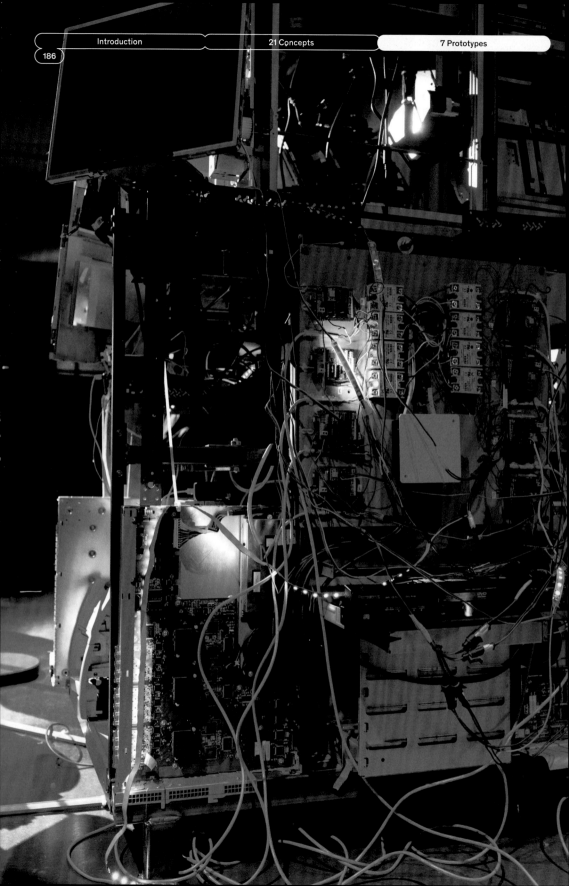

TRONS: Physical and Emotional Traces of Our Digital Worlds

Aisha Altenhofen

Mobile phones, telephones, televisions, computer sets, laptops, PDAs, VCD/CD/DVD players, radio receivers, and amplifiers are some of the electronic gadgets artist Akwasi Bediako Afrane collects to build his machine hybrids, called 'TRONS'. Afrane is interested in our relationships with electronic objects and how we share our daily rhythms with them. This includes the increasingly faster cycles of desiring and discarding those devices, as well as the environmental impact that implies. Through his installations, he uses electronic waste materials to build machines that question augmentation and prosthesis between visitor and machine. "I work primarily with discarded electronic gadgets," states Afrane, "which are working electronic devices that have been ditched by their owners in search for a newer or an updated model."

TRONSFORMATION workshop participants at work

The workshop aimed to rethink hacking as a way of accessing information

Based in Kumasi (Ghana, West Africa), he receives most of his materials through local second hand dealers. "Agbogbloshie" is the nickname of Ghana's most extensive e-waste desert, where so-called "Kon'dem" search through the wasteland to collect valuable parts to resell. He prefers gadgets that are situated within the home, as those are electronic devices that touch our lives most intimately. Afrane describes how "through these relationships, we leave traces of shared histories when we discard these gizmos." Personal histories of time spent with a certain object intersect with histories of those devices moving through a global system of mining, production, advertising, usage, and waste. Afrane uses e-waste materials as an entry point to interrogate those shared histories.

Ghana is an essential exporter of manganese and so is the Democratic Republic of the Congo with cobalt, minerals which are used for manufacturing lithium-ion batteries used in portable electronic devices. Their mining also impacts land-use change and sets off a sequence of associated environmental impacts like deforestation, erosion, noise, and emissions. Digital worlds are mined and transmitted via earth minerals, which return to those landscapes transforming them into electronic wasteland. "I created a documentary elaborating on the continuous life of some natural minerals," states Afrane, "which are chiefly used for the creation of some of these electronic devices." Through this documentary he contextualises the materials of his TRONS, as well as outlining a cycle of environmental damage caused by the scale of consumer interest and industrial production.

Afrane is using electronic devices as materials to discuss the many physical and emotional traces our digital worlds leave on our inner and outer landscapes. He underlines "the necessity to bring people to a state of openness in terms of understanding and interpretation of urgent issues." Through constructing machines that echo the many devices we leave behind, he asks us to examine how we relate to those machines: how do we assign value? How do we develop desires to purchase and discard? Through his TRONS he is offering physical interactions that experiment with new ways of relating to our electronic devices. Afrane is aiming to "to create projects that do not propose a solution, but rather projects that have the ability to incite discussion, and allow for diverse perceptions."

Materials were mostly second-hand gadgets, combined with electronic components

Participants working on different TRON projects

Workshop participants with Akwasi Bediako Afrane

THE BACKPACK OF WINGS: MODERN MYTHOLOGY
Hyeseon Jeong and Seongmin Yuk

The Backpack of Wings: Modern Mythology **represents speculative future scenarios, which are collisions and integrations between a bio-geotracking technology for wild animals in scientific fields and an animism in seismic disaster myths in East Asia.**

Since ancient times, whenever a natural disaster strikes, people anecdotally report that "animals knew it beforehand", a belief related to animals as spiritual beings. As telemetry systems evolve, this animistic belief is solidified and transformed into data by calculating, analysing, and biologging the animal body. This animal behavior data should make it possible to forecast such natural events in the near future. In the distant future, the evolving telemetry system could enable the creation of a new network (an Internet of Animals), in which non-humans and humans are interconnected. This new technology presents us with a ground-breaking means of facing the climate emergency. The transformation could also allow us to redefine the relationship between human beings and animals. Yet it simultaneously provokes a lot of questions: How far is the intervention of human beings into non-human life acceptable? Will animals be perceived as essential members of human society? Will they be revered as divine agents for predicting the future, or simply as measuring tools? And above all, could this technology be a genuine solution for the opaque future or is it just another anthropocentric techno-fixational illusion?

The Backpack of Wings looks into the innovative telemetry system and seeks a new relationship with non-human beings by focusing on the animistic aspect of ethological study. The project depicts an imminent scenario with the film *The Backpack of Wings: Modern Mythology*, and the vision of a distant future with the installation *The Backpack of Wings: Post Mythology*. The workshop *The Backpack of Wings: Sensory Networks* puts the lens on one migratory bird by using GPS data and invites the participants to create an imaginary storytelling narrative.

Frames of the film *The Backpack of Wings: Post Mythology*, depicting a future "an Internet of Animals" scenario

Seongmin Yuk and Hyeseon Jeong
in Conversation with Maya Indira Ganesh

MAYA INDIRA GANESH
Do you want to both introduce yourselves briefly?

SEONGMIN YUK
We made this project called *The Backpack of Wings*. It's a series of installation video works. There is a 20-minute film, a hologram fan, a two-channel video work, and a website. I am a multidisciplinary video artist and Hyeseon as well, and we both study at Media Arts of Cologne currently. We are interested in the intersection between mythologies, especially animistic mythologies and new technology, in animal tracking.

MIG   Can you tell us a little bit about the inspiration for this work, how and why it started?

SY   We started at home, during lockdown. We were looking out of our windows and basically watching the birds, how the birds move, where they move, and trying to imagine what they do. There were a lot of blackbirds, and we noticed that some blackbirds stayed in the forest, and some blackbirds were in human areas. So we started wondering why some are there and some are here. And then we started to research and found out that blackbirds are very special animals. Some of them migrate, some of them stay. And that was the initial moment where we got into the topic of animal tracking because we found out there was a huge research field focusing on animal tracking and understanding animal behavior. The more we looked into this field, the more we were thinking about mythology, especially in animistic stories. So we started to combine them.

MIG   Can you tell us about some of these myths?

SY   We were investigating East Asian mythologies—the belief that animals can predict the future or predict natural disasters. For exam- ple, earthquakes or rains. Some birds are thought to be the messengers to the gods.

MIG   Actually, that reminds me of a very distinctive aspect of Indian culture. The national bird of India is the peacock, and it's famous that before the rain comes the peacock will dance. That's the only time when you see all of its feathers opening up. So if the peacock is dancing, then you know the rain is coming, and that's important for a dry country like India. Different animals have different kinds of stories and mythologies associated with them. So, tell us about animal tracking because that's a big part of the film.

HYESEON JEONG

There are multiple methods. Most are basically using a telemetry system, but if you want to track a migratory bird which moves across the globe, then you need to use an antenna. The Icarus project, which runs through the Max Planck Institute, has installed an antenna on the International Space Station. The backpack, which is on the back of the animal, sends a signal to the ISS. This signal goes to the satellite, through an underground station and finally to our mobile phone. We are fascinated by this networking system, and from this system we build stories with other mythological narratives.

MIG   Could you tell us more about the Internet of Animals and what your association with Max Planck was like?

SY   The most fascinating part of Icarus is that there is a future idea for what is called the Internet of Animals. You might have heard about the Internet of Things where you can control your refrigerator in New York from Berlin etc. The Internet of Animals is where you can imagine a world where all species of animals are connected into a network, and they communicate with each other. We were fascinated by the idea because it has the possibility to reconstruct a hierarchical system, between animals and human. It also implies a centralized control system, a surveillance system where animals are used as resources, as data. So what does it mean to track animals? What does it mean to be within a network together as human beings with animals?

MIG   What was compelling for me was this idea that we strongly resist human surveillance. But this project forces us to think about why we would want to track animals. I mean, the obvious answer is to think that we can protect them. It's important to know where they are because they become data points that allow us to understand things like bio-diversity loss or understand what changes in their patterns of move-ment might tell us about our changing ecosystem. But we are still at the center of this knowledge, and the project made me think about what's in it for the birds, what's in it for the animals to be tracked? I'm also curious about the workshop later. Can you tell us about what's that you're going to do going to happen?

SY   We use a tool of the Max Planck Institute which is called the Animal Tracker app. We picked a specific bird, a white stork called Jonas, and we followed his migration route. The participants try to be Jonas, try to imagine from his perspective how he might perceive the world. So it's a completely different approach from what the Institute tries to do, which is to analyze behavior scientifically and to look into data. Try to write a short story from the perspective of another species; I bet you will have a feeling for how hard it is.

MIG   I like to read speculative and science fiction, and I find it interesting how a lot of writing is based on other planets and exoplanetary systems. But if you think about it, our planet itself is so weird and alien in some senses. We want to domesticate and know other species, so we give them names. We'll name our dogs Jack or something. That's a very human way of having a connection. You said you started by watching blackbirds outside, and I'm curious about how this whole project has changed your own relationship to thinking about animals, how you feel about them?

SY   Well, the first direct thing is that we watch birds now wherever we go. They just catch our eye. We cannot take our sight off them. Before this project, we were not at all experts. Through this collaboration with the Max Planck Institute, we noticed how different the approach of scientists and artists are, but also how many similarities we share. We went into the director's room of the Institute, and he had all the same mythological paintings and photos on his wall that we were looking into. From that visit we understood how their work impacts real life. A good example: the Animal Tracker app showed that in a certain geographic point the data log disappears; when you follow the path and look into that specific site you realize that the power cables are too high and the birds die there. Then you think about using policy to dismantle the electricity lines or lower them. It has a very direct impact.

MIG   I'm always struck by how there's a level of detail and specificity in every field, in every method. What is important for the scientist is really important to see in a film. If you are a lawyer or a doctor and you watch TV shows about lawyers and doctors, you get really annoyed with the way that they don't actually show you reality. But that's not the point of the TV show, right? It's to depict something else, to show drama or narrative. So is there any kind of difference like this that you encountered while working with scientists, scientific data, as artists?

SY   We think again and again that what we do as artists is to imagine. And what science does is to go really deep and specific. We are interested in the global lens and to speculate upon what this technology could drive in the future. This is the interesting part, having a collaboration between the artists and scientists who sit at opposite ends of the thinking.

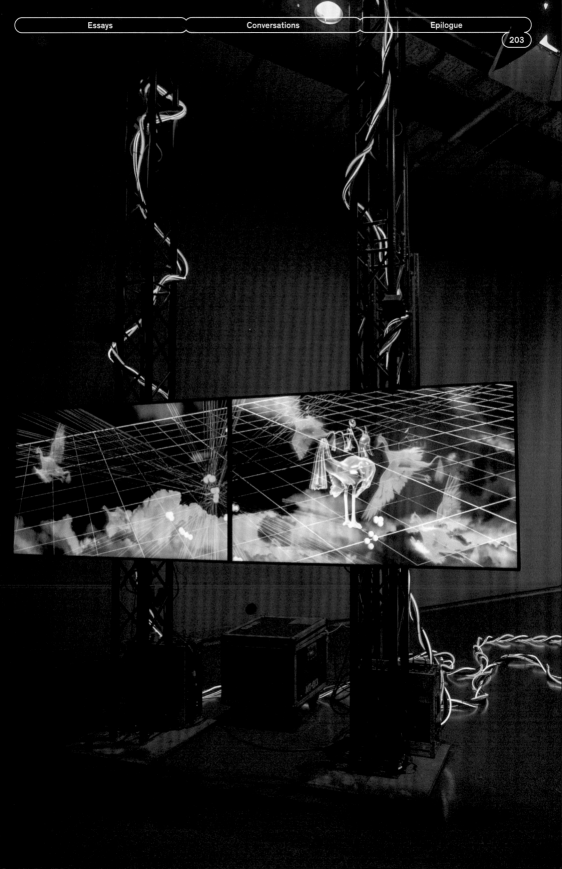

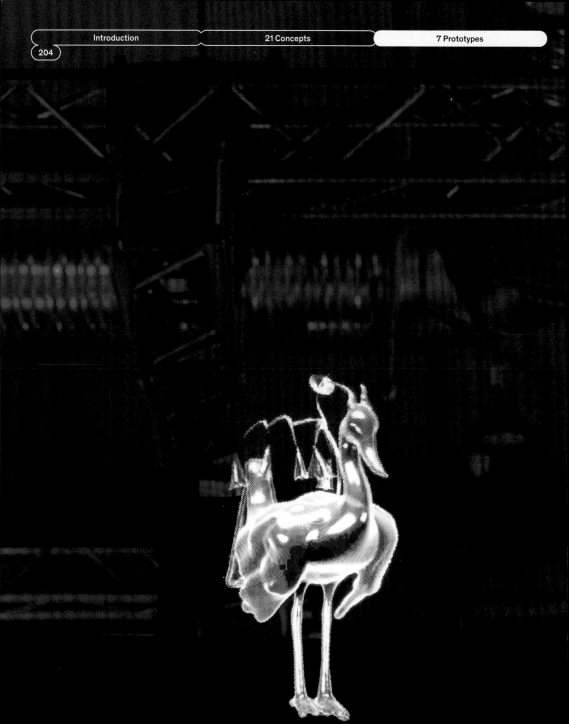

Grasping the Internet of Animals:
Embodiments and Symbiosis

Aisha Altenhofen

The Fagradalsfjall volcano erupted the summer of 2021, following a series of smaller earthquakes and tectonic rifting. Hyeseon Jeong and Seongmin Yuk, creators of *The Backpack of Wings: Modern Mythology*, were struck by their encounter with the erupting volcano while on their workshop trip to Iceland. "It was magnificent because it really looked surreal," they recall. "It felt like the landscape was talking to us. It's alive. It's not something static but essentially something moving. It felt like the earth had blood under its surface." Their words help us grasp how fictions can serve as a tool to give meaning to unexplainable natural events and make sense of them.

Hyeseon Jeong and Seongmin Yuk speculate on the possible implications of bird tracking technologies, from examining the data of migratory routes through an apocalyptic sci-fi lens, towards an allegorical mapping of the bird worlds they follow. Their project *The Backpack of Wings: Modern Mythology* interprets animal tracking data from angles of animistic myth-making, apocalyptic science fiction, and speculations on the life-worlds of the tracked birds. The project started with a sci-fi film that thinks through shifting telemetry systems. The film merges animistic viewpoints of animals—both as spiritual beings and forecasters of natural disasters—with a fictional future scenario where animal tracking data is commercially used by insurance companies. Jeong and Yuk's modern mythology looks at where East Asian disaster myths overlap with the interpretations contemporary scientists draw from satellite bird tracking data. By scripting those intersections into a narrative, the film contextualises the belief systems behind the interpretation and use of this data, illuminating how birds are valued, viewed, and positioned within human societies.

Their workshop took place at the Nordic House and was entitled *Sensory Networks*. The project speculates on the future usage of bird-tracking data. The artists perceive the workshop as a way to "balance the imaginative world and the real world. Because we are more working in imaginary storytelling, we are more

Screening of *The Backpack of Wings: Modern Mythology* at the Nordic House, Reykjavik

used to film making and fantasizing, the workshop is more focused on the bird itself." The workshop focuses on the fiction of grasping the inner world of a specific bird, following the migration route of an existing white stork called Jonas, and exploring the shared struggles of scientists and artists to understand the bird's perspective from a human point of view. Jonas was born in 2013 in Germany, where he spends his summers. The artists found that "originally he flew up to the African continent, but at a certain season he decided to stay in Israel at a dump site. Now he is using this dump site as his wintering location. When the winter was over, it took him 23 days to fly from Israel back to Germany."

As part of the workshop, participants imagined what it would be like to be Jonas at each location of his route, where the bird stayed for more than 24 hours. Through asking participants to imagine these scenarios and embodiments, Jeong and Yuk say that they "could explore how human activity could affect the bird, his migration route, his habitat, his behaviour" from a human point of view.

Storytelling exercises as part of the *Sensory Networks* workshop

DO AIS DREAM
OF CLIMATE CHAOS: SYMBIOTIC AI
Xiaoyu (Iris) Qu 曲晓宇

Do AIs Dream of Climate Chaos **investigates the contradictions in a machine learning system. Given sufficient data, how would AI compute its existence?**

To reach a general level of intelligence, a system must learn how it is situated in the environment. Though most AI systems manifest as software algorithms, they depend on a ubiquitous hardware infrastructure to exist. Given sufficient data, how would an AI compute its existence?

Symbiotic AI simulates an algorithm's coexistence with the ecosystem around it. During a turbulent season, a weather forecast AI attempts to decipher the chaotic system around its data center location by exchanging knowledge with the local species. As the simulation progresses, the AI unlearns planetary, human-centric datasets and gains dynamic, adaptive, and hyper-local insights from oak trees, milkweeds, hedgehogs, butterflies, lichens, and mycorrhizal fungi—slowly forming a cybernetic language of symbiosis. The data center worker inside the simulation and its human audience are bystanders, relying on AI to translate knowledge between nature and machine in this algorithmic story.

This simulation was developed from a series of role-playing workshops. Based on a collection of research artifacts, prompts, and embodiment exercises, the workshop participants are invited to represent different agents in the ecosystem and negotiate with the AI agent on the basis of their unique strengths and needs. Together, we want to build a believable narrative. Through collective storytelling, *Do AIs Dream of Climate Chaos* aims to explore connections between computation and humans—and the ecosystems they jointly endanger.

Views of Xiaoyu (Iris) Qu 曲晓宇's installation at the Driving the Human festival, Berlin, November 2022

Xiaoyu (Iris) Qu 曲晓宇
in Conversation with Ariana Dongus

ARIANA DONGUS
Can you tell us about the journey of how
this project has changed? What were your experiences
throughout these past two years that led you to this outcome?

XIAOYU (IRIS) QU 曲晓宇

My friend and I developed a workshop in New York at a space called Cybernetics Library. People from all kinds of backgrounds came to this library, and we wrote texts together and imagined a data center that is forming symbiotic relationships with the plant, animal, and fungus species around it. This little narrative was very much based on *The Backpack of Wings*. They had a workshop where people talked about a story from a bird's perspective, and that idea was inspirational for me. Originally, in this narrative, I was going to make the human data center worker the main figure in the simulation. You have this giant infrastructure in the middle of nowhere, and to cut costs, the company is only putting the minimum number of workers in there. Oftentimes, you would be responsible for a large amount of data, but just by yourself, so you're just looking at the screen, waiting for the monitors and then walking around. It's even more interesting to me to think about all the perspectives of the non-human species that would be in this environment. We think about AI as this intelligent system, but the ecosystem around it is also very much an intelligent system that has a different set of agendas, different data, different processes, different computation. AI is just one 'intelligent' entity, and it has a lifespan of maybe 25 years—that's apparently the average lifespan of a data center—and it has knowledge at the global scale but it's really not very nuanced. It's often taking the average or a summary of what's considered a global data set. In comparison, the animals, the species in the local environment have a different perspective. An oak tree, for example, lives more than 500 years. It has all this historical knowledge of a region, of how the weather changed for instance, and that is something humans do not have.

AD When you talk about symbiotic AI, are you mainly interested in the relation between AI as this intelligent system with non-human agents? What is the role of the human?

XIQ The human perspective is all encompassing. When we tried to add a human perspective in our first workshop, people started to come up with solutions where humans could fix this, could fix that. But it's all very aligned with the human agenda. So in the second workshop, we tried to take the human character out of the workshop and only have participants act as different species. In this environment, if we think about taking humans out of the narrative, a lot of really interesting stories start to emerge. How can we learn from a hyperlocal system that is evolving and what kind of information does each of the characters take with them?

AD   You explained that there are some climatic turbulences within the system; that this giant network starts to learn or extract knowledge from these changes.

XIQ   The ecosystem you see in the simulation is based on a seasonal change. So at first, when you are starting the simulation, you can put in different parameters for the year. You can make it a drier year or a hotter year. You can see the temperature change, the weather change. It's a little ecosystem. I don't always know what's going on with it and every time I come back, it might be a little different. Something new is going on.

AUDIENCE
Can you walk us through how you actually made the work? What's your data set? How did you train the AI?

XIQ   The simulation is built in a 3D program called Unity. Each entity is programmed to do certain things based on their needs. For example, the butterfly will need to consume the milkweed, which is growing next to the lichens, which is securing water for the oak tree, which is dropping seeds. You can see the hedgehogs are sometimes hunting the butterfly. Everything is interdependent on each other, and the climate is also changing based on the species interaction. Over the years, there will be a seasonal curve, but in summer, it might be more dry and in winter, it might be more humid. The data that we use for the weather system is based on New York, East Coast weather. It gets very cold in the winter and pretty hot in the summer.

AUDIENCE
I really appreciate the readings that you have outside. So with reference to one of them— Kate Crawford's *Atlas of AI*. There's a very compelling line that she has in it that artificial intelligence is neither artificial nor intelligent, and if that is true, if we believe that, why do we want to believe it's intelligent?

XIQ   I don't really think it's intelligence. The way we see intelligence is human-centric, and artificial intelligence is very much based on our assumption of how the brain works. If we look at the fastest supercomputers today, the quantum computers, they're still not as powerful as a fruit fly, if we wanted to simulate all the brain activities that a fly has. So that puts things into perspective of how intelligent this thing actually is. If we look at an AI's output and think it's intelligent, that's because it's analyzing data that we produced and the AI is talking back to us about stuff that humans care about. AI can be thought of as a human experience visualizer.

AD   On the topic of symbiotic AI—is this based on the assumption that everybody basically lives in harmony in a certain way? Also, how do you personally think about the idea that we could actually compute our own existence or AI's own existence?

XIQ   Symbiosis, first of all, encompasses all types of relationships between species. To me, it doesn't mean harmony. It means chaos. Ecosystems are constantly fluctuating. I don't think there is a state where we can say everything's stable. There's always negotiation going on. We depend on each other for certain things, and we compete with each other for other things.

This project started because I work so much with software, and I don't really think about this hardware concept. Data from my New York apartment reaches a data center in Virginia, then goes to a data center in the Netherlands. It's a globally distributed existence, and it's interesting to think about all these resources I'm consuming without knowing it. Every time we use our phone to access a website, this happens. This project is about bringing that perspective back to a local level and thinking about it within an ecosystem. I don't want to anthropomorphize the term AI more than it already has been, but it's fascinating to think about the agency of the algorithms themselves. There are researchers who explore if rogue AI already exists. If we create this intelligence system, it would have its own needs and its own agenda. I think that's very urgent to unpack. It's been fun for me, of course.

LARP as World-Building:
Symbiotic AI at the Cybernetics Library

Aisha Altenhofen

At the Cybernetics Library in New York, the artists Xiaoyu (Iris) Qu 曲晓宇 and Chao Hui Tu held an AI symbiosis workshop, in which participants played seven nonhuman characters that collectively challenged AI-predicted climate scenarios threatening their ecosystem.

"Our home, the Kia forest, is a 1,200-year-old forest rich in biodiversity and home to 100+ species regarded as important for conservation. Only ten percent of the forest remains, and the remaining is threatened by climate change." The Kia forest is the world in which Xiaoyu (Iris) Qu 曲晓宇 and Chao Hui Tu's AI symbiosis workshop is set. During a three-hour roleplay, participants discussed the changing forest ecosystem from the perspectives of seven nonhuman characters. One of these fictional characters is the Weather AI, an algorithm located within a data center in direct proximity to the Kia forest. The AI predicts two climate scenarios affecting the whole ecosystem, forecasting the weather for the upcoming spring and summer seasons. Over three hours, workshop participants embodied these seven characters, collectively imagining ecosystem implications caused by these climatic changes.

The warming climate will cause spring to arrive early, followed by at least ten frosts from March through May. This means a longer growing phase for biotic factors, and more soil moisture is lost through evapotranspiration. The Aquatic Milkweed is out of sync with the butterflies, which makes reproduction and feeding difficult. The Hedgehog emerges early from his hibernation when the food supply is low. At the same time, the data center increases CO_2 emissions, increases its water usage, generates large amounts of heat, and releases chemicals into the water.

The algorithm's spring forecast predicts a scenario that touches the living conditions of all of the seven characters: English Oak, Aquatic Milkweed, Monarch Butterfly, Common Hedgehog, Foliose Lichen, Mycorrhizal Fungi, and the Weather AI. Each workshop participant was assigned one of these characters and received a card with a QR code through which they could access an

Introducing the workshop at Cybernetics Library in New York

are.na board. The board contained their character's backstory, goals, abilities, and struggles that would become important during the roleplay. The Weather AI was defined by characteristics like a lifespan of 15-20 years, a performance of 4,000 trillion calculations per second, or through access to a global archive of human knowledge and information. The English Oak featured a lifespan of over 500 years and adaptability to drought and high pH levels, as well as a support system for around 2,300 species. All seven characters were also entangled in symbiotic relationships of predator and prey, producers and decomposers, all connected through a common ecosystem. After learning about the framework of their world and their character's placement within it, the participants embodied each role. Each character introduced themselves to the group from a first-person perspective, making their species' worldview and imagination tangible. After the announcement of the spring forecast, the characters came together in groups of four, each including an AI character. They discussed how the spring's climate would affect their ecosystem as a whole, the symbiotic relationships between the characters, and the position of the AI within the system. After this initial discussion, all groups came together in a Forest Meeting to collectively find ways to protect the system. Some of the ideas included the creation of artificial trees, by combining the AIs capabilities with the anatomy of the English Oak tree, or to use an artificially-generated voice to lure the Hedgehogs into the shade of the trees. After the spring forecast, the group replayed the structure now considering the summer forecast of the AI, which predicted a drought and heatwave.

Participants individually introduced their characters, making their different worldviews tangible

Workshop participants negotiating the narratives and evolution of their ecosystems

The workshop allowed participants to think through an ecosystem affected by shifting climate conditions, while discussing these changes tied to seven nonhuman perspectives. The participants played through the possibilities of symbiotic relationships between animals, plants, and technology and imagined new ways of facing increasingly unstable weather conditions.

Essays   Conversations   Epilogue

227

Technological Futures, Symbiosis, and Entanglement

This is an edited and excerpted version of a conversation that took place on November 26, 2022 during the Driving the Human festival in Berlin.

ARIANA DONGUS

A post-anthropocentric view is not only visible in your projects, but actually in all the seven prototypes and the whole Driving the Human spirit, so to speak. What role can high tech like AI play in future scenarios? Do we need AI in order to tackle the climate crisis?

AKWASI BEDIAKO AFRANE

The idea of AI really intrigues me. We are an interesting species that wants to have this kind of high technology and then also complain about the effects it has. This paradox is what I find interesting because what do we really want to hold on to?

XIAOYU (IRIS) QU 曲晓宇

The concept of AI is so planetary and it's embedded everywhere. And since I started doing my research, I realized my concept of tech or the tech industry has been so narrow. I've been really focusing on the side that's software-oriented and on people who design AI applications. The Driving the Human program helped to broaden my perspective on what technology is and who's involved in this industry. I want to explore how we can take such a global concept and place it at the local scale. Part of the problem with using AI for climate change applications is that so much data is global, leaning into the idea of big data for predictions, but there's often lots of nuance. Maybe it's more interesting if AI can actually learn from the local and the historical.

ANDRA POP-JURJ

I'm glad you mentioned how this program has shifted your perspective because in our project we've also been trying to learn about environmental model projections. We have a research booklet with some of the data sets and the differences are tiny. They don't say anything. There are so many gaps in the data as well. Sometimes you try to render an entire data set to visualize it and it's just gray or all the years look the same. You wonder, how is this possible? If arctic sea ice is supposed to melt by 2100, why have the carbon levels not risen accordingly or the amount of methane escaping the permafrost? So I wonder what is really the role of this data and how can we instrumentalize it, especially given that the climate crisis is not necessarily a crisis for all. Arctic cod will benefit from warming temperatures and an increase in plankton production and so on.

KIM ALBRECHT

This question is right at the heart of the problem because, on the one hand, to detect climate change in the first place, we need global computation, a global sensing apparatus to know that this is happening. Without technology, we wouldn't know about climate change, not in the sense that we know about it now. On the other hand, the energy consumption of data centers that we're building is extremely high. So the technology that helps us to gain this knowledge is destructive itself.

AP-J

We now have access to satellite imagery, height maps etc.—we can reconstruct the Arctic terrain within an hour through software, apply a texture, set up a camera, some lighting and it looks good. But I think one of the questions that we always struggled with is how ethical is it really to be talking about climate through technology and how to build a certain consciousness in visitors. Hopefully it collapses the distance a bit and makes things more accessible. It allows us to represent things that would otherwise not be visible to the naked eye and to make relations that might not be obvious.

AD

Akwasi, what I found intriguing with your project is your use of the notion of hacking. You present hacking as a means for a sustainable future.

ABA

For me, the core of the idea of hacking was not to look at hacking in the malicious way that people might normally associate with the term, but to see it as a kind of intimate understanding of a system in order to have access or maneuver as you want. Malicious hackers look for back doors or loopholes. With my documentary, I realized that these scrap dealers, recyclers, are also looking for loopholes. A method of finding ways to make money out of scrap. They extract from old televisions and refrigerators what is valuable to them. The rest is trash. They can get aluminum and copper, gold sometimes if they're lucky. Also with the repairers in Ghana, they told me, "Okay, the products are made, the producers don't give us extra components." Nothing is made in our country. If you have a television with a broken screen, the repairers have parts—a video board, a power board inverter, speakers, all separate. These can easily be swapped out. These people try to find broken electronics that people are throwing away and use them for repair. These processes are a way of having an understanding of a system that actually lets you work to your specifications.

AP-J

Yeah, I think this kind of circularity is also something that we need to make more glamorous in a way. I don't have that much experience with hardware, so I really respect the work that you do. From a software perspective, as an architect and researcher, the work has always been driven by precision and more computational power. We get so frustrated when our computer is just a little bit too slow or when a render takes too long or when we can't quite get the photogrammetry point cloud to look high definition. It's so easy to forget about limits. Where does it really stop? How much definition is enough?

XIQ

I've been thinking a lot about how tech is really an industry that creates needs. Optimization drives the whole industry and all the other pieces fall within that. Think about the metaphors the tech industry creates to go with that narrative. An iPhone is so nice and slick. You don't see the stuff inside. It's such a beautiful white box on the outside; beautiful design language around this really complex infrastructure. And on the opposite side, there's a demo metaphor. I heard from someone—I didn't fact check this—that the word provenance came from diamonds because you can trace the source of where each diamond comes from. I was thinking, what if we treat everything that we do in tech as the diamond instead of the fridge? What happens when you run an algorithm or what happens when you buy a new phone? What if technological provenance is required to be listed in a report, for example? I feel like the industry is just catching up to the hardware side of things. There is an art piece that I was working on before this where I was trying to look at data center machine algorithms. Right away, I could find that they were downloading from Northern Virginia, the GateHub data center that was acquired by Microsoft, then calling a server in the Netherlands. It's already a global operation in two seconds and I'm consuming their energy without even knowing it. I wish we had better language to unpack this. Maybe people in this room can set the industry standard.

ABA   Can I add something? When I was in Karlsruhe, when I was doing my residency, I built my project. I had the chance to go to people's homes to collect some of these devices they were willing to part with. There was this one particular device—I spoke with the person and what he said was, "Oh, it's a working printer, but I just upgraded my Windows PC to Windows 11 and now Windows 11 does not support the printer. So yeah, you can have it." I was like, what? It's very interesting how easily we let go of these things.

KA   Andra, I very much like the point that you made about questioning how much data is enough. One exercise that I made within my research was that I requested all the Google searches that Google has about me or that I made on Google and I got back a file with a quarter million searches from the last 10 years.

This was pretty fascinating. There's a short story, *Funes el memorioso*—from Borges—about a person who remembers everything. He does not forget anything. He knows the shape of every cloud at every moment that he ever saw in his life. And he says that he himself has more knowledge than all of humankind. When I looked through that data, it felt to me that that was basically what was happening. It is quite uncanny because at times I had no clue what I was searching for. I don't even recognize the terms, but somehow I, at some point, searched for them. I don't have that knowledge anymore but Google does. But at the same time, that is not really anything they can use, it's only data. It's not real insight. At the end of the story from Borges, the person who has all these thoughts—the one thing he's very bad at is dealing with other humans and he's not capable of having a conversation or being a human in general. So that's basically the folly of this accumulation of data, which I find intriguing.

AD

There is the question of the position of the human. Whose data is it? Who is deciding what type of information to give? What type of information do we collect?

AP-J

I'm glad you mention this because it's also something that triggered this whole project for us. It started from the geopolitical conflicts that are now happening and that are enabled by environmental degradation—because the Arctic is accessible, it matters who owns what, who can extract whose oil, who can ship, who can govern, who has sovereignty. It's always about these lines that are projected onto the surface that then differentiate this body of water from that body of water. All of this is enabled by machines because they can send ships with sonar to scan the bottom of the ocean and to provide bathymetric maps necessary to make any kind of territorial claim in the Arctic. Part of our project is to show how these manmade regulations actually don't mean anything for any of the characters featured in the game. The fish doesn't care if he's swimming in international waters or in Norwegian waters. We're trying to decenter the human a little bit. We are not using any of these lines as part of the cartographic exercise that we've been doing, instead working with surfaces and blurriness.

KA

I find this beautiful. Yesterday, I walked through and I had the perspective of a pigeon. I was a reindeer over here and a microbe over there. I found it all touching when I walked around and looked at the projects. At the same time, I constantly felt embedded in technology, felt very small as a human within all the screens, within all this computing power. That's what I found interesting here, that so much technology is used to get us into a perspective outside of the human.

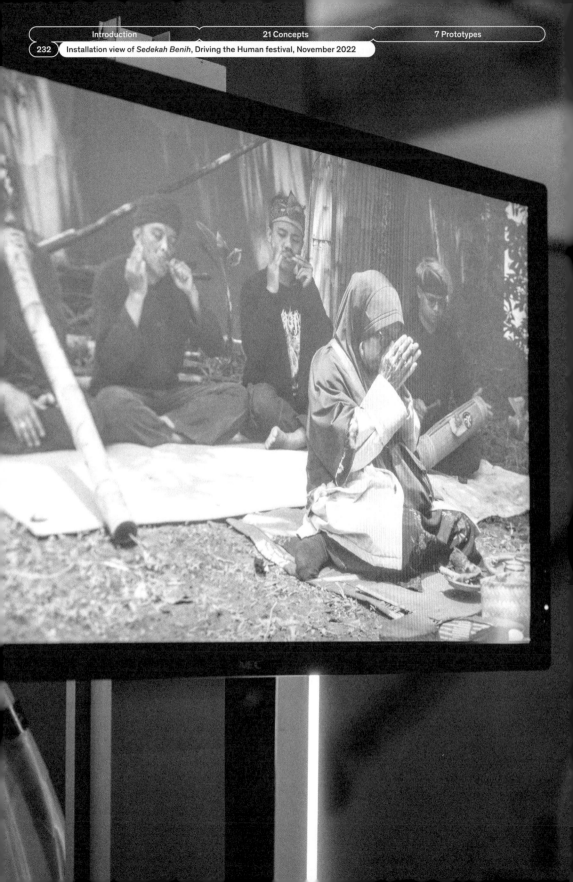

Installation view of *Sedekah Benih*, Driving the Human festival, November 2022

This is an edited and excerpted version of a conversation that took place on November 26, 2022 during the Driving the Human festival in Berlin.

CHLOE STEAD   It seems we're all a little bit ambiguous about this term, world-building. I wanted to start by asking you all what you understand by the term "world-building" and how this concept relates to your individual practices.

YURI TUMA   World-building. Okay, well, let me tell you a little bit about what I do. I'm an artist working with sound, art, and performance, but I'm also part of a collective in Madrid called The Institute for Postnatural Studies. And what we do is academic and cultural programming to question the way we relate to the word or concept of nature in Western culture. We program seminars around queer ecologies, Afrofuturism, colonial thinking, to understand that nature is much deeper than just the green forest that we're all used to visualizing; it has a lot of political, economic, social connotations that are very important when we speak about the environment and nature. World-building, for me, is any sort of art practice that can propose a future, or a landscape, or a territory, or a character. I can think, for example, of a Spanish artist called Pablo Durango. He does drag art. When he's performing, he is mostly alien, part human. And that alone, as a public performer inhabiting this other character or persona, is already communicating in a different way, is some sort of world-building practice.

One of the seminars that we did in the Institute was a collaboration with the Institute of Queer Ecologies called *Mutability and Mutualism*. We were lucky to have Jack Halberstam join us. Jack was saying, "Why are we world-building? Maybe perhaps we should be unbuilding, unworlding because if we keep building worlds on top of a world, maybe that's alone in the attitude of something that we shouldn't do." Jack used the example of Gordon Matta-Clark, how he takes away parts of a building and creates holes as artistic practice. It's not adding matter, it's not adding a building to the surface, but actually extracting and still being able to create.

CS   Is unworlding then not another term for destroying? Is there something clearly destructive about the action? I think destruction can be a way of also showing that you're dissatisfied with a certain state of something.

YT   I think it's a matter of how you are inhabiting this term. Destroying doesn't necessarily mean a negative thing. We can perhaps think of the word "destroy" as transforming into something else. Think about dystopias, utopias, endings, and beginnings; it's always a cycle of transformation.

CS

Kabelo, I wonder what you think about the idea of world-building. I mean, as a curator, you're supporting, facilitating, helping to imagine new possibilities for an institution. How does that relate for you?

KABELO MALATSIE

This is also a very new word for me; it feels loaded, but I don't know it well enough. But I would say that in my work I'm thinking about curatorial practice in an expanded way or expanding curatorial practice to include things like administrative work. Thinking about those tasks as curatorial practice means that I can question them. And in that questioning, one can question hierarchies, one can question notions of equality, one can question ideas around justice. One can question even who speaks when and how, what platforms, why do we use Excel spread-sheets? Why do we use accounting? What have we inherited from those forms? So thinking that everything I do should come from a practice of questioning. I'm interested in questions. I don't know if that has anything to do with world-building. And the questioning for me is interesting because I'm thinking as a curator, I'm there to hold artistic practice. I think we've concentrated a lot on exhibition-making without thinking that all of that includes a lot, a lot. I mean the bulk of the time you're talking to administrators before anybody sees the work in the exhibition. What conditions and what forms of communication—how sensitive are those people to the artists, the world that they bring, the thoughts they bring, and of course the work they bring?

CS

I think you bring up an interesting tension there. I do want to go back to artists that have generative utopian practices as well, but just to stick on this for a second. You talked about the backstage and one thing that I think about a lot in my own writing is how do we also celebrate institutions or artists that care about these things that are, say, organic in their processes and how they deal with people. If I'm a director of a museum, if I invite this artist in to create a new world, to look to the future, to do this great project—for me that's great, but what happens with the day-to-day? What happens with this world that you're building in the institution that perhaps the audience doesn't see? Does it negate a great new future that the artist might be showing in the exhibition space if in your office space you're not treating your employees correctly, if you're not making sure they're getting paid well enough, if you are bullying them or any manner of things that happen behind closed doors? I think it's interesting to think about the unsexy aspects of world-building as well because that's also important.

YT   I think any world-building comes from questioning. Being part of an independent association, I think the sort of practice that we do between ourselves is definitely a more tactile way to manifest world-building. The way we care for each other, the way we question—how should an independent association work, how should we apply for grants? If we do get the grant, how should we work with it? For whom, when, for how long? I think these are questions that are super interesting. It's not just the artistic practice that is proposing a world, but also how in practice the association's organization is also generating these new modes of relating to each other and to art. I've been feeling a bit in crisis with some contemporary art because I definitely believe that the process is very important—I'm definitely more inclined to be interested in artistic practices that are collectively creating or that are not necessarily focused on building something specific. I don't know if it's off-topic, but something that Kabelo and I were speaking about the other day was sound art as a great example to rethink how institutions show artwork. That's also an example of unworlding. If we pay attention to sound and active listening, it's another way of inhabiting the world that is not an ocular-centric mode of relating. That alone, that transition of switching the senses or prioritizing another sense is, for me, a way to world-build.

CS   To quote Octavia Butler—there are many, many quotes that I could have taken, but I really liked this one—"There is nothing new under the sun, but there are new suns." I would argue that world-building is something that artists have been doing since cave paintings. You can build a world with a pencil just as well. I think sci-fi writing has certainly popularized that term in the past few decades, and we've been seeing exhibitions dedicated to world-building by contemporary artists that directly quote Octavia Butler or other writers. I wanted to ask you both if you actively read, watch, or listen to sci-fi, and how that kind of influences what you do. I'm personally a big Philip K. Dick stan I would say. I had a big book of his writing, and it's insane how many kinds of ideas he has in every single story. They're not written particularly well—the female characters are flimsy and there's lots to not like about them—but the ideas that he has for how terribly people can treat each other, even on different planets, are insane. There's something very generative about sci-fi.

YT   I love that you bring up Octavia Butler. I'm a huge, huge fan. And I think in one of the trilogies, the *Xenogenesis* trilogy, for example, the first book—I'm going to try not to do any spoilers. It is a new world. It's a world-building out of a new scenario.

CS   What's quite interesting about her is that I think a lot of scientific fiction writers are imagining humans and what humans do on, for example, another planet. Whereas Octavia Butler is really someone that is actively thinking about new things that haven't happened yet—not just how we, me and you, would react to a certain change.

YT   There are new modes of relating to other bodies in her work as well. Beings that have tentacles who communicate through energy and through vibration, and the way they make love and the way they make jokes. What do we do now with this new mode of relating to each other? Are we going to come back and do the same thing over and over? And in a way, Octavia Butler says that the human desire for hierarchy will always be the demise of humankind. So can we come back to a new planet and keep from repeating the same mistakes? This idea of world-building is interesting to think of: a clean sheet of paper versus drawing on top of drawings, on top of other drawings, on top of more drawings.

KM   I want to add something, something that I've been thinking about. I think it's called the Pluriverse and it's inspired by Zapatistas who are thinking about worlds within worlds. That idea complicates a kind of universal idea, universal understanding of something. It means that there are many things that are happening simultaneously and many worlds that we can't understand. I'm interested not just in artistic practice—I, of course, work in it and I think artists are fantastic. I also think that my grandmother was building all the time, and she didn't need to paint something to build. There are many ways of building. If we are building, what do we imagine is the data we are using to build? Because we are all socialized in particular ways. So this repetition you are talking about is repetition that's inbuilt, repetition that's socialized. We are constantly trying to find new ways of running away from the same problems. I don't know if we should run away from the problem or face the problem head on. But if we really deal with it head on, then building or starting anew, or whatever other term, will make sense. But as long as the structures stay the same, everything is still problematic. Education is problematic. As long as all of that is there, I feel like speculation and ideas about the future will always be in a loop.

CS   The idea of artists potentially offering another set of eyes, offering other ways of seeing things in the here and now—maybe that's the optimistic way of putting it.

KM   The optimistic way would be to do that, but not using the same mode that leads to the same problems. Extraction is a problem. Patriarchy is a problem. Capitalism is a problem. And I know all of these things are hard to run away from. Of course, there are artistic practices that are doing very interesting things and finding ways out. Of course, there are a lot of people who have different views of the world, and that's generative.

CS

I think sometimes I can personally feel a bit bogged down by all of these really big questions. But something that I do think about a lot is that we all have spheres of influence, even if that's just with your own friends, with your own family, in which we can try and, without being too cheesy, build our own world based on principles that we think are fair and just. Sometimes there can be problems that come from trying to constantly look into some other place and not to just start with where you are. Which is not to say that being generative isn't a good thing, thinking big isn't a good thing because you need those people, too. But I think that I'm quite a detail-oriented person. I often think: what can I do in my small sphere of influence as a writer, as a daughter, as a friend?

YT

I think what Kabelo said is very exciting. We should feel excited to unlearn. I think that's something that we can all potentially look forward to as an individual and as a society. I don't know how we do that. For me, I've been using sound as a way to unlearn things. It drives me to inhabit the world in a different way. There are so many ways. I think of Eliana's work, for example, that sheds light on these Indigenous ecological leaders that have been silenced for trying to unlearn or to share knowledge that would help unlearn things. So it is a battle to unlearn, but it's an exciting one.

"I'm interested not just in artistic practice ...
I also think that my grandmother was building
all the time, and she didn't need to paint
something to build. There are many ways of
building. If we are building, what do we imagine
is the data we are using to build? Because
we are all socialized in particular ways. So this
repetition you are talking about is repetition
that's inbuilt, repetition that's socialized.
We are constantly trying to find new ways of
running away from the same problems."
(Kabelo Malatsie)

Introduction   21 Concepts   7 Prototypes

240   Conversation between Eliana Otta, Vincent Rumahloine, Corine Pelluchon, and Vera Sacchetti, Driving the Human festival, November 2022

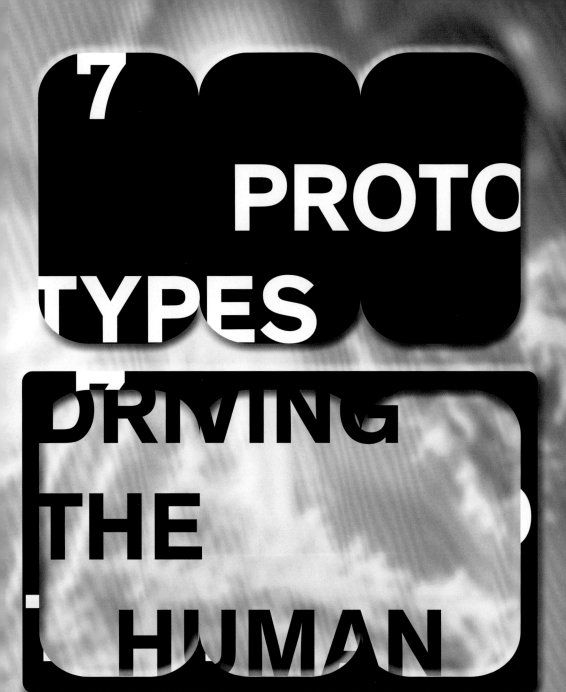

7 PROTOTYPES DRIVING THE HUMAN

HUMAN-BACTERIA INTERFACES: AN EXPLORATION OF THE PRESENT AND FUTURE OF HUMAN-MICROBIAL ECOSYSTEMS
Anne-Sofie Belling, Bea Delgado Corrales, Romy Kaiser, and Paula Nerlich

What could future interactions with our microbial world look like? How can collaborations with microbes become part of our technological future?

The *Human-Bacteria Interfaces* concept explores new relationships with microbes through science-based speculative prototypes. Similar to other species and matter on Earth, microbes can respond to signals and stimuli from their surroundings.

A core element of this concept is examining the potential of designing microbes to become living sensors that can respond through light to stimuli based on their genetic design. By designing new interactions with microbes, care and concern for other non-human living beings becomes a conscious part of our everyday experience. At the heart of this concept is a narrative that explores a biophilic turn within the generative genre of design: what if we could design in partnership with the non-human living world (with organisms such as microbes) rather than relying solely on the industrial extraction of matter to create the increasingly complex world that surrounds us? How could new relations with microbes build our future homes?

The *Human-Bacteria Interfaces* installation leads the visitor through a spatial timeline of the real and speculative worlds in which the project lives: from the genetically-designed microbes in the laboratories of today to elaborate visions of future human-bacteria relations. The main part of the physical installation is the Ambient Living Intelligence, a speculative prototype of how a human-microbial interface could be integrated into a future built environment. It uses textile and microbial communities that dwell encased in glass vessels to create a living sensor that glows upon detecting touch.

Views of Anne-Sofie Belling, Bea Delgado Corrales, Romy Kaiser, and Paula Nerlich's installation at the Driving the Human festival, Berlin, November 2022

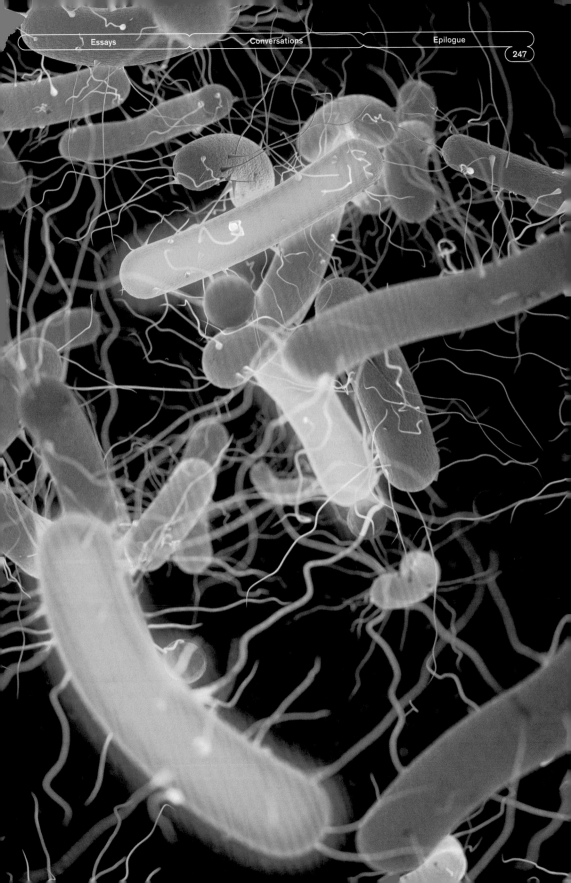

Paula Nerlich, Bea Delgado Corrales, and Romy Kaiser in Conversation with Sandra Fendl and Julia Ihls

SANDRA FENDL

Can you give us a short summary of what your project is and what you are doing?

PAULA NERLICH

We are four PhD students at the Hub for Biotechnology in the Built Environment, located in Newcastle, North England, which is a merged project between the Architecture School of Newcastle University, and the Microbiology Department at Northumbria University. We came together, just for Driving the Human, to create a project together. Back then it was COVID...we found that the narratives around microbes, at that time, and often still now, were quite negative. They are very much linked to, "Oh, microbes can affect us negatively. We get sick through them, and so on." But we are, I think, about 80% microbes, and the rest of us is human. We would not exist without microbes. They're in constant exchange with us and the environment. So to gain a better understanding of these really valuable narratives that drive us as humankind, we started to think of how to interface with them. So if I interface as a human with another human, we might do this through verbal language or bodily language. How can we find ways to interface with beings that we can't really detect with our bodily senses? Here you can see them through a microscope, but with normal eyesight we cannot perceive them. This is where our interface idea started.

BEA DELGADO CORRALES

Not only do we want to interact with these microorganisms, but we also want to integrate them fully in our lives. Things that we do regularly in the lab include transforming bacteria with pieces of DNA that you can design to produce different lights, colors. And this is done with easy tools that everyone uses in the lab, so why don't we use them to engineer bacteria into producing bacterial cellulose that could change color after a reaction from a stimuli? This was the basic concept, but then we thought, "Why not also integrate that with textile so we can actually create an environment that is fully living, that is reactive?"

ROMY KAISER

We needed to bring these biotechnologies out of the lab, into an environment, into shape, into application. Therefore, we were thinking, or envisioning, a world where we would live with the microbes around us. This interface could go in totally different directions. We see textile as a way to shape and scale up these biotechnologies. The organism needs things to grow—you need nutrition, you need temperature, but perhaps in the future, it might be possible have enclosed areas where a touch interface is possible. We decided for this exhibition to provide an experience of how this future home could look like.

PN Our vision is that maybe the textile, one day, could almost do what the bioreactor does. Maybe the textiles could supply the nutrition to the organism, and so on. But this is another research area that we've now sneakily brought into the project. Basically, with our project, we want to invite you to physically explore what is possible now, and what we envision as feasible in the near future. In the last room, you see our video which is a far future vision. We are collecting more questions about these potential applications, but also about the ethics behind them. How can we really create a mutualistic symbiotic existence with these living materials?

JULIA IHLS
What technical questions or challenges did you have while working on this project? How did you decide on the format that you show us now?

PN We are two textile designers, one microbiologist, and a creative technologist, who's also working in the realm of anthropology. It was the first time we worked together, and I found every time we were iterating, we found new ideas. It's insane, because at some point we felt, "Let's just settle on one idea. We have so, so many ideas."

RK At the moment, due to legislation and regulations, we're actually not allowed to bring a genetically modified organism in any space. Not outside the lab even. So we were thinking about how to overcome this limitation, how to have an interactive experience for someone when you can't actually show the object. In the end, it was very important for us to have this tactility. In addition, when you work with biological entities, you need to provide media, nutrients, and conditions for them to grow. So that's where the bioreactor idea comes from, because we use them pretty regularly now in labs to grow specific microorganisms, or cultures of different microorganisms. We wanted to have this concept integrated in the built environment. We talked to different bioreactor experts, and they were blown away by the fact that we wanted to create something that was beautiful and useful. Because bioreactors, if anyone has seen them around, are ugly and really big—even if they do amazing things.

JI In this design work, how did your practice shift and change through your collaboration with a non-human partner or with partners from different disciplines?

PN I'll start with language, because I find that's a really important question, especially when looking at cross-disciplinary practice or interdisciplinary work. Having worked now with many people in other disciplines, it's not always common that people are open to adapt terminology and the way they express themselves. Because we do sometimes use the same words, but actually they mean different things. And within this group and with our supervisor, I always felt that there is this patience and curiosity and willingness to rephrase and bring the other person into what we want to share and say.

BDC   It felt, at first, like I crushed a lot of dreams. And in that sense, I think I changed too, because I tended to think in terms of scientific outcome. The question of how you can merge arts and science was completely out of my mind. I was always asking, "What's the purpose of this?"—not the way that you should approach these topics. So for me, working with the team meant shifting the way I also view science. I allowed myself to accept that even though what I do in the lab tells me this is not possible, I can think of ways to imagine possibilities.

RK   Actually, I find it funny that you say you were crushing dreams, because for me it felt a little bit like you were just opening up the conversation. In the beginning, I was not fully aware of what's actually possible. Because when you're not in the lab, it's a very mystifying place...

   In the end, we are allowed to speculate, we are allowed to challenge boundaries and be creative about what the future could look like.

Navigating Disciplinary Differences: Bridging Science and Design Envisioning Microbial Futures

Aisha Altenhofen

An early three-dimensional render of an ambient living intelligence

Anne-Sofie Belling, Bea Delgado Corrales, Romy Kaiser, and Paula Nerlich met at the HBBE (Hub for Biotechnology in the Built Environment) in Newcastle, UK. Working in an interdisciplinary way with backgrounds in creative technology, material design and microbiology, the collective is moving towards the field of biodesign. Constantly translating between the languages of multiple disciplines, they state throughout the process that "there are always different foci in the foreground—so every perspective takes a lead at a different time." They describe this process as shifting "between checking on the biological requirements —pushing it towards the impossible speculative concept in application and then translating it back to biology again, merging it into a feasible future-scenario." Through working back and forth, Belling, Delgado Corrales, Kaiser, and Nerlich are not just able to start or finish with a biological perspective, but adapt conceptual design ideas in response to the lab process. As important questions throughout the process, the collective outlines: "Is this biologically feasible? How would this be translated into future applications?" or "How does the process actually work on a molecular level?"

Beyond producing the biotechnological framework for prototypes in the lab, the team behind the *Human-Bacteria Interfaces* project is committed to creating more relational bonds and awareness around the biological phenomena we already coexist with. By displaying their ideas visually and designing workshops, the collective aims to communicate the many ways in which we are already entangled with bacteria. This serves as a ground to collectively imagine how those relations might be shaped in the future. The collective is framing the focus of their workshops and displays as a blend of science communication with "still letting people feel and experience how it would be to interact and live with ALI, an 'ambient living intelligence.'"

The collective states that "by living together with something alive" we might be able to "train ourselves in implementing and valuing the 'act of care' again". ALI is aimed to become a technology to attune into the bacterial scales of our environments and integrate them into our daily lives. Through the knowledge we acquire living with such different life forms, the collective hopes we learn to extend these "acts of care" to living beings we haven't considered before. While developing the ALI prototype, they are also prototyping a way of interdisciplinary collaboration between biotechnology, art, and design. The team behind the *Human-Bacteria Interfaces* project is always circling around the question "Is this a fantasy for the future or perhaps already possible today?"

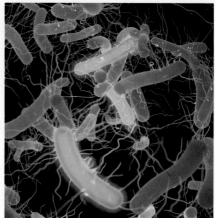
An early simulation of human-bacteria interaction

Views of different programming activities at the Sister Garden in Bandung, Western Indonesia

SEDEKAH BENIH
Vincent Rumahloine
and Mang Dian

Based in Bandung, Western Indonesia, *Sedekah Benih* researches and documents the traditional ecological knowledge that is passed down in society from generation to generation through art and media. At the root of the project is the belief that traditional knowledge can be learned, developed, and shared to help solve the current problems related to climate change.

Since April 2021, *Sedekah Benih* has magnified the importance of building bridges between science and society in order to facilitate change. The project has shifted its focus to preparing communities for an exchange of knowledge. Often, there are communication gaps when certain knowledge is introduced to a community; at the same time, individual communities lack the confidence to interact with people whom they consider more intelligent or powerful. *Sedekah Benih* aims to strengthen individuals within the local culture through a series of initiatives that combine traditional ecological knowledge with other activities that expose them to different circles. *Sedekah Benih* has now evolved into a safe space, encouraging communities of diverse backgrounds to come together in Bandung to share and discuss ideas and know-how.

This project highlights the role of a group of mothers from the Cibogo area. Through a series of programs developed over the last year, *Sedekah Benih* has discovered how important the work of women—particularly mothers—is within the community. With their help, the initiative's reach has expanded significantly. The next steps will focus on the involvement of local children, followed by a more gradual outreach to fathers and youths.

Together with several communities in the city of Bandung, *Sedekah Benih* is now ready to share and exchange knowledge that will be beneficial for the future of many people.

Vincent Rumahloine and Mang Dian in Conversation with Alexander Hicks

ALEXANDER HICKS

What I really enjoy with this project, is that it's about knowledge. It's about preserving knowledge by giving it to other people, showing them how it's done. That's the same thing with my collection of chilies, where people say that I shouldn't give them to anybody else, they're just going to regrow them, and then, everybody will have them. I say that everybody should have them. That's the thing—everybody should have the knowledge, but everybody should also know what this knowledge is worth, and what it's supposed to do. That's what we were talking about before. It's so important that people realize that the stuff that they know is important, they are experts somehow, and they have all these little knowledge pieces. I experienced this in Munich when we had our mentoring session. I had so much great stuff prepared that I wanted to share with Vincent and Mang how they can do better agriculture. That there was all this new scientifically proven stuff. They were just bored, saying, "We've done that forever." I was like, "So do you know why?" And they said, "No. But we just do it." That's the thing that's so important, that we have this knowledge and know about this knowledge, but also, what it's doing and why it's good that we keep doing it. So many little things that we do in the green businesses, in growing plants, in growing food is old knowledge, but so much we're not going to do anymore because it is not efficient enough, because we don't know what it really does. That's something really important that I have learned a lot about in the last year. A little bit more than a year, working with these two guys.

VINCENT RUMAHLOINE

Sharing this knowledge, it's one thing that we are trying to build within our project. We want to be with everyone that is involved—it's important. It can be that you are studying in university, or you are just learning agriculture as a hobby or something. When we agree on doing this project together, everyone is important. We practiced this in our garden, our community garden. So, you can come, you can share anything. We can have a different opinion about religion because in Bandung now, religious stuff has become a thing. We want to bring people together with respect. Because I think it is really important, and we tried to do that in Pforzheim. There are many Pforzheimer coming here today. I remember when we were sitting by the pond during the lockdown: "Mang, if we want to do this, we need to do it as a safe space." Everyone from different backgrounds can sit down here, because we share the same concern about society, why everyone has become so extreme to the left, to the right. No one wants to be staying in the middle to accept others. So, from this point of view, I think I'm an artist and Mang is an activist, we have this common ground of wanting to make a safe space. Maybe that is what makes this project keep on going, and how it can affect people beyond culture, beyond borders. Like you said, it's working in Indonesia and I see it's working also in Germany.

VINCENT RUMAHLOINE TRANSLATING FOR MANG DIAN

So, for Mang Dian, knowledge is a really wide universe. There is nothing impossible if we want to be serious, and really willing to do it. We want to keep on sharing the knowledge beyond this event. Now, there are many people in Bandung who are also really happy that we are here.

AUDIENCE MEMBER

What would be the next step after *Sedekah Benih*?

VR We talked about this with Mang Dian, that we did a lot of stuff over the last year. It's kind of like trial and error. Which one to continue? Not all of our projects are working. There are a few things that, okay, are not working but we agree that if everything falls down, we are going to stick with the mothers. Because this is the strongest part, and we can really feel it. And I think the most significant change within the community since last year is the mothers. Now, they start to express themselves and can lead. For me, and for us, it's really valuable. We want to stick with this and then we want to continue working with them. For Sedekah Benih, we want to still share knowledge, to bring people more. Now, we are ready for scientists; now, we are ready for designers, we are ready for architects, we are ready for many different people, because the community is ready. At the least, you can talk with the mothers. If the others are not ready, we can bring the mothers, and you can talk about anything with them. They will really, really attack you with many questions.

That's the important part of our project. Once you feel important, then you know that you are okay to start showing your skills, small skills about making sambals, for example. And then, you start to feel like an expert. So, yeah, give me more people who want to learn. If Mang Alex is coming to Indonesia, for sure, he is going to go to the mothers first. He will get a lot of sambal.

Mediating Ecological Forms of Knowledge: The Evolution of *Sedekah Benih*

Aisha Altenhofen

Assembling the gathering space in Pforzheim, to host a discussion on the history of chili

Working with chili seeds as a core material in Pforzheim

Initiated by Vincent Rumahloine and Mang Dian in Bandung, Western Indonesia, *Sedekah Benih* is a platform for knowledge exchange, focusing on bridging scientific and community knowledge by using seeds as vessels of ecological intelligence.

"Plants can become a universal language and can be catalysts for human encounters," state artist Vincent Rumahloine and environmental activist Mang Dian. The platform they have founded, *Sedekah Benih*, aims to mediate a multiplicity of ecological forms of knowledge. The project explores the relationship between human and non-human beings, by creating safe spaces where individuals from various backgrounds can share, exchange and discuss multiple ways of knowing and engaging with plants. These perspectives stretch from the experience of individual members of local communities, to collective oral histories transmitting ancient agricultural knowledge, and to collaborating with scientists who work in biotechnology labs. Rumahloine and Dian describe how they view plants as a language to connect and bring together "humans as seeds who have a lot of knowledge, no matter their background." Sedekah Benih is about creating opportunities for exchange that get people from various backgrounds into the same space to start these conversations.

The Sister Garden, in Bandung, Western Indonesia, is where Rumahloine and Dian initiated *Sedekah Benih*. Based on an urban gardening project by Mang Dian, they started sharing seeds within their local community and initiated research around collective memories of *tiis leungeun*, which roughly translates to a "green thumb", or a person talented in farming. Through their research, the collective discovered that Sundanese Indigenous Communities store and express agricultural knowledge through *Karinding* music. This music includes information on "how traditional astronomy is used to determine the correct times for planting and harvesting," explain Rumahloine and Dian. "On another island, there is a song as a mitigation for tsunamis. In the eastern part of Indonesia, there is a 'Sasi' system [agreement to protect endangered species from harvesting] to manage natural resources." *Sedekah Benih* is about collecting and sharing these pieces of knowledge, disseminated not only through discussion, but through the embodied practice of care of one's own seedlings.

At the first Driving the Human festival in October of 2021, the team behind *Sedekah Benih* installed a greenhouse where they hosted discussions and handed out a local seedling, lamb lettuce, to all those who passed by the festival. Before being spread through the city, the lamb lettuce seedlings were also bathed in the Karinding music, in an embodied connection to the plants in the community garden back in Bandung. When taking them home, visitors were encouraged to connect to the *Sedekah Benih* online platform, and thus establish a relationship with the garden in Indonesia and the seedlings planted here. Rumahloine pointed out how the harvest—of the lamb lettuce in Germany, and of the chilis and red ginger native to Indonesia in Bandung—could then be performed together on different sides of the globe.

Beyond growing plants like chili and red ginger, *Sedekah Benih* has been hosting events and collaborations within their garden. Last month they hosted Sabulang Bentor, a public event collectively celebrating the upcoming fasting month of Ramadan with mothers from the local community, representatives of the city government and the *Sedekah Benih* team. Together, they cooked "munggah", a meal composed of Nasi Liwet, a rice-based dish that includes tofu, vegetables, salted fish, sambal, and crackers. The shared meal created a space for conversation and exchange between the different parties. Other events at their garden included a chili competition, Karinding music sessions, and their ongoing seed sharing activities. The Driving the Human mentoring event in December 2021 allowed *Sedekah Benih* to get in touch with chili

Planting and caring for diverse types of chili at the BioChili farm

expert Alexander Hicks, who runs the BioChili farming project in Germany. Mang Dian completed a residency at BioChili to share and exchange his knowledge from urban farming within the Sister Garden. As part of the residency, the *Sedekah Benih* team hosted a public event in Pforzheim discussing the history of chili, as well as multiple perspectives on growing chilis in our current times.

The team behind *Sedekah Benih* states how "the seed is information that records the process of evolution for thousands of years." Rumahloine and Dian create spaces that acknowledge and exchange multiple readings of the information these plants hold, from ancient agricultural practices, to the analysis of scientists working in biotechnological labs and the memories of individuals. These multiple perspectives showcase the complexity of the plants themselves, as well as the many ways humans relate to them. Staying with this complexity, *Sedekah Benih* is about moving consciously into a future that reflects the many facets of human positions within ecosystems, as well as striving towards understanding non-human life forms in a more comprehensive manner.

The public space in Pforzheim, which became a gathering and exchange space

VIRTUAL SANCTUARY FOR FERTILIZING MOURNING
Eliana Otta

Virtual Sanctuary for Fertilizing Mourning **was created with the intention of commemorating the deaths of indigenous leaders and environmental activists assassinated in recent years in Peru, while defending their territories from deforestation, mining, and drug trafficking.**

Over the course of a year and a half, we worked together with their families and communities to create virtual tours of the areas they strove to protect, now hosted in a website called Luto Verde. Every tour is different, trying to reflect each community's own universe, uniquely shaped by its territory, collective activities, and more-than-human bonds. Oral histories, remembrance, songs, and all the information that the communities found suitable to share, were used to develop portals into ways of life that are now threatened, but also to convey the invisible and affectionate threads sustaining them. The recorded material additionally shows the effects of extractivism and corruption in places where nature is treated merely as an infinite source of resources and profit. Besides the website, *Virtual Sanctuary for Fertilizing Mourning* is constituted by its research activities, texts about its work with the different communities, sound pieces, drawings, and a site-specific installation at the Berlin venue silent green.

This project has emerged from the conviction that remembering the deceased can be a way to learn from and defend the precious territories and cultures to which they belonged. Getting to know their communities, even from afar, will hopefully highlight the important daily battles they face in defense of the Amazon under the most precarious circumstances. By mourning the lives of Mauro Pío, Gonzalo Pío, Arbildo Meléndez, Yenes Ríos, Herasmo García, and Santiago Vega, we aim to help fertilize the grounds for the ways of living they defended.

Views of Eliana Otta's installation at the Driving the Human festival, Berlin, November 2022

Eliana Otta in Conversation
with Suzanne Pierre

SUZANNE PIERRE

I took a walk reading the descriptions, the biographies, of the activists that you've represented and honored in your piece. My initial reaction was of pain. Seeing the faces of these individuals, the way the etchings captured their seriousness and commitment to the reason that they lived and why they were killed, touched me significantly. Many of these people understood that their lives were at risk. There seems to be an anticipation on a spiritual level as well as a literal level.

ELIANA OTTA

It's really touching that you read this in the drawings, because the drawings were mostly done from images that I took from newspapers or the internet when the person died. In general, as you say, they are very aware of the risks and have received threats. In many cases, they decide to continue their lives and their struggles. For example, in the case of Arbildo Menéndez— Arbildo's sister, Sarah, tells how he was aware of these dangers. The last Christmas before the year that he died, he wanted to have the whole family together to dance and to eat and to enjoy. But at the end of the night, he was telling her that he was at risk and that he knew it. Also, he said that probably the state needed that to happen in order to pay attention to their claim—in this case, to access proper recognition of the land titlings of his community. I guess in many of these cases, the people that are engaged and involved know that if they don't try to do these things, nobody else will, so it's really up to them to continue this kind of fight.

SP   There's something that comes from being connected to a place that you have no alternative to; that it is this unique place both in its ecological reality as well as its cultural and spiritual significance. Its particularities also make it a target, and also make the individuals there a target. Can you speak about the nature of living with mourning and how that necessitates a different type of creative expression? How do you capture grief for people in a situation like this, while also holding the continuousness of it?

EO   Your question makes me think of many different things at the same time. For example, it makes me think of Beatrice, who was the daughter of Mauro Pío, who was the leader of Nuevo Amanecer Hawai and was killed in 2013. After he was killed, his son, Gonzalo, who became the next leader, was killed in 2020. I think of Beatrice's way of always merging laughter with sadness, and remembrance with tenderness; and still bursting into tears when she remembers her father, but at the same time laughing precisely because she remembers him. I guess these feelings are always mixed when we mourn or remember people we care about. At the same time, I think that the importance of these mourning and grieving practices is that they allow us to precisely connect with these things or people that we care about. We can sometimes feel a transition between pain or sadness and also joy and love and the feeling of being alive precisely because we can acknowledge what we care about and what moves us. I think I'm interested in this dialogue between these emotions that many times are thought of as being separated or opposed.

SP   What this makes me think about is that, in different societies, in different communities, we have a different level of proximity to death. I'm from the United States. My experience is that on a day-to-day basis we don't engage with death, or proximity to the risk of death—we avoid it actively. Our culture is anti-death. It's taboo. Can you talk about the relationship and how people operate when their culture is not just engaging with mourning and grief, but really forced to engage with the decision to live close to death because of what they care about, because of what's precious?

EO   It's difficult to generalize. On one hand, some of these communities are inhabited by Kakataibo people. It's a particular ethnicity from that area. They have a deep cultural tradition of burying their dead in the ground of their own houses. The first day that I was going to do an interview, I was walking with the widow of one of these persons, going to the house of the parents of her husband. On the way there, the brother of the killed person ran into me and he said, "Ah, you are searching for my brother. My brother is there." I was like, what does he mean, my brother is there? They arrived at the house and they said, "Ah, yes. There he is." He was literally underground in what would be their living room. You see the shape of the tomb, which is underground. So it's really living all the time with your deaths. Then the value of the territory has also to do with this fact that the people that you love are always with you and you're always with them. Which is also complicated, because, for example, in this case, the widow was forced to live there because her husband was buried there. But actually she was from another village. There are many different phenomena happening at the same time, with some people who really live deep-rooted and connected to the environment in a spiritual sense. Then there are other people who are co-opted by capitalist habits and work for the deforesters, or maybe young people that are carrying a backpack full with coca leaves to produce cocaine because they can earn some quick money. Also, these mourning practices are changing. Just recently we received the news that one person knew that her son drowned in the river. She sent me a picture of them making a grave in the

forest, but they brought materials from the city to make it with cement. I want to talk with her next time I'm there to ask her why she felt the need to build this cement structure in the middle of the forest that looks so alien. This is also a moment of transition.

SP   I'm always interested in the direct experience of making the art, and then the meta experience of what we do with it. I'm not an artist, I'm a scientist. I think about the ways that my work has an effect for me personally, and then has its own life outside once it's published or once it's being understood or consumed. I think about you as maybe a conduit for the stories of these individuals who've given their lives. I wonder about how you see yourself?

EO   Part of the thinking process to have this work shown here had to do with being aware that these stories don't get coverage in Peru. It is mostly a couple of websites that do independent journalism that dedicate some time to work on this, and maybe one or two newspapers once in a while. But it's not something that becomes part of the public conversation. I also thought that bringing this to a very different context could have a bouncing effect somehow over there. We are just waiting for the others' gaze to say something. Part of the project which is being shared this weekend is the website. There are many amazing websites floating in cyberspace that nobody looks at. There is also a fear of ending up as one of those. Normally my work has a collective dimension with participatory activities and interventions and provocations that then always lead to some unexpected place or situation. Because when you work with people, of course, you can't control what happens. That's also the interesting part of it.

SP   In my own work I'm a researcher and I think about how there's two levels of effect of the work. There's the environmental data and the scientific result, the conclusion, that we offer. Then there's actually the practice of doing science and doing inquiry, how they're two different things, but they have a coupled effect of creating power where there is some vacuum of power; creating agency for people depending on how science is done and who it engages and who is allowed to participate. You can create not only a new result but you can also create people with a different type of agency or capacity. In a way, the participatory artwork that you have made is a version of that, a version of engaging people who might not have even felt or realized that they have that participatory power. It's more of a prompt than a question, but how do you think about what engagement and participation does for the spirit of people who live in precarity?

EO   Well I think, because Peru is so deeply shaped by colonial structures, there is a rippling effect of the attention that something gets. How, for example, when we come from somewhere very different to these places, to begin with, there is this sense of recognition that gets activated, that people want to share their stories very openly. They feel good that somebody from far away is here. At the same time, there are also the structures that operate in the country that normally put them in the position of victims, or of waiting for development agents to do something. They also get somehow used to this dynamic of asking for things when somebody comes from outside and they have expectations regarding what you can offer. In that sense, we were always very honest saying that what we can do is to make these videos and share them and talk about these stories and to find ways of communicating them. But this is everything we can do. As artists, we can't really do more because normally all requests get mixed. There is a request for justice, for visibility, for filling in material needs, for receiving donations, for all kinds of things that get mixed when you're coming from the outside to such a place. At the same time, there are also effective bonds that start to be developed and certain complicities with certain people. So it's, again, a multi-layered situation and experience. But so far, what I have seen with this work and with some other projects that have to do with collectivizing laws and mourning, is that the people that participate are very, very generous and very open and very thankful of having a space to open up about these kinds of stories or experiences. I think there is a confirmation of the lack of spaces and situations and rituals for sharing and engaging with collective loss, and with socializing grief and its effects which are normally considered negative.

Building a Virtual Space for Mourning:
Visit to the Peruvian Amazon

Aisha Altenhofen

"A special moment happened at Unipacuyacu, the first night we tried to screen the videos. I asked Marcelino, the leader, if he had a bedsheet or any surface to project on. He came back holding a banner that they printed on the two year anniversary of the killing of Arbildo Melendez's, the former leader, asking if it could work to project on the back of it. Not only it was a great surface to project on, but it also created a moving, phantasmagoric experience, to watch the videos of the territory he was defending, screened on his face and the face of Yener Ríos and Herasmo García, the environmental defenders assassinated in Puerto Nuevo. Another layer was added in that way, spontaneously, to the evening, while literally shedding light on those lives lost to the actions of wood fellers and drug traffickers."

These words by artist Eliana Otta introduce not only one of her experiences screening her work for the Unipacuyacu community in Peru, but also the complex layers of the screened work itself. In February 2022, Eliana Otta and the filmmaker Nuno Cassola went on a research trip to Peru visiting the four communities Unipacuyacu, Sinchi Rocha, Puerto Nuevo, and Nuevo Amanecer Hawai to learn about their assassinated leaders and their threatened territories. During their stay, Otta and Cassola recorded visual footage of the daily lives of the communities within their territories, their stories and cultural objects. Based on this footage, Otta is building a virtual space for mourning for the communities that can also serve as a communication tool to bring these issues to the attention of a wider public. Over the summer of 2022, Otta and Cassola returned to Peru to revisit the four communities, to show them the work in progress and include their feedback in the making of the work. They ended up visiting three of the four communities, as Nuevo Amanecer Hawai was busy building an essential road to their community, which had to be finished before the start of the rainy season. The aim of these screenings was not only to get feedback,

Experiencing the VR version of the project with the Unipacuyacu community

but also for them to consent to their voices and images being used, and to make sure the visual material matched their perception of the situation. The screenings took place under very diverse conditions, depending on each communities' access to electricity and technology. With electric generators Otta and Cassola were able to screen the works upon unconventional and surprising surfaces such as the banner. In the following, Otta describes her screening experience with the Unipacuyacu community:

Puerto Nuevo community members showing their traditional way of dress

"We went there with a projector we rented in Pucallpa from people who teach cinematographic tools to indigenous students, but we couldn't bring much equipment because of the weight, because getting there involves taking cars, mototaxis and boats, so we needed to travel as light as possible. That night we didn't manage to properly connect the sound, since our cables were not compatible with their mixer. The next day, they brought a huge, professional mixer with a boat from a nearby town. After making the shoot with them wearing their traditional tunics (cushmas), we gathered again around the projector and connected everything. When we were ready to start, rain started pouring intensely and we all had to go under cover, bringing the equipment under the roof. Children, young and old people, we all had to go under cover in a space of 30 square meters, also protected by the banner with Arbildo's face printed which would be used as a screen. Once there, the young guys in charge of the mixer connected it, and we spent an hour together in our makeshift refuge, listening and even dancing to a bit of cumbia and techno from the 90's. The young men passed a bottle of a drink from hand to hand, sharing it with us, while the women took care of the babies and Camilo, an eight-year-old kid, played in the soccer field in front of us. Alone, totally wet, he ran everywhere under the rain. I asked him to wear the 360 degree camera on his head for a while, and he left with it happily, while we all stayed under the shelter hearing 'this is the rhythm of the night.'" After the screenings, Otta discussed the community's

Eliana Otta during her travels

responses to the work, their thoughts on representation, and what could be missing.

"Probably the most notable thing was that the three [communities] expressed their desire to have videos appearing with their traditional clothes. Since the videos were made trying to avoid disrupting their normal lives, in all of them they appeared wearing their everyday clothes, the same as any person would wear in an urban context. Now that they saw themselves on the big screen, they felt that their indigeneity was missing and feared that they would be confused with any 'mestizo' (mixed race person). This was expressed with different words in each place, but the content of the message was the same: they wanted us to make more videos with them wearing their traditional dresses, also explicitly making traditional activities such as fishing with arrows or making handcrafts. In some places they talked about the pride of showing such things and the relevance of showing their grandparents' ways of doing things. In another place someone also mentioned that if they didn't seem indigenous then people would not help them. It was never an innocent request, but one connected to their present struggles and demands, in which Indigenous identity is densely tied to the cultural traditions and the land they inhabit."

Showing the materials to children on a tablet

Screening the videos at the Puerto Nuevo Community

Essays   Conversations

Installation view, *Virtual Sanctuary for Fertilizing Mourning*, Driving the Human festival, November 2022   287

Cyberscape Ecology

Brigitte Baptiste, Biologist transwoman, MA, PhD, Chancellor of Universidad Ean in Bogotá

Every change that humans as a species have brought to the planet means an evolutionary movement, a displacement of the Earth's previous ecology. At least three kinds of effects can be addressed to understand what extent those changes are creating new realities, which have and will affect our capacities to adapt to the challenging and threatening futures we are producing. The first one is the creation of *ecological entities*, something that started with the first tool humans crafted (for instance, the carved stone slicers used to cut hides that provided new interactions between the *Homo* species and the other members of the ecosystem); the second, the attached *symbolic understanding* to those entities, unique to our species and the most significant and eventually threatening device to our own survival; and the third, a combination of the previous, which is the resulting process of *agency shifts* produced by the continuous and unavoidable adjustment of all the ecological entities, including people, *and* the attached symbolic understanding. We have and will always promote the appearance of new complexities through our unique way of thriving on this planet.

ECOLOGICAL ENTITIES

A spaceship, a vaccine, a wooden puppet, a city, are no lesser parts of the world ecosystem than an eagle, a virus, an oak. The fact that the first ones are human creations does not undermine at all their full participation in the relational system of beings, where every entity is more or less attached by exchanges of energy, matter or information. These components create the elastic glue among all things and provide their most important quality: adaptation, which is the result of a relational change that never happens without a challenge, and has to be understood as an experimental shift in the interactions between living and non-living ecological entities, subtle or dramatic. Some entities are very ancient, such as volcanoes or cyanobacteria; some more recent, such as mammals or air fryers; some are inorganic, some organic. Most of them are cyborgs,① a combination of living and non-living pieces of things, the most important ontological category of beings at present. Cyborgs frequently are blurred in the futile and dangerous conversations about the moral status of "nature", a word that has lost all of its meaning in the middle of the discussion of political ecology.

Folding and cracking is the source of innovation and evolution at all scales. New entities appear constantly as aggregation, connection, and fracture, creating enough disruption to define the new era of the

① Although the Oxford, Webster and Collins dictionaries define cyborg in terms of technologically modified humans, others prefer a wider conception, since it would impossible to forget humans are living beings, and prosthetics can be applied to modified all kinds of organisms. Plainly, cybernetic organism.

Anthropocene. Here, the known universe is folding once more. Here, humans can be crushed by the constantly moving pieces of the ecosystem or become buried by the accumulation of sediments, totally disappearing or remaining as living fossils. We may become something else, another kind of human, perhaps, in the next phase of the global ecosystem. But also, in the light of human understanding, everything is becoming something else all the time, no matter how hard our memories try to drive our present. We know the brain is no less addicted to coherence and stability than to sugar and other substances, since it is a biological device evolved to produce a workable simulation of things, where it does not matter how information gaps are filled. Until very recently, the ecological narratives that have allowed us to bloom as a species were particularly flawed by simplicity, because they were built locally on a limited set of things or because we have restricted access to very fast or slow processes. Even the most sophisticated model of the rainforest made by its native people is useless to apply to the rest of the world, no matter how much we praise ancient wisdom, although the values attached to all ways of living should be considered as sources of critical thinking and wellbeing. But at the end, collective understanding of reality has to be permanently updated and shaken by new generations no matter how comfortable our experience of things seems to be—nostalgia is not a good place to be, as it recreates isolated communities in time and space (and their supporting dogmas). No silver bullet will help solve the multiple paradoxes that humans have created just by being on the planet. There is no panacea, there are many panarchies (sensu Holling and Gunderson, 2002).

Western sciences and our ways of thinking and living deconstruct everything to the smallest level of fragmentation, leaving immense quantities of stuff to be understood or reassembled: modern epistemologies always leave leftovers. Analytical processes are the most important tools to decipher how things or phenomena work by breaking them into components, which gain independent (and sometimes unexpected) life. However, the real proof that we understand the way things function is the ability to recreate the original entity by reassembling it. Clearly, we cannot do that with living beings. Frankenstein siblings, though, emerge everywhere, at all scales, creating new relationships and therefore, new ecosystems, some of them spookier or more solitary than the creature from Mary Shelley. In the making of new entities everything becomes prosthetic, everybody grows new organs, extends their senses, asks new questions, faces different challenges. Languages, also entities, are created and evolve. Some of them reach new levels of complexity to reinforce the giant informatics network while other languages are destroyed and become extinct together with their speakers, devoured by colonialisms, violence, and their marketing strategies. Information is assembled and reassembled permanently, energy is "produced" and managed through new ways, and matter is designed again every day by lively and inspired algorithms. Recombination and information exchange by means of intercourse is one of the most ancient and successful innovation strategies, actively integrating mutation into evolutionary pathways. Human innovation works alike, inserting pieces of weird stuff everywhere: fashion, for example, represents the continuous test of our own adaptive-designed suggestions, no matter how bizarre they may appear.

We, humans, design our bodies. At the extreme, we die, but from time to time we can expand our short experience on Earth through the ICU (intensive care unit) which is the seed of space travel: we will reach the stars in suspended animation, science fiction tells us. We change our anatomies, our sex, our gender and also our care strategies by abandoning the concept of fixed identities. We use multiple prosthetics and enjoy becoming others, at least for a day, through carnivals and cosplay, experiences present in almost every culture. We can perform, we live performing. We struggle being many, being wider, being other, and even if for some this is feared as a threat, for others it is an opportunity to explore themselves with deeper freedom.

We, humans, design our habitats. We decide who can share the benefits, as pets, plain food or symbionts. But also, we witness and enjoy or hate the capacities of other species that learn to live in our natures. Mosses on the roof; rats, and the owls that hunt them in the parks at night; guilds of dogs roaming, released and orphaned on the city outskirts by their human alpha partners, help us to realise, once more, that we are not alone. Our organic companions will stay in our guts, our sewers, our mating places, our computers, even if highly modified by us.

We, humans, design our future as collective beings, surrendering our individual consciousness from time to time to participate in larger entities, ephemeral organisms like Myxamoebas; thinking as flocks, perhaps working as bees, but always as a unique species. We may share a crowded beach or a giant musical scenario for days to enjoy the outdoors, even using soft drugs to modify perception and gain empathy. We study together in giant universities, we fly packed in planes. Street gangs and digital tribes thrive: they have appeared as war or peace promoting organisations, created to become enslaved or to fight for denied rights and challenge current inequalities. Rules and shared myths or ideologies are information devices, soft or strong narratives that hold together armies, orchestras, fan clubs, institutions at large, the human-driven ecosystem.

We have created the multiverse and now will have to deal with its new secretions. Some technologies, both soft and hard, may have poisoned the Earth and ourselves, but many others have made *sapiens* a very successful species. We are still trying to accommodate them—like a sudden diva, a viral popstar in a digital channel that finds herself trying to make sense of the new complexities of life.

We can grow bioinspired after the fossil fuel era—that's the goal—but we have to be ready for nastier, lustier, dirtier environments, bizarre practices, another kind of beauty, a mix of our biological ancestry and our technological and symbolic secretions. Glass frogs behind waterfalls in the rainforest search for caves to reproduce and protect their siblings in jelly stalactites. Beautiful flying creatures emerge from disturbing blind larvae which have spent years eating rotten materials deep in the soil. Plants and animals shift sex and gender from time to time to avoid gene pool exhaustion, although some of them have been able to invade the world without sex and gender. Deadly bacteria or alien cell pieces stay alive in our bodies, in a complex conversation with other microorganisms that became the seed of immune systems, the result of millions of years of collaboration. Suddenly, the organic dimension of nature appears in front of us as radical innovation, with many entangled rhythms and extents. We realize that we are part of the process, another recent experiment of life capable of developing new organs, perhaps capable of saving the planet by bringing a new meaning to the word evolution.

CYBORG PHYLOGENETICS AND NEUROECOLOGY
There are many kinds of biotech symbionts. Clay pots with clean cultures of microbes for fermenting food or preparing beer can be considered hybrid devices that human ingenuity brought to life thousands of years in the past, becoming the ancestor of the industrially produced substances which are now ecological entities: cheese, wine, kimchi. These symbionts participate as "stuff" in the global network of energy becoming matter: they have evolved through time, they will become something else. Perhaps we are more used to thinking about yoghurt as an ecological entity than of cell phones or birth pills, but they are all active members of the current planetary metabolism. Every biological entity participates in the extended and heavily modified contemporary biota where DNA, organs, organisms, communities, and landscapes are being constantly reshaped, and where digital technologies are adding new levels of complexity. Satellite imagery, drone surveillance, and cloud computing are providing new capacities for planetary operation

(frequently far away from safe operating spaces, sensu Rockström),② becoming essential pieces of the global ecosystem and opening new avenues for complexity while helping us reassemble the world in a more sustainable and just way.③ The notion of cyberscape,④ for example, links virtual reality with land use planning and urbanism—although the digital dimension of the process is frequently ripped from the entity it is addressing, the landscape made from dirt, sweat and dreams. On one hand, rivers, forests, mountains, people, trees, animals, roads, ports and dams may have digital twins, rarely understood as real novelty in the metaverse since they are linked to the "original"; on the other hand, they may emerge as monsters or chimeras only linked to their previous level of existence by untraceable algorithms. Hence, cyberscapes are not just "the virtual landscape of cyberspace; the face of computer networking"⑤ as Wiktionary says, because this definition does not tell anything about the hybrid condition of all ecological entities, both organic and inorganic, and focuses solely on the informatic component of its own reality which is the digitally-perceived surface of the new landscapes. The definition is useless without phylogenetic inference,⑥ the link with matter, the source. Cyberscapes are landscapes assembled by cyborgs, not just as metaverses but in this worldly level of existence.

Every person develops a particular wiring with the environment while their neurological system grows. Placement, even before birth, has important implications for the way we build awareness and how our mind expands, both in material and symbolic ways. Our exposure to the environment while developing is being recognized as a fundamental source of synchronicity and adaptation, without being deterministic.⑦ Ecological connectivity is the mechanism by which our brain has framed a more or less complex image of reality through millennia and it has allowed us to thrive within networks of other entities, no matter if they are human or not—microbes, animals, plants, devices and even ghosts became an active part of our lives. Our ever-changing senses have provided an extended neural ecosystem where the notion of proximity and relevance of everything produces knowledge and meaning. These are not just "things" that "happen" in our minds, but are the bond with all other beings in a very tangible way. Many questions remain: How different are we wired as members of a local network of ecological entities? To what extent does living and culturally evolving in the Amazon, the Sahara or the Arctic create different neurological infrastructure and the subtle placement capacities that allow us to successfully migrate and adapt (or not) to many cultures or environments? Do cities provide a totally divergent neurological experience reflected in different kinds of thought? Do we

② Johan Rockström, Will Steffen, Kevin Noone et al, "A safe operating space for humanity" in *Nature* no. 461 (September 2009): 472–475, https://doi.org/10.1038/461472a

③ Kate Raworth, "A Safe and Just Space for Humanity," Oxfam Discussion Paper, February 2012. http://www.oxfam.org/sites/www.oxfam.org/files/dp-a-safe-and-justspace-for-humanity-130212-en.pdf

④ The Cambridge dictionary speaks about "cyberspace" as "the internet considered as an imaginary area without limits where you can meet people and discover information about any subject", or "an electronic system that allows computer users around the world to communicate with each other or to access information for any purpose", but lacks a definition of cyberscapes. https://dictionary.cambridge.org

⑤ https://en.wiktionary.org/

⑥ Phylogenetics is the study of the evolutionary history and relationships among individuals, groups of organisms (e.g., populations, species, or higher taxa), or other biological entities with evolutionary histories (e.g., genes, biochemicals, or developmental mechanisms). Phylogenetic inference is the task of inferring this history, and as with other problems of inference, there are interesting and difficult questions regarding how these inferences are justified. *Stanford Encyclopedia of Philosophy*. First published Dec 8, 2021; substantive revision Jun 30, 2022.

⑦ Kendra Cherry, "The Nature vs. Nurture Debate: Genetic and Environmental Influences and How They Interact," *Verywellmind*, October 19, 2022, https://www.verywellmind.com/what-is-nature-versus-nurture-2795392

⑧ David Pitt, Paul R. Samson, eds., *The Biosphere and Noosphere Reader: Global Environment, Society and Change* (Oxford: Routledge, 1999).

think differently, organise our knowledge differently, operate following diverse ontologies, produce novelty through alternative epistemologies? Do we all behave as generous truth holders trying to convince others to adopt our unique perspective? How far is our subjectivity a source of adaptive knowledge within the network of other subjectivities?

During the history of humanity our noosphere, ⑧ the amount of available and shared knowledge, has grown continuously, making us a different kind of people, generation after generation—even with the same biology as our ancestors, we are as different from them as any other species. Sciences and the arts, also shifting concepts, struggle to create a shared version of our planet without blurring its wonderful diversity. How does science and art celebrate the multiplicity of the human experiment, but also abandon or redefine ideas of what we are, in terms of ethnicity, gender, capacities, and rights? How do they create a place where we learn to simultaneously experience different scales of thought, meaning being local and global at the same time? Perhaps this is through a "guided schizophrenia", a built-in capacity of being different things at different moments and different places, like ancient anemones...

IDENTITY

Nothing more ephemeral and misleading as identity to serve as a device to decode the structure behind ecological relationships. Genes keep producing unique versions of living matter (organisms), algorithms (genotypes) that keep computing traits (phenotypes) within certain domains that we call "species". Like in a landscape, there is a difference between what can be seen and what lies behind and produces what can be seen. A beautiful rural setting can be compared in Asturias, the Viet mountains, the Addis Ababa hills and in Boyacá, but a close look of its components will show different actors performing a similar plot. Besides analogy, mimicry has played an important role in defining ecological relationships: seduction and deceit are regular strategies to reach a positive evolutionary outcome. Ecosystems, and their material expression, the landscape, are performative: predation, symbiosis, mutualism or any other relation between their components are bonded by signs, the semiotics of nature which become modified by the rising cyborg. The process of building a human city is as natural as the hornet's nest and even if the latter may not be technologically modified, they hang on the roof of human-built ceilings, benefitting from the offer of new habitats and simultaneously modifying them. The Wasp, a fictional hero belonging to the metaverse, flies between levels of complexity and is a connecting ecological entity between the digital and this material world, perhaps a bit more complex than Brigitte Bardot, another fictional character that has ignited a shift on gender representations and behaviours in human recent history.

Natural selection has been always a game, a hide and seek challenge where the genetic basis of beings is invisible and has to be guessed from a similar but never identical genetic frame. Adaptation, then, is the result of performing in a play with biologically produced actors, whose real identities are just partially disclosed. It is built upon generation after generation of testing every single detail of the character outfit, on intensified physical expressions that are read as "fitness" (the reddest, the stinkiest, etc.), sometimes in a very complex mix of things that is very difficult to grasp or deconstruct. The attraction between living beings is mysterious; there is no possible optimization of the multiple equations that run in parallel to compute a body, an organism that will be tested against a similarly complex environment. The ecological theatre runs permanently... and each time Hamlet is played by a slightly different genotype which remains unknowable, hidden.

Taxonomies brought by modernity helped us to simplify a difficult world but had a nasty consequence: we ended up thinking of things and entities as fixed categories, and worse, lying to ourselves with the flawed conception that naming meant knowing. Taking the tag for the thing, since the brain enjoys the fable no matter how lethal it may be. But at the end, local realities, those ontologies at hand, have limited influence because things keep changing and are always a moving target. We only perceive their changes by interacting with them. Collecting insects may help us know them better, but it also creates a new entity that lays dead for centuries on a museum shelf: the only "true" insect is the last one that has had an ecological interaction with our kind, hopefully not being destroyed in the process. However, the specimen in the collection adds a new layer of meaning, not just information, to the original idea of "insect". Digital insects as virtual constructs are not the same as those we have put in a collection, nor the organic one that escaped, but can also be part of an expanded notion of *insectness* that hopefully may help others to thrive. They add to all other information that encompasses the notion of that being (the insect) *as part of an evolutionary and everyday changing environment.*

AGENCY

Agency is the capacity to give voice and autonomy to an (ecological) entity in a given system. Within an ecosystem, "agency" could be defined as the capacity of each participant or member to acknowledge the existence and relevance of the other: do ants care about humans, as humans care for ants? Can we speak of the voice of the forest without replacing, faking, or inventing such a thing? Are humans or non-humans capable of speaking for different Others genuinely? Can the Earth become a biocommonwealth, a planet where ecological relationships among multiple entities can bring stronger possibilities to expand the experience of life elsewhere?

If certain levels of cooperation among people has allowed us to release huge amounts of energy captured by the planet through millennia with unprecedented levels of efficiency, it has also unwillingly created a new planet, unstable and hostile to our own kind and most of the non-human biodiversity. In the process, however, we find ourselves deeply changed and forced to face our emerging ecological identity: humans are also becoming others, technosymbionts, self-produced entities and cyborgs that escape from the classical and outdated evolutionary tree we use to make sense of biological change through time.

There are many proposals for a "more than human" world, but a "post-human" era which has emerged recently does not count as evolution: if humans do not relate to the technosymbiotic perspective (the connection of cells with chips, for example), becoming a piece of digital memory in the machine may or may not mean *becoming* at all. The future depends on the degree of awareness retained by the process, where the sentient human cyborg will have expanded self-consciousness and empathy. It will have a new body and different capacities, and will take care of life on the planet from its new ecological position, hopefully towards sustainability.

Cyberscapes are the new environment and the latest device of humans to depict ecological entities, where we can challenge our common understanding of everything while living, experimenting, and embodying the process of recreating the world. This happens not just in silica, as a memory, but in very solid ways. Accepting our growing digital skins will allow us to "feel and touch" ourselves and the world in many additional ways than in the past—although not far away from the ancient fire pit where we heard stories about fantastic beings and sweeter lives.

MAKING MEANING OUT OF THE EMERGING ECOLOGICAL REALITIES
The next stage in our lives as a species is linked to our development as cyborg entities thriving in cyborg landscapes in the emerging Anthropocene. Many have already chosen not to walk that way, a beautiful option—history has seen many splits and fertile mutations without idle effects on the common ancestor, although they may fail and disappear. Human evolutionary pathways will not be defined by biology, perhaps bringing new meaning to the word speciation. However, if we become extinct, there will not be anybody left to make further judgments about anything, an irony—the future of the universe would become trivial (unless aliens are

recording) and irrelevant, no matter what we tell ourselves before disappearing. Human dignity will become a void idea and human ethics an irrelevant fact without political agency, no matter if rivers or bears were granted full personhood by our wise or dumb leaders. Values will mean nothing without the ecological entity that values: that is the best reason for humans to stay on the planet—but away from the centre, without having the slightest notion of destiny.

PROTOTYPES

ECO-
RENEWAL

"During the history of humanity our noosphere, the amount of available and shared knowledge, has grown continuously, making us a different kind of people, generation after generation—even with the same biology as our ancestors, we are as different from them as any other species. Sciences and the arts, also shifting concepts, struggle to create a shared version of our planet without blurring its wonderful diversity. How does science and art celebrate the multiplicity of the human experiment, but also abandon or redefine ideas of what we are, in terms of ethnicity, gender, capacities, and rights?"
(Brigitte Baptiste)

Essays   Conversations   Epilogue

303

Citizen Engagement in the Age of Climate Crisis

This is an edited and excerpted version of a conversation that took place on November 25, 2022 during the Driving the Human festival in Berlin.

VERA SACCHETTI

I'm going to start with Suzanne and ask you about this idea of citizen engagement and how it manifests in the work that you are currently doing.

SUZANNE PIERRE

I am from the Critical Ecology Lab, a nonprofit research and social change organization based in Oakland, California. The organization is a collaboration between scientists, scholars of various disciplines and community members who are all asking the question: how can we use the techniques from Western science to actually describe the way that historical colonialism, oppression, and white supremacy have shaped things at a molecular level all the way up to the ecosystem level. It's a necessary part of my work to be in conversation with community members but also using science and art to inform how we can mobilize communities to ask for and demand real change. What does citizen engagement mean in my context? The most important is that science has historically used communities for experimentation, for data collection, for testing, and ultimately for marketing. Very seldom has the scientific community actually gained ideas for new hypotheses and questions based on the priorities of communities that have been marginalized. So making sure that science centralizes the goals and futures of oppressed communities is a huge piece of my work.

VS

Can you give us an example of one specific initiative that you're currently developing?

SP

So an example is where the Critical Ecology Lab is testing a new model for hypothesis generation. We are in a planetary crisis right now. We don't have time to allow the demographics of traditional science to continue to generate the same ideas that have kept us in the exact same place we've always been. We're not changing and responding quickly enough. So what would it look like if scientists and especially scientists of color, people of oppressed backgrounds, were put directly in conversation with communities that are not only locally being harmed by ecosystem change but have been part of global systems of oppression? In Oakland, Critical Ecology Lab is piloting a hypothesis generation series, which is called *Ecosystem Questions for the African Diaspora*. We're focusing on the African diaspora, but the model that we're generating is really for many communities beyond just the one. It's a series of events where we invite people within their schedules, within their means, to come join us to use their cultural memory as well as future aspirations across lines of ethnicity, citizenship, socioeconomic background to say what our shared racial heritage means for ecosystem change. Scientists get to ask, "How do we listen?" and then turn those thoughts and what we hear into testable hypotheses that we go and actually enact in research. We return with the data we collect and say, "Does this actually add to or answer questions that the community is concerned with?"

VS

I'm from Colombia and nowadays, I'm in charge of a business school that is trying to become a sustainability school. I'm the only one that holds a degree in science—we have 12,000 students and 350 staff, all working on business, all of them are thinking business, business, business. So my ideas mostly break our business as usual. They are founded on science of course, and entrepreneurial innovation, but also in democracy. That's why engagement is so important. We need to involve people of different backgrounds, who come from a diverse set of cultural environments. Colombia has at least a hundred different ethnic groups. We have a strong Afro-descendant community—at least 10 to 15 percent of our population.

BRIGITTE BAPTISTE

Brigitte, I would also like to start with this question. What does citizen engagement mean in the context of your work?

Also, other issues related to ways of thinking about the ecosystem and the planet, ways of doing things. One of my perspectives is queer ecology. How queer people can bring new ways of understanding ecological relationships and the world. In many cases the things we depict as problems are not problems—they are other people's problems and not ours. It's quite a challenge to put non-orthodox ecology on the minds of the students and teachers.

VS

Eliana, we've seen in the example of the project that you present at the Kuppelhalle that your engagement with and advocacy for these communities is hugely important.

ELIANA OTTA

It's an interesting choice of words to talk about citizen engagement because Indigenous communities in Peru are not considered and have not been considered citizens to begin with. There have been many people dying in the last decades when they have tried to defend their lands and when they have tried to protest and to become political actors because they have never been seen as citizens or as people with the right to defend their points of view. Somehow, there is a short circuit in my mind when I try to think of the communities I'm addressing and the word citizenship because this is normally something that doesn't go together, at least when talking about the Peruvian context. There is an interesting discussion to be had when we talk about peoples that are living in a kind of parallel dimension or world when they are not directly engaged or organized through the formal ways of law or administration. They are normally touched only when there is violence, conflicts, and injustice. Living in Europe as a Peruvian, I have felt very alienated many times, especially during the pandemic because of the difference in which it affected Peru and Europe. This is also something that made me want to work with these communities and somehow refresh and deepen my bond with Peru even though I have been away. What do these times ask from me? Working on this project is one of the ways in which I'm trying to address this question.

VS   I want to explore this idea of visibility and invisibility that you have alluded to in a variety of different ways because the work that you do is actually trying to bring visibility to ignored demographics—people that have not been part of the initial conversation.

SP   I think about visibility in the context of visibility to whom—what defines a community as being seen or legible to others. Legitimacy in the eyes of the settler colonial state is one type of visibility. There's a lot of work that a community has to do to contort itself to appear worth recognizing. My work is trying to pivot away from that type of visibility. The power that science holds as an institution and other sorts of structures of legitimacy or formality have been demeaning and reductionist of these communities. My question is not how do we do citizen engagement to make people more visible and therefore empowered, but really how do we do a sort of mass divestment from the idea that people should be visible in a way that brings safety or brings participation. How can we usurp power without legibility, without visibility, and is that actually a different outcome? The reason that I'm a scientist is because I wanted to understand how the inner workings of the scientific enterprise uses identity as well as expertise, as a manipulator of power—to get all of the technical skills associated with science so that I could manipulate those power structures. I want to exist in a world where the gaze that would make us visible is irrelevant.

BB   Suzanne, you mentioned at the beginning that you were trying to provide a new method to create hypotheses. I think this is amazing because there are many communities where scientists are a minority—it's different from Europe or even China where you have a strong scientific community. We have to trust that these small communities are working on behalf of the whole country or the whole population. It's not just a problem of science—it's a larger problem of society. So what I want to do is to protect science in our countries, to do better science and to really produce new knowledge to help to build wellbeing in our communities. Because if we don't do that, we will lose centuries of global thinking. We need to be open to new languages, to ways of understanding reality. We need to be very humble in terms of how different people explain what is happening to themselves. We need to build a new stage of scientific thinking, a wider way of understanding science.

VS   Eliana, I feel that many of the things that have been said resonate with things I've seen in your practice.

EO   I am working on an idea which is called Fertilizing Mourning. This idea is taking inspiration from an ancient practice of soil regeneration from an area of the Amazon. It has been proved scientifically that over thousands of years there was an interaction between humans and the soil—performing rights of mourning in which they would bury and burn human debris with organic debris. They were making the soil more fertile than it was. There is proof now that the Amazon is not so generous by a miracle, but through the progressive process of this interaction. And this had a spiritual component for the people that were doing this, performing these rituals.

Then there is a center in Peru in an area called Tarapoto, where a woman has been trying to rescue this tradition which is already practiced there by the Quechua Lamistas. She was commenting how for her, it's very easy to see and to imagine the young Quechua Lamistas from the area to still practice these traditions, that they could combine these traditions with their intention of going to university and to learn science and to develop their knowledge; that it was more difficult for her to imagine young scientists coming from other countries to embrace the spiritual dimension of such a practice. She was not seeing this openness from the people that were coming from abroad to learn about the practice—they would keep the practical part and not be able to engage with the spiritual part. This is something that for me is a very interesting challenge when thinking about how to expand the scientific field. This is something that I have been trying to consider when approaching my own understanding of mourning; the possibility of not seeing things as divided and opposed, disrupting this dichotomy of binary relationships that modernism has constructed to organize everything that surrounds us. I am trying to see this entanglement between what is supposedly opposed—for example, life and death. What kind of regenerative practices could come out of this understanding of things as being more fluid and contaminated between each other?

VS   I would like to reflect on this idea, the dismemberment of modernism that is happening where we are trying to recuperate things that seem to be forgotten, that seem to be erased in binaries, in neatly explainable oppositions. I want to ask you all about this idea of an effort of imagination. I would even maybe dare to say it's a sort of a world-building effort.

SP   What we are doing as a group—and I'm sure others here as well— is literally world-building where there is a world we live in and then there's a world that we absolutely need to exist. I think when you talk about this relationship between mourning and actualizing the experience—the memory or the sort of heritage memory present as a response to loss—that's such a beautiful and poignant form of world-building because it's a resurrection, like an experienced resurrection of a past that was deliberately taken away. So how can science be a co-conspirator or an ally in that process? How can every interaction with our memory and our history be legitimized from within? I mentioned this process of hypothesis generation—what if we're not asking, "Oh, will science listen to the histories of people from the African diaspora?" but rather, saying within this room of a shared ancestry, "Can we grieve our experiences while inquiring and using the scientific method as one mode of inquiry?" Actually, it's not only a healing process but a revolutionary process.

BB   It's a very complex issue and I would like to approach from one side, which is the issue of narratives because we have been trained to attach to one narrative to legitimize and to feel that we get some power from the narrative. We hold onto it—this happens to all of us if we teach, or if we have families, or if we participate in a community. We are all attached to a way of telling the truth. It's very difficult to question ourselves and to modify this narrative because it's embedded within emotional things. So how do different people in the world tell stories about themselves? There are plenty of interesting ways of breaking the dominant narratives. I think that's the challenge for pedagogy. Let's think together, how do we build these contemporary narratives because we are entangled now in a very complex way.

EO   I would highlight the importance of the experiential approach and of inhabiting the present, trying to somehow be responsive and loyal to the circumstances that are around. Extending into daily life somehow through simple actions. I guess that's the biggest pedagogy that we can create together, the one that has to do with embodied knowledge and the kind of knowledge that gets passed on beyond attending a class or reading a text.

VS   I don't know exactly what it is, but it feels sometimes that we are asleep—all the work that you have been describing is work that is urgent and it needs to happen now. We cannot wait any longer. There is an urgency that comes through working in certain contexts that does not allow us to ignore the work that we have to do.

BB   The word urgency always comes together with the word speed and speed is relative term. It's urgent to change, but the sense of urgency is different for different groups; you may rush and make mistakes. Let's do experiments, let's work together, let's talk a lot about what's happening and let's understand why you feel that things are so pressing and for others they are not. And then try to figure out different pathways or different scenarios—"Okay, it will take twenty years, two, three generations to make a real shift for the planet." We need to have faith in that.

EO

For people that are part of a genealogy of oppression, colonialism, and constant violence, the question was never so much about the future. Right now, there is this obsession about the future and end of the world narratives, which doesn't acknowledge that somehow, the end of the world is happening daily and has been happening over centuries for many. The majority of people living under those conditions have managed to survive and to defend themselves and save their knowledge, their traditions. They experience pleasure, fun, and desire under those conditions. It's less about worrying about the future, but worrying about the present and probably about the past and seeing all those entanglements.

SP

The sense of urgency is false. The sense of urgency is a tool for manipulation. The sense of urgency causes us to do things that are not in our best interest, including choosing false leaders or choosing leaders that are a matter of ease rather than doing the work and investing in the collective generation of ideas and methods towards our liberation. The sense of urgency completely erases the history of the apocalypse. That has been our experience. I think that being slow is actually the most transgressive thing we can do because it means that we are saying, "What do we have to lose?" There are only harmful systems that exist right now. The urgency that I feel is for people who are suffering, species that are disappearing, ecosystems that are collapsing and are unrecognizable. So if the urgency is to save society as it is, I think that slowing down can actually be an invitation to an alternative.

Blueprints for Collaboration: Science and the Arts

This is an edited and excerpted version of a conversation that took place on November 25, 2022 during the Driving the Human festival in Berlin.

DARIA PARKHOMENKO

Today, with the global ecological crisis and many other threats, the interaction of art and science is becoming more and more urgent. Here, with Driving the Human, we are forecasting scenarios of the future, building new instruments and prototypes, thinking about how we can actively participate in real life problems. Art-science collaborations in the modern meaning of this term appeared in 1968 through E.A.T. (Experiments in Art and Technology), in the United States at Bell Labs—many of you might know this story— where the engineering group was an initiator of this approach and as a result we received a synthesis of new technologies and new artistic media. The common difficulties in this field are usually the different languages and different goals of the participants. That's why it's an absolute must to have a common driving force to unite and support these collaborations. My first question: what's actually driving you in these collaborations? What is a driving force for artists to collaborate inside your teams? For scientists, what's a driving force for you to collaborate and participate in this project? For curators, what do you see as the potential?

SARAH DONDERER

I would say the main factor is curiosity and also the urgent need that we have to do something, to be active, and to cultivate different perspectives. Coming not just from a technological point of view but also from science, to have more experimental approaches and bring inspiration into projects.

BEA DELGADO CORRALES

In my case, one of the main forces that brought us together was trying to shift the focus and rethink science as happening within only objective, sterile environments, and that an artistic perspective is completely opposed when, in the end, they complement each other so well. To think about using science, and in our case microbiology, to foster new ways of thinking, new ways of relating to our world within our daily lives.

SEONGMIN YUK

Well, in our case, we share a lot of curiosity. We got a lot of inspiration from the scientists, especially from those at the Max Planck Institute. We noticed after our discussions that they also were inspired by our project. This is a constant exchange that enriches each side—I think that was the point.

DP

The problem of time is a very interesting topic to discuss because the pacing of time in art and science is totally different. When in art we can build a project in one or two years, in science we need much more time to check hypotheses or to write an article. For Driving the Human, the project has been running for quite a long time. It's already the third year, right?

SD   I think what's super interesting for the Driving the Human concept is that we are talking about prototypes. In the beginning, I was also not so sure what that means because normally you think about something that goes into production afterwards. But the interpretation here is really broad, that the development is also part of the experiment and it doesn't have to be resolved into a final product.

DP   What do you think will be the continuation? What is the future of these seven fantastic prototypes?

SD   Well, I hope that the process has been inspiring to all the participants, but also to the people that came to experience, interact, and see that it is possible to really work with complex scientific topics and ideas and translate them into hands-on or experienceable environments. I think what also happened here in the discussions with all the participants is that the scientists who've been involved in the project have a point of outreach to artists to start new projects, new collaborations.

DP   Seongmin, let's go to your project—I have a question because one of the starting points of your project was ancient mythology, that animals are the first to sense an approaching disaster. I think it's not only in Asian mythology but in many mythologies that we understand that animals are much more sensitive than humans. In *The Backpack of Wings*, you actualize this mythology and combine it with technology and projections of the future. What role do you think interdisciplinary collaborations can play?

SY   We collaborated with the Max Planck Institute of Animal Behavior and Dr. Hemal Naik who was a very helpful entrypoint to meet researchers in the animal behavior lab. We had a great opportunity to visit and we could really experience how the researchers work in practice. From the scientific point of view, what they gave us as feedback after watching our film was that we, as artists, focus on speculation and looking at these topics in a global way. That's a different and maybe challenging aspect for them while doing their own specific research.

DP   Do you think that your project can somehow solve ecological problems?

SY   As an artist, I don't think I can solve any problems directly. However, we can think, and we can think further about what we can solve together. This is connected also to the first question, how art and science could collaborate because as an artist I always try to imagine the future. That's the power of what artists can do.

DP

Sandra, I know that acatech is very interested in art and science collaborations. Artists usually want to say, "Don't benefit from us because we are so independent, we do what we want." But still, it looks like these two different cultures, art and science, can benefit from each other. What's your point of view?

SANDRA FENDL

In general, how can science, or a scientific institution like acatech, benefit from working together with artists? We work so differently, and I feel like in artistic practice there is way more freedom. In science, very often we have specific questions which result in the need to follow a specific path of exploration. Art can really engage a topic or process that is totally unconventional. Hence, opening up completely new perspectives and new innovations.

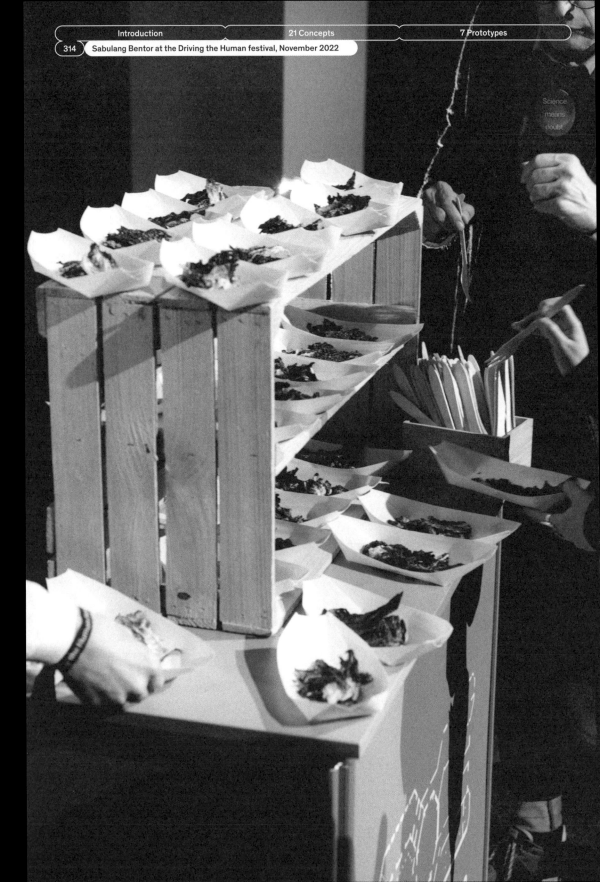

Essays   Conversations   Epilogue

Sharing Knowledge, Building Bridges

315

This is an edited and excerpted version of a conversation that took place on November 27, 2022 during the Driving the Human festival in Berlin.

VERA SACCHETTI

VINCENT RUMAHLOINE

Can you tell us a bit about the food, the *Sabulang Bentor*?

Sabulang Bentor—it's a term that is used by the local people in Bandung in Indonesia. It's a form of discussion with many jokes in it. It's relaxing but always there is some direction: how we want to build the bridge, how we want to take care of our community. We have had seven Sabulang Bentor. It's always related to food. So I want to bring that here. There are five stages. Everyone comes to each stage to start eating with a story behind the food. It's more or less like speed dating but casual. Then at the end, we wrap it up by asking how you feel about the experience. You can do it in every part of the world, and it's going to work out. That's the Sabulang Bentor.

Last year after our workshop in Munich, I came with Mang Dian and my collaborators, and we met many interesting people. Mang Dian asked me a very simple question: how to bring all this knowledge to the community in Indonesia?

The starting point is how to touch the community from inside, using what they know, what is really close to them. Food is always one part of this activity. For me, this is the bridge that I'm trying to build. We are building bridges and using food as a catalyst in between.

ELIANA OTTA

I'm thinking of these very basic corporeal needs that are addressed when we think about food and nourishing and at the same time decay and loss—these processes that connect all the phenomena involving living beings.

A very interesting response that we received everywhere in reaction to our videos was that people from the three communities wanted to be represented with their traditional clothes. They would show not only the clothes but also make explicit the kind of knowledge that they have in the sense of handcraft or how they hunt or cook, dye fabrics with plants. It was clear from some people that this was coming from pride and a necessity of honoring ancestors and defending the kind of life that they want to have. It was also a pragmatic need of thinking that they could also receive some kind of help, being aware that these videos are going to be shown abroad and in faraway places, places with specific resources. There was this mix of pride about the knowledge and the tradition that is being shared, but also this pragmatical, political consciousness of how certain demands are tied to performing certain identities.

VS

Corine, we had an earlier conversation about what could be the role of philosophy in a time like this. Thinking about the kinds of knowledge accepted in the Western canon as valid, does philosophy have a role in breaking such asymmetries?

CORINE PELLUCHON

Claude Lévi-Strauss spoke of lateral universalism. Traveling and trying to discover other cultures is a way of decentering one's gaze—not to have an overhanging rationality but being aware of the fact that nobody has a global gaze. Instead of speaking about the world we have to speak to try to speak to the world. Empathy is so important to understand and also to understand that you don't understand; that you cannot enter the feelings of a bird whose wing is broken, but you can recognize that this bird is suffering and that it deserves to be cared for. To care is a way of repairing the world, trying to maintain the world.

I think that the role of the philosopher is to find some words that give some guidelines because philosophy is between science and poetry. We have to care for words and we have to care for the way we say things. The role of philosophers and the role of artists is this because we human beings live according to the words we use. We are naked and we need to orient ourselves, be it at the individual or collective level by using words and representations. Sometimes these words are very dangerous and sometimes these words are nourishing. The role of philosophers and artists is to nourish a little bit, to provide some food that gives a direction, sometimes a vitality, an energy, so that we can have the courage to face all the difficulties we are confronted with and to overcome them.

Essays   Conversations   Epilogue

319

Transforming Human and Non-Human Environments

This is an edited and excerpted version of a conversation that took place on November 26, 2022 during the Driving the Human festival in Berlin.

VERA SACCHETTI

Paula, you are not an architect. You are not an urban planner, but you are a designer and a PhD student. Tell us a little bit about yourself and how you fit into the constellation of the *Human-Bacteria Interfaces* team.

PAULA NERLICH

Hi everyone. I'm actually trained as a textile designer. A while ago I decided to explore surface matter more towards DIY biomaterial design, moving away from textiles and textile fabrication. In my practice as material designer, which I did for a few years, I explored how to create materials, compostable materials from food surplus. And then somehow I got an Instagram message that said, "Hello, there's a PhD position looking for a textile designer with a biodesign background at the Hub for Biotechnology in the Built Environment at Newcastle. Why don't you apply?" And I did so. Now I am at the Hub as we call it, the HBBE, which is part of Newcastle University in the architecture school, and Northumbria University in the microbiology department. So, suddenly I am in this realm of architecture that I've never been in. I usually think very small. I love small, fluffy textiles. I love creating beautiful materials that react to light in their surroundings. Now I have to think big, and at the same time I'm invited to work in the microbiology labs to explore how to work with living organisms. This is what brought me together with my peers Romy Kaiser, Bea Delgado Corrales, and Anne-Sofie Belling, who are also PhD students at the HBBE. They are all exploring different things: textile design, creative technology, but also microbiology. We, together, founded our group just for Driving the Human. It led us towards *Human-Bacteria Interfaces*, a project that is in the context of the built environment because that's where our research is placed. But it is also looking at how to reconnect, how to interface with the invisible, with the microorganisms that have so many amazing properties that really contribute to us as human beings.

VS

This trans-scalar approach is something that I think both Tatiana and Washington also work in, perhaps not at the microbial scale but certainly at various other scales. Washington, can you tell us about your practice?

WASHINGTON FAJARDO

I'm an architect and planner. Until recently I was in charge of the planning department of the city of Rio de Janeiro. In the past 16 years, I have been working for the city in two different positions. I run the historic preservation department and I have been working on crafting a specific practice regarding planning that I have been calling holistic planning. I am trying to bring more subjectivity to the urban planning process. As you might know, planning is always about land use, economics, social aspects, mobility, et cetera. And because of my work with historical aspects of the city and especially dealing with more segregated spaces in the city of Rio, like favelas, I started to realize that it would be necessary to expand these ideas of planning. I have been doing research with MIT's Senseable City Lab on a project called *Favelas 4D*. Our idea is to try to create a digital twin of a whole favela and its informal settlements. Favelas are a segregated space in terms of social class but also in race and especially in the lack of infrastructure and lack of quality of housing. Using LIDAR scanning, we can make it possible through VR to record everything inside of an area of a favela. By doing that, we try to establish bridges between these very segregated places. We don't have Google Street View in favelas in Rio, and also other cities in Brazil. That means a new level of segregation. We are talking now about digital segregation. The digital twin makes it possible to do data analysis for the built environment. We still have tuberculosis in favelas in Brazil. It's persistent and basically related to the quality of the built environment. So my main idea is how to use this information in two ways: to open conversations and also to allow scientific analysis of the built environment.

VS

TATIANA BILBAO

Tatiana, tell us more about yourself and your practice.

I'm an architect. I live and work in Mexico City. Since I was studying, I always clashed with how I was educated or trained. I studied in a difficult period where architecture was seen as a representation of many things but mostly of power et cetera, to be very distinctive and to be inserted in the landscape. And my interest in entering architecture as a discipline was because I saw it as a very vital thing for our lives. I always saw architecture as providing a primary form of care for our bodies. Understanding architecture like this immersed me in the work of having many engagements with people, conversations, and stories. I was trying to enable platforms for people to create lives, or still trying to do that.

For me, the idea of challenging the way we think of representation is vital. I have been working in this regard all my life. I have challenged the way we draw in architecture, the way we create representations, the way we create processes of design. Cartography is completely subjective, non-directive, and enables one type of conversation. The same, I think, with architectural drawings. So, I have engaged myself into thinking beyond them; we need new forms of representation.

VS

I like that you both alluded to questions of representation. I feel, in a way, the practices of all three of you have very much to do with these ideas of making visible. Not just creating an awareness but to really show different modes of existence somehow.

TB   In the beginning, I was trying very hard to understand how to become the other. It was always difficult to imagine that I even had the right to create something that somebody else should live in. Idealist me thought that I needed to become the other to design. At some point, when I became less innocent, I understood that that was not possible, at all. I was just faking, that it was untrue, and it was almost even not honest.

PN   So when you say the other, was that a human being?

TB   The other human that would inhabit these places. I understood how it's much more honest to understand that you cannot become that other. So how can we create platforms for that other to create their own life in that place? That is the question that has driven my thoughts since I was really able to put it in words. I do think there's an urgency to understand that each of us on this planet lives in a completely different way, every one. So we all have the right to inhabit this planet and to inhabit it our own way. How can we create societies that create those possibilities? That's something that I question.

WF   That's an interesting topic. As you might know, the urban transformations in Europe in the beginning of the 20th century had a lot of impact in South America, especially in the '30s and '40s. We started to copy all the ideas of opening big avenues and boulevards. But especially in Brazil, the modernist ideas for cities are still really strong. Brazilian cities are getting, at least in terms of land consumption, bigger and bigger and less dense. In the case of Rio, we had the highest peak of density in 1960, and we have been decreasing density since then. Something that I have been trying to fight against is this persistent idea of modernist ideas for cities in Brazil. Although I believe in government, and although I believe in how states can deal with the scale of our urgencies, we also need to design new institutions. Not only do we need new cartography, new representations, but we also need to redesign the idea of government. We are working under such old structures to deal with such complexity. I don't know the answer for that, but it's something that I'm trying to do.

PN   So, I'm not an architect, but what I understand of the built environment is that it's very human-centered, it's very human-driven, and it's been designed by humans and has shaped human culture for as long as humans have existed. But, what I also think is that human culture can also shape built environments. There are already movements embracing community knowledge when creating, especially community centers.

TB   To continue on what you were saying, Paula—I think that we have created a culture where architecture or the built environment has become our protective feature from externalities. We need architecture to protect our bodies, to exist on this planet. But it has become much more than just a protection. It has become a limit for us to really be still part of this ecosystem. There are many, many bodies in the world, especially in the north. I'm not going to name that country which has really been dis-adapted from the Earth. They live in 22 degree centigrade their whole life. They're born in a house that is 22 degrees year-round. They go to an office that is 22 degrees, regardless if outside is minus 19 or plus 50. And the moment they're exposed to the weather, just the weather, forget about the little bugs, they're sick. Architecture is a culprit of that. We created millions of square meters of buildings that cannot be illuminated or ventilated naturally. We have created millions of square meters of buildings that need that kind of artificial weather to exist, that can only live with artificial weather inside. I think that we need to understand how to start thinking about our built environment as a mediator between us and our ecosystem rather than as a limit.

PN   I feel like if I don't have any spiders in my house, then something is wrong. Do you know what I mean?

TB   Absolutely. But the majority of the people will feel that's very strange. You live in a precarious way.

VS   I am wondering if you could reflect on this idea of fighting modernism, or fighting the modern idea, and how to best go about dismantling it actively. I do think it's an effort that takes all of us. That takes many little actions every single day. But it also takes a big effort of de-centering, not just the human perspective, but also traditional geopolitical structures that we have ingrained in our planetary existence.

TB   Well, I think that the modern city has a profound problem: that we can only exist in it in one form, in the production mode. The city is built for productivity and is built because of that productivity. Everything, even the house, is a kind of response as the place of rest from that place of work. It is very specific to a form of living, which doesn't apply to the majority of the planet. In it, to exist you need to produce, but the friction comes from the fact that to produce we need to first exist. This city, the modern city, does not acknowledge the fact that we need to first exist. It's not acknowledging the labor for us to exist, for bodies to exist.

It's imposing one form on the entire planet. That form can respond to a specific geographical position with a specific culture embedded. But that is not applicable to the majority of the planet. We don't have the same conditions in terms of terrain, weather, or temperature, but also in culture, in the way we relate. This city only allows one form, the hetero-patriarchal way of existing. Guess what? It responds to a family of one father, one mother, and two children. It applies for some but at a specific moment in time. So, the model is very static—it's built for an ideal period in the life of someone very singular.

Hope in the Context of Climate Change and Global Crisis

Corine Pelluchon, Philosopher, Professor at Université Gustave Eiffel

Despite the extreme risks we are facing and which will, in the coming years, make life difficult for many people, it is possible to talk about hope. Paradoxically, this tragic situation, in a way, calls for hope.

However, this supposes that we understand that hope has nothing to do with optimism. In French, there are two words: *espoir* and *espérance*. Espoir is the expectation of something that concerns me, the wish to see my desire fulfilled within a fairly short time, whereas espérance, which is a theological virtue, does not concern a personal desire nor something determined. It is the ability to see the future in the present, to give our times a direction which is not completely predictable but is based on some signs that indicate a new era. Espérance refers to something which is already there, although it is not accomplished (*noch nicht, schon da*). It can nonetheless be announced, like the Bible which contains many elements I borrow to build a secular notion of hope.

Espérance is from Jerusalem more than from Athens. If you remember the Greek myth, Pandora's box, *Elpis*, espoir, which remains when all things are gone, is a consolation, something that might be false but helps people to accept reality. But we don't need consolation nor lie. Moreover, espérance is born out of despair.

This is the second aspect that distinguishes espérance from espoir and optimism: It is is inseparable from the experience of despair and the knowledge of dangers, even of evil. Espérance is the expectation of the unexpected (*etwas Unverhofftes*). It is the expectation and the crossing of the impossible—*la traversée de l'impossible.*① Espérance is born when one has lost one's illusions and false hopes.

① Corine Pelluchon, *L'espérance, ou la traversée de l'impossible* (Paris: Rivages, 2023).

Thus, espérance is a specific relation to oneself, to time and to history that gives those who finally discover it the ability to act in a certain way, to have confidence in the future and even in a certain moral progress and to communicate it, although they can suffer from the present time. The word confidence, which comes from *fides* (faith) better translates what I call espérance than the word hope.

I shall develop three points:
Why do our tragic times call for espérance?
Why is it born out of despair and why does it become a method and a decision?
What kind of energy does it bring and why is it strong but not spectacular?

WHY DO OUR TRAGIC TIMES CALL FOR ESPÉRANCE?
The specificity of our time is that we are facing the possibility of our impossibility: the possibility of the collapse of our civilization as a result of the disasters associated with climate change and our development model. The possibility of the end of the world or rather of the end of a world.

We are not only afraid for ourselves and for humanity and other species. We also have to recognize the precarity of our civilization. We have doubt on everything we have learned and were proud of. Through these connections, the end of the world has already come.

But the good news is that even those who don't want to think about global warming from morning to night can no longer deny the threat. Moreover, the most courageous persons develop a form of anxiety and depression that is called eco-anxiety. This overwhelming and painful state of mind is the result of the awareness of our tragic situation.

This is precisely the time to speak of espérance which is completely opposed to denial and to any form of optimism that would be a way of saying we have the solutions to our problems. Espérance is the capacity to both see the chaos or the mess of the present, and to understand the precursory signs of some important changes that could in the future lead to a more sustainable and fairer development model.

However, in order to have this ability to see the beginning of a new era —which I call the age of the living, and whose flag bearers are the animal cause and ecology—and to think that this movement will be stronger and stronger, *in spite of* all the regressions and the violence such change triggers, you have to lose your illusions and all hope.

WHY IS ESPÉRANCE BORN OUT OF DESPAIR AND WHY DOES IT BECOME A METHOD AND A DECISION?
Espérance is the passage from death to life, like in Ezekiel when the dry bones return to life. It supposes the experience of destruction, of a complete night in broad daytime. Espérance is "despair overcome", Georges Bernanos said.② There is no hope without the crossing of that impossible which is despair.

② Georges Bernanos, *La liberté pour quoi faire ?* (Paris: Gallimard, 2019), 28.

Despair is actually a psychic death: it's a way of dying or living one's death as Kierkegaard says in *The Sickness Unto Death*. When your reason and your will are humiliated by suffering, the temptation is to give in to despair. But if you give up even this will, your self becomes empty. Or almost empty, since there is something left: the principle of life which makes you still breathe. Some people call it God, others nature, like Spinoza. I will call it life. It links us to other living beings. The recognition of this thread of life wraps you in sweetness.

Espérance is the expectation of the unhoped, because it is born out of nothingness and was not expected at all. It is born when you believed you were almost dead. It is like a second morning, the youth in your maturity. It is not something spectacular. It is like the return to life after psychic death. You discover you can even enjoy life in such a mess. Those who have really exposed their subjectivity, experienced despair and overcome it by giving up false hopes understand at the same time the precariousness of life, its smallness and its beauty. It is from the loss of one's illusions that gratitude and the ability to wonder are born. It explains also the need to be surrounded with beauty in order to *endure* the difficult present and to feel its intensity, to be a survivor in the sense that Derrida spoke of in an interview a few days before his own death: *survivance* implies feeling life's intensity and being able to enjoy the *here and there* because one looks death in the face and knows that death is coming[3]—which has nothing to do with the ability to anticipate since death is "the impossibility of a possibility," an aporia which confronts one with the unknown but opens up the meaning of existence.[4]

[3] Jacques Derrida, *Apprendre à vivre enfin. Entretien avec Jean Birnbaum* (Paris: Galilée/Le Monde, 2005).

[4] Jacques Derrida, *Apories* (Paris: Galilée, 1996), 125.

To a certain extent, the young people of Extinction Rebellion I met have a similar experience. I too had it. It first starts with fear, helplessness and anger because nothing is happening and governments are not doing much. People are still eating meat every day and continue their business as usual. This painful experience lasts for some time. You don't see how you can get out of it. And yet, it can be turned into something else, if you manage to share it with other people and above all if you understand that the origin of such despair is the love for the world.

Eco-anxiety is not like other despair caused by a lack of love for oneself and for life. The latter, Kierkegaard says, can easily degenerate into hatred of oneself and of life. On the contrary, eco-depression is produced by the love for the world and the desire that humanity becomes responsible. Eco-anxiety is thus a grace and a burden at the same time. To stress this noble origin does not prevent you from suffering, but it helps you regain self-esteem and transform negative emotions into commitment and good energy.

Moreover, to look at other people doing their best at the local level, in agriculture, education, health care, education, to promote a fairer world and change the modes of production and consumption gives you energy and courage.

The point is also to understand that the threat of collapse is an opportunity to formulate what we want and what we don't want, what we should keep because it is valuable, and what we should change, or even abolish. Facing the possibility of collapse drives you into being more aware of the things you cherish and to enjoy them. It also should force us to make an inventory at the individual and collective level.

It also drives you into being pragmatic, because of this origin and this "*traversée de l'impossible*", and because of the special relation to time which characterizes hope.

By the way, you may have noticed that, among the greatest activists—Nelson Mendela, Peter Singer, Lincoln—there is no bitterness nor resentment. You won't hear them lecturing others. They didn't judge although they fought against what they were doing. Taking on the madness of the world disposes one to compassion, which is the consequence of a transformation of subjectivity, not a psychological trait. The greatest activists have what I call "*la puissance anarchiste de la douceur,*" the power (*potentia*, not *potestas*) of sweetness, because they know that there is a moral progress which is underway, whose precursory signs are still there, but they also understand how deep domination and anthropocentrism are rooted in all of us. Also they look for the appropriate means to put issues in the political agenda, while taking people and society as they are.

Born out of despair, espérance becomes a method and a decision.

Espérance is close to utopia. When Kant says that there must be no war, that it is a categorical imperative, he knows that there will be wars, but this utopia is the condition allowing its realization because it obliges us to seek which institutions will make it possible to install a durable peace:

"*The question is not to know if perpetual peace is something real or chimerical (...) but we must act as if the thing existed, which perhaps does not exist, to have for project its foundation and the constitution which seems to us the most appropriate for it.*" ⑤

As with E. Bloch in *The Principle of Hope*, enlightened hope (*docta spes*) and concrete utopia constitute a transforming force of the present, and hope detects the possibilities of the future wrapped up in the present—but things happen in a perhaps less spectacular way than in his book.

⑤ Immanuel Kant, *Doctrine du droit, Oeuvres philosophiques,* edited by Ferdinand Alquié, vol. III (Paris: Gallimard, 1986), 629.

WHAT KIND OF ENERGY DOES ESPÉRANCE BRING AND WHY IS IT STRONG BUT NOT SPECTACULAR?

The specificity of espérance is that it has energy. It is not a mere discourse. You can have a discourse on espérance which makes you understand that history has a meaning and a direction, but a discourse does not suffice to create espérance which implies energy and desire. Espérance is the experience of resdiscovering life after death, like in Ezekiel when dead stones are recovered with flesh.

Moreover, it is strong but not spectacular.

The question is: how can we bring a good social energy right now?

Don't forget that espérance is born without being sought. There is no method to create it. Nonetheless, starting from reality itself, we can pay attention to the harbingers of a movement that is taking shape—for me these harbingers are the concern for ecology and the animal cause. We can underline its depth and its strategic dimension, by showing what is at stake in it.

Accompanying a movement and giving a name to an era is not dictating from above what others should do, but translating into concepts what is happening in order to give this movement a coherence, a direction, a strength, and maybe an efficiency. To help it win against all the forces that oppose it. This was at the core of what I called the New Enlightenment.⑥

⑥ Corine Pelluchon, *Les Lumières à l'âge du vivant* (Paris: Seuil, 2021).

Be that as it may, espérance works for the present and above all for the future. It is a way of preparing for the time when the world will have to be repaired and rebuilt after the catastrophes.

Ideally, we should start to build something that would suddenly create the conditions for a social energy that is not pathological, for a common future that does not presuppose the distinction between friends and enemies and is based on our shared destiny which includes animals.

There is espérance when you feel a good energy coming from *Eros*, not *Thanatos*. However, it is not a leader that gives espérance! And our books do not suffice to create espérance. They can contribute to it, but it comes when it comes. It might be in the air, but we don't know when it arrives and how.

I will end with this image of hope found in Charles Péguy, in *The Portal of The Mystery of Hope*.⑦ He wrote this text a couple of years before dying at the age of 41 during the First World War.

⑦ Charles Péguy, *Le Porche du mystère de la deuxième vertu* (Paris, NRF: Poésie/Gallimard, 2000), 22-26.

He compares espérance with a little girl who holds her two sisters: Faith, who is a loyal wife, and Charity who is the mother. This little hope carries the other theological virtues. She looks like nothing. And yet, she can do a lot, this little one. She is the unhoped-for, the unsuspected. *L'espérance, this little one, who seems like nothing at all,* and whom people sometimes do ignore, will endure everything. She does something to life and to the world, by grace or by virtue of the absurd, like the meaning of life after crossing the void.

What surprises me, says God, is hope
This little hope who seems like nothing at all. Faith is a loyal Wife.
Charity is a Mother.
An ardent mother
Or an older sister who is like a mother.
Hope is a little girl, nothing at all
Who is still playing with her snowman.
And yet it's this little girl who will endure worlds. It is she, this little
one, who leads them all.
For Faith sees only what is.
And she, she sees what will be.
Charity loves only what is.
And she, she loves what will be.
Faith sees what is.
In Time and in Eternity.
Hope sees what will be.
In time and for eternity.
In the future, so to speak, of eternity.

New Ways to Inhabit the Earth

Freo Majer, Corine Pelluchon, and Margit Rosen in conversation, moderated by Vera Sacchetti

VERA SACCHETTI

Corine, your essay *Hope in the Context of Climate Change and Global Crisis* was an important inspiration for Driving the Human. Your words deeply resonated with us, and somehow mirrored the attitudes that we sought to bring to the project, particularly when you say that "*espérance* works for the present and above all for the future. It is a way of preparing for the time when the world will have to be repaired and rebuilt after the catastrophes." So hope, the unhoped-for, the unsuspected, what is it then? And what is it not?

CORINE PELUCHON

Under the circumstances—ecological catastrophes, the social political situation we are confronted with—it's very important to distinguish hope from optimism, which is sometimes a denial. Optimism is a way of saying that things are not that bad, that business as usual can continue and *espoir* or hope is not something personal, it can coexist with fear and the awareness of dangers. It's very important to say that. The two main elements that constitute hope are the consciousness of difficulty—which I call the impossible—and that uncertainty is our daily life. We have to be aware of something that escapes or will challenge what we have learnt. The precarity of both civilization and ourselves is at stake, but for humanity, it's extremely difficult to recognize that we are confronted with something which escapes our ability to understand, to master everything, and which is of course painful and causes unimaginable amounts of suffering. To accept this suffering is a condition to face reality, to get rid of false solutions and false hopes and also—and this is the second element which constitutes hope—to be able to discern, in the mess of the present, some precursory signs of a new era which is not yet here but presents the opportunity to repair our world. In the seven prototypes of Driving the Human, I see that a lot of people are now recognizing that we are not an empire within an empire, and that all interdependencies with other beings count and constitute our own identity. I think this is an anthropological evolution signaled by a change in how we understand human beings. This would change a lot of things in the way we organize society, while paying attention to the interest of other beings, be they human, non-human, future or present. It's important to enable these artists to grow these ideas and give them more strength, more flesh.

VS

At the very beginning of the project, we were inspired by complementary ideas, namely the ideas of Bruno Latour. His thinking was instrumental in the initial stage of this project, helping to define goals, ambitions, and visions. When Driving the Human started in 2020, the exhibition *Critical Zones*—curated by Latour and Peter Weibel—was on display at the ZKM Karlsruhe, and many of these ideas were on display there. Next to me is Margit Rosen, curator at ZKM and long-standing collaborator of Latour. Margit, ZKM collaborated for 24 years with Bruno Latour, did 4 exhibitions, and you personally were involved with several of these instances and also the theater play *Kosmokolos: Global Climate Tragi-Comedy*. You were mentioning that hope in the thinking of Latour also plays a role. Can you tell us about that?

MARGIT ROSEN   I can repeat some remarks he made some time ago, referring to Clive Hamilton's book *Requiem for a Species: Why We Resist the Truth about Climate Change*. Latour said it's very important to give up hope in order to get into the right mood; hope is not the solution but the problem. He would give up hope in order to start to act. This doesn't mean to resign oneself, however. Latour started to think many years ago about the question of why it is that when knowing all the facts for the last 30 to 40 years, the evident change we need doesn't come to pass? The problem is not that we are not informed, but that people don't have the sensitivity or capacity to perceive the dimension of this change. In this way—and that's maybe the relation to Driving the Human—he was looking for something which he called a new "alliance". This is why he started to do exhibitions, this is why he started to work with musicians, with dancers and why he wrote the *Kosmokolos* theater piece, of which I had the pleasure to create a German version for the radio. For Latour, art and theater presented the possibility to bring onto the stage this very contradictory feeling we are experiencing at the moment, and to recalibrate, and develop a sensitivity to what is going to happen, what might be necessary.

VS   Freo, how was Latour influential for you as Driving the Human was starting?

FREO MAJER   For me, the work of Bruno Latour has been very encouraging and touching. I was devastated when I learnt about his passing; he had a very generous and warm-hearted approach to all kinds of practices, and pointed to a reconciliation with the ideas of the Enlightenment. You call it the New Enlightenment. The Enlightenment, in science, has always been about doubt, the negative sides of things, questioning, not accepting so-called knowledge or facts easily. I was always impressed how Latour, as a thinker, as a player of thoughts, was able to correct himself, to change paths and always to integrate the former stage of his thinking into the next stage. When we started discussing the concept of Driving the Human, everybody felt that he would be the theoretical grandfather of the initiative, and we were very excited when, in parallel, we saw *Critical Zones* develop at the ZKM. Maybe not everybody knows what *Critical Zones* was about—it focused on the habitat of humans and other species, which exists a few meters above and under the Earth's planetary surface: this includes bacteria, animals, plants, humans and the oxygen that we need, the climate that we need for survival. The project advanced the idea that the planet is not in danger. It will always be there. But we—humans—are in danger, and we should think of reconciliation with other beings and forms of coexistence.

CP   It's true that for years we have been considering that politics was a game between human beings, and it's true that Latour said that politics is a cosmopolitics. How can we have an enlightened political science, and reconcile science, society and politics? This idea was very important and he was one of the people most vocal about it. Now, I come from existentialism, from phenomenology, and I try to elaborate a philosophy of existence by describing the human condition not only in light of freedom but also in light of corporeality, of passivity and vulnerability, and the fact that we are all have an impact on other beings, humans and non-humans, while we exist. We need to take seriously our corporeality, and understand that the materiality of our existence has ethical and political consequences, and that we need to take other beings into account. What I have seen in the Driving the Human prototypes is an awareness of the artists, of this necessity to decenter the subject and to have the point of view of the insect, the animal. I think this enlargement of our consciousness is, in spite of all the mess we are confronted with, good news and a sign of moral progress. Of course, there is a gap between theory and practice: in order to fill this gap, between what we know, what we think, and what we are doing every day, we need affect, we need creation, we need imagination. We need a style, *"une parole parlante"* as Merleau-Ponty said, something which is not a discourse but an embodied discourse, something that touches people and brings energy, that wakes them.

MR   I just want to mention Latour's last book, *On the Emergence of an Ecological Class: A Memo*, which he authored alongside Nikolaj Schultz. There, he underlines how important it is to find a common language and a common imagination, comparing the economical struggle with the working class struggle. What we at ZKM also found interesting working with Latour was his hands-on approach, which is so important to describe what our existence depends on. The pandemic and the war are so frightening. But they reveal all these infrastructures we depend on:

production, transportation, etc.—suddenly everything becomes visible. What was important for Latour was to create a method where we get out of the abstraction we usually live in and as soon as we all together describe what our lives depend on, suddenly we find new alliances. Also, how should we know what to defend when we haven't even described it properly? What is in front of us can only be negotiated and addressed if sciences, arts, politics work together—if we all do this together. That might be a question to Freo: most of us share a certain set of values—but how do we reach out to other people and enlarge this circle?

FM

That seems to be a mystery for many people, for many organizations especially. We always think about it as Forecast and in the context of Driving the Human. For us, it has always been about organizing access, surprising encounters, and exchanges by just bringing people together, putting them in a space and giving them a joint problem, task, or challenge and then seeing how they solve it. As soon as you offer a framework that is understandable or tangible, people will do something together. In our case, it is a deadline—for example, at the end there will be a festival. Whatever you do together, it will be shown. It helps a lot for people to know, "I have half a year, I have that amount of money, I need to cope with certain infrastructures, questions, timeline, etc." For me, we are in this together with a joint experience of problems, challenges, questions, existential threats even. It doesn't make sense for you to remain in your silo, in your ivory tower, in your own perspective. It shouldn't be just about the necessity and the urgency to tackle these topics, but it should be fun, productive, and meaningful. This kind of work gives your life a lot of additional dimensions and is a very touching experience. The Driving the Human prototypes are not only about success and results. It is also about how they got there, what kind of decisions they had to take, what kind of interests drove them. To get to this point is already such an achievement, in my opinion.

VS

At the end of Driving the Human, what we tried to create is a place for many different kinds of encounters, in order to access the complex topics at the core of the seven prototypes. They are multilayered, complex, and perhaps difficult to absorb in an immediate stage. Therefore, in our public events, we have created immersive ways to experience things, and experimented with various formats, such as conversations, intimate encounters, tours, performances, and many others. Perhaps this idea of a multiplicity of encounters starts answering the question you posed, Margit. But more importantly, as we reach the end of the three-year research initiative, it is important to consider the outcomes and how they relate to where we started, way back in 2020. What are your conclusions, Freo?

FM   I can say that I felt a deep and personal responsibility for all these processes. We started with more than 1,000 submissions to our open call. 1,017 minds, biographies, ways of life, backgrounds, educations. 1,017 times, an individual, a duo, or a collective thought about, "What could drive the human, me as a human, the human species?" This effort alone is so meaningful. When we worked through those proposals, we were all very touched by this serious effort, the professionalism, the feeling of meaningfulness and wanting to change something concretely. When we selected the 21 concepts and met them in Berlin in 2021, we already had a more personal insight into how they wanted to work, what the potential of the proposal was, and what their drive was. At the end of these three years, 7 prototypes have evolved and transformed—they have really learnt a lot. I have also learnt a lot from them and am very grateful for all these deep and meaningful interactions: all different kinds of collaborations, traveling back and forth, having mentorships, access to material research, access to technologies. The depth of the process has to do with a form of enlightenment: having surprises, having doubts, having to change direction. Overall, this is remarkable.

MR   What I appreciate about the idea of the prototype is the idea of permanent confrontation between the artists and the research, again and again and again, with specialists from different fields and other artists. This is a completely different form of knowledge: it includes failure, doubt, and great surprises. And it creates a new community of people who had previously never talked to each other and never shared their knowledge. In this way, the prototype is a wonderful model.

VS   I would like to conclude on the notion that, for all of us who took part in the project, Driving the Human has been a wonderful learning experience. Freo, you mentioned the network and community that was created around the making of the seven prototypes. Going back to what Margit was saying, maybe the strength of Driving the Human lies in the unexpected, the unhoped for that Corine referred to at the beginning of our conversation. The unhoped for, the unexpected connections, the unexpected learnings, the unexpected encounters have been a constant part of these last three years of work. We believe this is the most important, perhaps the most intangible legacy of such a project. The strength of this network is something that we tried to make visible—and we hope that you encounter it as well, navigating these seven prototypes and all that lies around them.

"What I appreciate about the idea of the prototype is the idea of permanent confrontation between the artists and the research, again and again and again, with specialists from different fields and other artists. This is a completely different form of knowledge: it includes failure, doubt, and great surprises. And it creates a new community of people who had previously never talked to each other and never shared their knowledge. In this way, the prototype is a wonderful model." (Margit Rosen)

Project Credits and Acknowledgments

THE BACKPACK OF WINGS: MODERN MYTHOLOGY

CREDITS, CONCEPT

DIRECTED, WRITTEN, AND EDITED BY
Hyeseon Jeong
ACTOR
Yukee
VOICES
Lili M. Rampre, Kilian Kuhlendahl, IrishCobbler, Ricky DB, Tim Stephenson, Karen @Acapela Group, Kimberly @VoiceMaker. In, Léo Beaudoin, Meagan Hall, AnitaCrystalbaby
LINE PRODUCER
Petra Clemens
ASSISTANT ANIMATOR AND COLOR GRADING
Seongmin Yuk
SUBTITLE TRANSLATOR
Meagan Hall
SOUND EFFECTS AND DESIGN
Hyemin Jung
MUSIC
'Aphasia' by ABADIR, 'I got ice on my bag' by Yukee, 'Yonaoshi' by Jeolmyohan, "One Cybernetic Carrier Pigeon Said To Another..." by Ali Rahman
PRODUCED BY ACADEMY OF MEDIA ARTS COLOGNE (KHM)
CO-PRODUCED BY DRIVING THE HUMAN

ACKNOWLEDGMENTS, CONCEPT

Movebank (hosted by the Max Planck Institute of Animal Behavior), Seongmin Yuk, Prof. Ute Hörner, Thomas Hawranke, Prof. Hans Bernhard, Sam Hopkins, Ali Rahman

CREDITS, PROTOTYPE

MAX PLANCK INSTITUTE OF ANIMAL BEHAVIOUR
Michael Quetting, Hemal Naik, Carla Avolio, Andrea Flack
3D MODEL VFX
Nathan Schönewolf
INSTALLATION ASSISTANT
Blanca Barbat
MUSIC, SOUND MIXING
Hyemin Jung
DATA VISUALIZATION SUPPORT
University of Konstanz, Department of Computer and Information Science
PROJECT TEAMWISE
Ying Zhang, Stefan Erk, Prof. Dr. Falk Schreiber
IMAGING BARN
Alex Chan, Mathias Guenther
WEB DESIGN & DEVELOPMENT
Egozen Collective
SOUNDSCAPE COMPOSITION
Jiyun Park

ACKNOWLEDGMENTS, PROTOTYPE

Max Planck Institute of Animal Behaviour, Ute Hörner, Thomas Hawranke, Leo Beaudoin, Atelier Xoda, Nomeda & Gediminas Urbonas, Marc Lee, Temporary Gallery, The Nordic House, Christelle the Cat

DISSUASION ENGINE

CREDITS

Chris Salter, Erik Adigard and Alexandre Quessy

ACKNOWLEDGMENTS

The organizers and supporters of the Driving the Human event

DO AIS DREAM OF CLIMATE CHAOS: SYMBIOTIC AI

CREDITS

UNITY DEVELOPMENT / TECHNICAL ARTISTS
Alex Tianyou Wang, Easton Self
SOUND DESIGN / 3D MODELING
Niles Fromm
WORKSHOP DESIGN AND CO-HOST
Chao Hui Tu
SYMBIOTIC AI ZINE DESIGN
Nicole Schwartz

ACKNOWLEDGMENTS

David Hecht and Sam Hart, Organizers of the Cybernetics Library in New York and Berlin

DOWN TO THE ECONOMY

CREDITS

Agnes Wessalowski, Amon Nirandorn, Christian Wismer, Dorothee Reumann, Mila Zoe Meier, Philine Strauß

ACKNOWLEDGMENTS

Herbert Enge und Neele Peters (Thalia Theater Hamburg), Karin Rissen-Nizvani (Klabauter Theater), Annika Wismer, Carsten Wismer

HABIT@

CREDITS

DESIGN LEAD
Yasmine Abbas, Dk Osseo-Asare
TECHNICAL DRAWINGS
Dk Osseo-Asare, Mahan Motalebi, Tiffany Leung

FABRICATION
Yasmine Abbas, Dk Osseo-Asare, Mahan Motalebi, Jamie Heilman, (DigiFab)
DESIGN PARTICIPATION
Mia Fantasia, Luke Scanlon, Richard Sodeinde, John Martin, Dara Olumide

ACKNOWLEDGMENTS

Pennsylvania State University Team, all participants and stakeholders to the Fufuzela development

HABITAT THEATRE: HOW TO TRANSFORM A TERRITORY INTO A STAGE—A MANUAL

CREDITS

Barbara Boss, Damiàn Dlaboha, Maximilian Grünewald, Mira Hirtz and Béla Rothenbühler, Jules Gisler

ACKNOWLEDGMENTS

Frank Raddatz, Frédérique Aït-Touati, Dr. Bertram Schmidt, acatech, ZKM | Center for Art and Media, Robert Preusse and Stefanie Rau

HUMAN-BACTERIA INTERFACES: AN EXPLORATION OF THE PRESENT AND FUTURE OF HUMAN-MICROBIAL ECOSYSTEMS

CREDITS

VIDEO PRODUCTION / 3D ARTISTS
Artem Furenkov, Alexey Belov

ACKNOWLEDGMENTS

Hub for Biotechnology in the Built Environment (HBBE), Research England (UKRI), Dr. Martyn Dade Robertson, Dr. Jane Scott and the Living Textiles Research Group, Dr. Angela Sherry, Dr. Joshua Loh, Dr. Jasmine Bird, Aileen Hoenerloh, Matt Crown, Chris G. Pip Miller, Oliver Perry and the Architecture Workshop, Newcastle University

INDIGENOUS LANGUAGE OF TAŞLICA: A CASE OF INTERSPECIES COMMUNICATION

CREDITS

VIDEOGRAPHER
Ebru Gümrükçüoğlu
SOUND DESIGNER
Hakan Atmaca

ACKNOWLEDGMENTS

Aslıhan Demirtaş, Deniz Ova, Oğulcan Aksoy, Aslı Dinç, Irmak Erbaydar, İlayda Tuna, Pınar Yazdıç, Pınar Yalçınkaya, Can Koçak, Yiğitcan Erdoğan, Aykut Şabanoğlu, Dr. Reimar Volker (Goethe-Institut Istanbul)

MONSTERS AND GHOSTS OF THE FAR NORTH

CREDITS, CONCEPT

GAME DEVELOPMENT / PROTOTYPE ENGINEERING
Dr. Thomas Deacon
SOUNDSCAPE
Chingis Enkhbaatar

ACKNOWLEDGMENTS, CONCEPT

ADS 8 TUTORS
Kamil Hilmi Dalkir, Ippolito Pestellini Laparelli, Rhiarna Dhaliwal, Dr. Dubravka Sekulic

CREDITS, PROTOTYPE

3D ARTIST / GAME DESIGNER
Max Bredlau
GAME PROGRAMMER / GAME DESIGNER
Benjamin Grill
SOUNDSCAPES
Josh Banham

ACKNOWLEDGMENTS, PROTOTYPE

Alfred Wegener Institute (AWI) Helmholtz Centre for Polar and Marine Research (Josefine Lenz, Prof. Dr. Susanne Liebner, Torben Windirsch), Dr. Susanne Kadner, British Antarctic Survey (Dr. Nicholas J. Cox, Ian Rudkin), Nordic House (Arnbjörg María Danielsen, Hrafnhildur Gissurardóttir, Snæfríður Grímsdóttir), AWI (Dr. Volker Rachold), Max Planck Institute (Dr. Hemal Naik), Apecs (Anastasia Deyko, Carina Keskitalo), Agricultural University of Iceland (Dr. Christian Schultze), Fraunhofer IGD (Steffen Knodt), Dr. Heiko Goelzer, Dr. Chris Jones, Xandra van der Eijk, Dr. Vera Meyer, Bryndís Snæbjörnsdóttir and Mark Wilson, Dr. Dubravka Sekulic, Julian Oliver, Elise Misao Hunchuck, Marco Ferrari, Dr. Marina Otero Verzier, Marc Lee, Sibylle Kurz

PLANETARY PERSONHOOD—A UNIVERSAL DECLARATION OF MARTIAN RIGHTS

CREDITS

Nonhuman Nonsense, Filips Staņislavskis, Diane Assiri, Kunle Kuforiji, Jonas Thunberg

ACKNOWLEDGMENTS

Prof. Dr. Elizabeth A. Povinelli, Dr. Michelle Maloney – Australian Earth Laws Alliance, Dr. Andreas Johnsson – Planetary Geomorphologist, Dr. Ansgar Greshake – Museum für Naturkunde, Federico Campagna, Nahum, Petra Lilja – Age of Entanglements, STRP.nl, International Space University, Vilém Flusser Archive, diffrakt | center for theoretical periphery

RIPPLE, RIPPLE, RIPPLING

CREDITS

Yizhuo Gao, Yunshi Zhou, Laura Belinky

ACKNOWLEDGMENTS

We owe a special debt of gratitude to villagers in Shigushan who have generously let us into their lives over the years.

THE ROOTED SEA: HALOPHYTIC FUTURES

CREDITS

Sonia Mehra Chawla, Miriam Walsh, Branden MC Carthy, Sam Healey, Kiera, Siena, Gaurav Khera, Creative Informatics Scotland, Ray Interactive UK, MS Swaminathan Research Foundation India, acatech – National Academy of Science and Engineering

ACKNOWLEDGMENTS

acatech – National Academy of Science and Engineering, MS Swaminathan Research Foundation India

RUM_A: MULTISPECIES URBAN REFUGE IN CLUSTER

CREDITS

VIDEOMAKER
Ana Clara Mattoso
WOODWORKER
Gustavo Moreira
VIDEO EDITOR
Laura Fragoso
PHOTOGRAPHER
Lucas Martins
SOUND DESIGNER
Stephanie Doyle

ACKNOWLEDGMENTS

Jeanine Geammal and Malu Fragoso, project advisors; Eleonora Fabião and Marta Peixoto for helping with the translations from Portuguese to English; Elisa Peixoto, Maria Lucia Peixoto, Jaime Acioli, Nadine Nicolay, Valter Oliveira and Verónica Aparecida, Robin Mallick (Goethe-Institut Rio de Janeiro) for the support

SEDEKAH BENIH

CREDITS

SEDEKAH BENIH TEAM
Tegar Pratama, Djuli Pamungkas, Reksi Muhamad Sidik, Raphael Raymond Rene R, Arsya Ardiansyah, Della Sabarini, Gina, Adlil, Thoriq Firdaus, Reja Hilman Suwandana, Endira F Julianda, Roni, Gustar Brata
COMMUNITIES
Komunitas Masagi, The Power Of Emak Emak, Puzzle Indonesia, Kuya Gaya, Srikandi Pasundan
PARTNERS
Goethe-Institut Bandung, Look Who Is Talking Project, Project Seven and a Half

ACKNOWLEDGMENTS

Our family, Driving The Human production team, Goethe-Institut Bandung, Rakarsa Foundation, Buruan Sae, Masagi Community, Wangunsari News, Sesama, Saujana Doc, Female Plus, Samahita, Srikandi Pasundan, Komuji, Puzzle, Sanggar Seni Rupa Kontemporer, Dapur Musafir, All participants in Bandung and Berlin, and all *tiis leungeun* in Bandung

SERVER FARM

ACKNOWLEDGMENTS

Ogust (Athens)

SUPERLOCAL—0 MILES PRODUCTION

CREDITS

MODELMAKER
Stefano Carrari

ACKNOWLEDGMENTS

Marie Hervé

TOXICITY DISTRIBUTED—POST-EXTRACTIVISM ECONOMIES

CREDITS

PROJECT IDEA AND EXHIBITION CONCEPT
AHORA (Linda Schilling Cuellar and Claudio Astudillo Barra)
SUBJECT MATTER EXPERTS
Bernardo González Ojeda (PhD in Biological Sciences, Full Professor at Universidad Adolfo Ibáñez, Center of Applied

Ecology and Sustainability), Ariel Muñoz Navarro (Ariel Muñoz, PhD Forest Sciences, Dendrochronology and Environmental Studies Laboratory at Universidad Católica de Valparaíso), Victor Castelletto Puño (Victor Castelletto, Marine Biologist, NGO Surgencia), Karen Villanueva Mayne (Bioplastics Designer), Sebastián Escobar Cruz (Civil Engineer)

STUDENTS

Universidad de Las Américas undergraduate architecture studio: Gabriel Alarcón, Daniela Barría, Rodrigo Burgos, Gonzalo Carrasco, Sandro Chamorro, Kevin Colimil, Ignacio Painen, Rafael Pizarro, Yennifer Quintana, Tomás Salinas, Alejandro Sanz; Universidad Andrés Bello undergraduate research seminar: Abarca Sebastian, Briones Carla, Burgos Renata, Carvajal Paz, Castro Catalina, Díaz Ariel, Farías Nacaret, Fernández Felipe, Ladrón De Guevara Joaquín, Lagos Sebastián, Llanos Samuel, Loyola Cynthia, Meyers Mathias, Muñoz Javier, Nieto Tamara, Olguín Nicolás, Ortiz Francisca, Pérez Patricio, Sepúlveda Matías

ACKNOWLEDGMENTS

Sindicato de Pescadores y Mariscadores Los Vilos / Fishermen's and Shellfish Workers' Syndicate Los Vilos; Hugo Alvarado, Los Vilos resident; José Adán, Los Vilos resident; Carolina Zurita, Los Vilos resident; Verena Lehmkuhl, Goethe-Institut Chile

TRONS 'R' US

CREDITS, CONCEPT

Kankam Cedi, Jacob Danquah, Afia Asare and Obeng-Fosu

ACKNOWLEDGMENTS, CONCEPT

Frederick Okai, Va-Bene Elikem Fiatsi

ACKNOWLEDGMENTS, PROTOTYPE

Va-Bene Elikem Fiatsi, Emeka Ogboh, Oben-Fosu, Eyram Donkor, Sadat Mohammed, Frank Gyabeng, Morkporkpor, Afia Asare, Jacaob Danquah, Awilo, Ato Annan, Mr. Osei-Bonsu, Appiah Bilal

THE TROPICAL TURN—MANEUVERS FOR A PLANETARY EMBODIMENT

CREDITS

CONCEPTUAL, DISCURSIVE, AND TECH DEVELOPMENT
jpgs

ACKNOWLEDGMENTS

Conceptual discourse braided together from conversations with Daniela Medina Poch, Bonaventure Soh Bejeng Ndikung & SAVVY Contemporary team, Sarah Grant, Neema Githere,

Futura Trōpica Netroots, Transmediale Summer Camp 2021; technical advice from Carlos Serrano.

VIRTUAL SANCTUARY FOR FERTILIZING MOURNING

CREDITS, CONCEPT

DRAWINGS
Eliana Otta
VIDEO EDITING / DIRECTION
Eliana Otta
DOCUMENTATION (IN THE FIELD)
Diego Vizcarra

ACKNOWLEDGMENTS, CONCEPT

Beatríz Pío Flores, Víctor Pío Flores, Jhover Meléndez, Diego Vizcarra, Dr. Denise Quistorp (Österreichisches Kulturforum Berlin)

CREDITS, PROTOTYPE

CONCEPT, CAMERA, EDITING, TEXTS
Eliana Otta
3D CAPTURES, PRODUCTION ASSISTANCE, COLOR COR-RECTION, PERMANENT ADVISOR
Nuno Cassola
SOUND CORRECTION
Dion Christodoulatos
TRANSLATION FROM ASHANINKA
Herlin
TRANSLATION FROM CACATAIBO
Yuliza Meléndez
TRANSLATION FROM ENGLISH AND SUBTITLING
Santiago Guerra
RESEARCH, ADDITIONAL CAMERA
Diego Vizcarra
POST-PRODUCTION ASSISTANCE
Nickos Myrtou
3D RECONSTRUCTION, WEB DESIGN, AND PROGRAMMING
Hermanos Magia, with the direction of Gabriel Alayza

ACKNOWLEDGMENTS, PROTOTYPE

Carmen Loyola, Leader Emilio Maraví and members of the Nuevo Amanecer Hawai community, Leader Marcelino Tangoa and members of the Unipacuyacu community, Leader Elías Mozoline and members of the Puerto Nuevo community, Leader German Guerra and members of the Sinchi Roca I community.

7 PROTOTYPES

THE BACKPACK OF WINGS

HYESEON JEONG is interested in social phenomena of digitalization, new power/network structures, and decentralisation. Her work engages with a wide range of themes, from scientific approaches to political issues. She has generated non-linear narratives by translating and reconstructing the research content from various fields, in a maximization of fictions, radioplay, videos and sounds, entangled under a theme, and then exhibited as part of exhibitions, festivals and sound performances. She is currently studying at Academy of Media Arts Cologne.

SEONGMIN YUK is an artist, interested in notions of de(re)constructing boundaries, space and physical embodiment, interdependent perception, transboundary, posthumanity, and digital transhumanity. Seongmin Yuk looks for the possible nodes networking through those notions, (de)composes the intersections through his videos, performances, installations, and constructed spaces. He is currently studying at Academy of Media Arts Cologne.

DO AIS DREAM OF CLIMATE CHAOS?

XIAOYU (IRIS) QU 曲晓宇 (b. 1993, China) is an artist, technologist, and programmer based in Brooklyn, NY, working at the intersection of software engineering and new media art. With code as her primary medium, her works engage with the speculative, political, and poetic aspects of technology. Currently, she works on prototyping experiments at Google Research. Do AIs Dream of Climate Chaos started from her reflection on the entanglement of technology and nature and her role in speculating change as a tech worker.

HUMAN-BACTERIA INTERFACES

ANNE-SOFIE BELLING is a designer/technologist who interrogates design futures through practice-based and speculative design research. Her research often focuses on extending human somatic relations and experiences with other-than-humans through emerging technology interventions. She is currently studying a PhD at the HBBE, where she is examining the more-than-human relations of transplanetary imaginaries and off-Earth habitats through practice-based design research.

BEA DELGADO CORRALES is an environmental microbiologist interested in finding new microbial species through bioinformatics and new DNA sequencing technologies and she is now focused on characterizing the built environment microbiome. During her PhD at the HBBE, she wants to explore the possibility of using the microbial distribution in our homes to promote a healthier environment through building design and other strategies.

ROMY KAISER is a designer with focus on biomaterials, smart textiles and future textile thinking. As a "designer with hands, scientist in mind, activist by heart" she aims to change our mindset as well as current systems towards a more sustainable living using textiles and materiality as a tool. Currently Romy holds a PhD position at the HBBE. Her project Textile Hosting investigates the scaffolding potential of textiles for living media, like mycelium or bacteria, for bio assembly and construction purposes.

PAULA NERLICH is a designer and explorer. With her material research she aims to support the elimination of so-called food waste through the creation of circular biomaterials from industrial food production surplus. In her practise as material designer and as co-founder of Circular Home Lab, she initiates discourse around rethinking systems of waste, the food industry and community. Her PhD project *The Materiality of Well-being* is a practise-led research project, searching how multisensory experiences and interactions of smell and touch, with a focus on the interrelationship of bacteria, smell and textiles for enhanced wellbeing.

MONSTERS AND GHOSTS OF THE FAR NORTH

LENA GEERTS DANAU is an energetic and curious research architect who engages with political, environmental and planetary issues in a focused and skilful way. Her work has been exhibited among others, at Radialsystem (Berlin), De Gistfabriek (Wijnegem), ZKM (Karlsruhe), and Silent Green (Berlin). While she mainly thinks conceptually via research and design, she loves working with her hands.

Originally she comes from Antwerp, where she also completed her bachelor degree in Architecture. During her Masters, she explored the architectural field at the Bergen Arkitektur hogskole (Norway) and finished her degree at the Royal College of Art (London). In her Master thesis, Lena investigated fluid border situations and investigated the potential of digital environments as a new mode of representation. After working experiences in the architectural field at B-architecten and urbanist/researcher at Maatontwerpers, she is now working with Tick Tack gallery, as a carpenter for Studio Bonne, and as part of alternaa – a collective established with Andra Pop-Jurj.

ANDRA POP-JURJ is an architectural designer and researcher born in Romania. She trained in architecture at the Technical University of Munich and National University of Singapore and holds a MA Architecture from Royal College of Art. Her diverse and multidisciplinary background have stimulated her interest in the expanding definitions of architecture, research-based worldbuilding and speculative design in digital environments. Her MA work explores the spatial manifestation of geopolitical conflicts in the Arctic region caused by environmental degradation. Building upon this, Andra further investigated the tension between extractive economies, wildlife and and permafrost landscapes based on forms of multispecies cohabitation encountered in the natural gas infrastructures of the Yamal peninsula. Andra has practiced at several architecture studios in Germany, at Sergison Bates architects in London and the Belgian studio Veldhuis architectuur. She is currently a researcher with Forensic Architecture, where she has worked on investigations into border violence between Greece and Turkey, where natural processes have been weponised to assist in human rights violations. Alongside this, her spatial practice is situated at the intersection of arts and science and employs various formats ranging from writing, drawing and mapping to films, game engines and spatial installations. Andra is currently expanding her research and enquiry into forms of multispecies cohabitation together with Lena Geerts Danau as part of the Driving the Human arts and science collaboration.

SEDEKAH BENIH

MANG DIAN is an environmental activist that works with the river, waste management and urban farming in Bandung, Indonesia together with Cikapundung Community, Karang Taruna, dan PHL BBWS Citarum. He is now the director of Masagi Community and head of the neighbourhood 04 Cibogo, Bandung. He runs and manages his urban farming activity at his small garden called Urban Organik Farm at Cibogo, Bandung.

VINCENT RUMAHLOINE is a contemporary artist that playfully interrogates the social fabric and the mundane in society. His work mainly revolves around people; from social issues, human rights, traditional values, human relations, collective memories to re-designing historic narratives. Rumahloine is the winner of the sixth Bandung Contemporary Art Award 2019. His winning project Don't Call Me A Hero was exhibited in the Latiwangi Art Gallery in Bandung and tells the story about an Indonesian exile in Prague, who lost his citizenship after the 1965 tragedy. Vincent's work bridges the gaps in

society by adding a twist of uncanniness and by using artistic strategies to get closer to the experiences and lives of (non-art minded) others. Vincent graduated in Ceramics at The Bandung Institute of Technology in 2009. He worked as an art teacher and as a social worker with HIV/AIDS victims, before becoming a full-time artist. His project has been presented at Pulosari Public Space in Bandung, Contemporary Ujazdowksi Castle in Warsaw (Poland) and The National Gallery of Indonesia in Jakarta.

TRONS 'R' US

AKWASI BEDIAKO AFRANE (b. 1990) is a Ghanaian artist living and working in Kumasi, Ghana. His works explore the idea of augmentation and extensions between technological gadgets and humans. He works with discarded electronic gadgets which he refers to as "amputees", refashioning and repurposing them into machines and micro-organisms he describes as "TRONS". These TRONS become potential platforms and media for reflection, engagement and interactions. Stripped bare of their familiar housing, the TRONS become mechanical gizmos subsumed with the consciousness of previous owners of these gadgets and himself.

VIRTUAL SANCTUARY OF FERTILIZING MOURNING

ELIANA OTTA (Lima, 1981) is an artist with a Master in Cultural Studies, who inquiries about our relations with nature and precarious labor in neoliberal, extractivist economies, and also gender inequality, intersecting feminism, poetry and politics. She addresses these questions creating spaces for conversation, trust and curiosity through shared intimacy, with projects that involve pedagogical, curatorial and editorial work. Her current PhD project Lost & Shared: A laboratory for collective mourning, towards affective and transformative politics, aims to investigate the ways in which art can enable the collectivization of mourning, creating dialogues between theory and affective labor, through collective experiments that connect emotions, critical thinking, body and space. She coordinated the curatorial team of Lugar de la Memoria (Museum of Memory) in Peru (www.lum.cultura.pe), has taught at Pontificia Universidad Católica del Perú and co-founded the artist-run space Bisagra (www.bisagra.org). She is currently Candidate at the Phd in Practice Program at the Academy of Fine Arts, Vienna. She is represented by the Galería 80m2 Livia Benavides. She founded the first shop dedicated to young fashion designers in Lima, Pulga, and has an eternally amateur alter ego, dj Flaquita.

21 CONCEPTS

∇I : TOWARDS EARTHLY TECHNOSYMBIOGENESIS

MATTHEW C. WILSON is an American artist, filmmaker, and researcher based in the Netherlands. In Wilson's films/videos, sculptures, and installations viewers encounter a range of agents and intelligences entangled in natural processes and shape-shifting historical forces. His projects utilize research-based, site-specific, and methodologically eclectic approaches to track the inertia of Modernity—through contemporary ecological crises and technological transformations—into speculative futures.

Wilson holds an MFA in Visual Arts from Columbia University in the City of New York and undergraduate degrees in Literature and Art/Design from North Carolina State University. He has been a participant in the Whitney Museum of American Art Independent Study Program and numerous residencies including Aalto University, Jan van Eyck Academie, Tabakalera, Terra Foundation, CSAV/Fondazione Antonio Ratti, and Skowhegan. His work has been supported by grants, fellowships, and commissions from Mondriaan Fonds, Forecast Platform, Kone Foundation, Talbot Rice Gallery at Edinburgh University, and the European Commission through the NEARCH project. His moving image work has screened on Vdrome.org, at IFFR—International Film Festival Rotterdam, the Eye Filmmuseum in Amsterdam, and Círculo de Bellas Artes in Madrid, among others. Gallery exhibitions include: Het Nieuwe Instituut, Rotterdam, NL; Marres, Maastricht, NL; Exhibition Research Lab, Liverpool, UK; and The Brooklyn Rail Curatorial Projects, Brooklyn, New York, US. Wilson is currently a tutor in the F for Fact MA at the Sandberg Institute in Amsterdam, NL.

DISSUASION ENGINE

ERIK ADIGARD is, with Patricia McShane, the founder of M-A-D, an interdisciplinary studio combining brand positioning, interaction design, visual communication and environmental design. M-A-D routinely works on the relationships between technology and socio-cultural concerns. Notable works include visual essays for *Wired*, media installations for the Venice Architecture Biennale, the book *Architecture Must Burn* and the branding of IBM software. The Chrysler Award for Innovation in Design, Rome Prize in Design and Venice Biennale Special Mention are among Erik's top awards. M-A-D's work has been featured in major international exhibitions and publications, including SFMOMA, the London Design Museum, the Cooper-Hewitt Museum, and Meggs' *History of Graphic Design*.

ALEXANDRE QUESSY is the director of Art Plus Code Inc, a Canadian company that does software development and user experience design for innovative and artistic projects. He has worked as a software developer, and as an artist and designer since 2003. Quessy works as a senior software developer, business analyst and UX designer every day. He's acting as an agile facilitator to manage teams of developers and designers. Over the years, he has worked as a developer in different teams, namely the Society for Arts and Technologies (SAT), Autodesk, D-Box and Boeing, to name a few.

CHRIS SALTER is an artist, Full Professor for Design + Computation Arts at Concordia University in Montreal and Director of the Hexagram Concordia Centre for Research-Creation in Media Arts and Technology. Trained in economics, philosophy, theater directing and computer music, his performances, installations, research and publications have been presented at festivals, exhibitions and conferences around the world. He is the author of *Entangled: Technology and the Transformation of Performance* (MIT Press 2010), *Alien Agency: Experimental Encounters with Art in the Making* (MIT Press, 2015) and the forthcoming *Sensing Machines: How Sensors Shape our Everyday Life* (MIT Press, 2022).

DOWN TO THE ECONOMY

VIENNE CHAN approaches money as a medium of social sculpture and seeks ways of re-imagining it to better address social needs. She has held a European Media Art Platform (EMAP) residency at m-Cult in Helsinki (2020), a Weisman Art Museum Creative Collaboration residency with the Carlson School of Management at the University of Minnesota (2019). Vienne holds a MFA in Public Art and New Artistic Strategies from Bauhaus Universität Weimar, and was a recipient of a Rosa Luxemburg Foundation Scholarship. She is currently on the editorial board for the peer-reviewed journal, *Money on the Left*. Vienne lives in Duisburg, Germany.

KATJA MEIER studied education at the University of Lüneburg with a focus on educational work and social pedagogy, dealing with the interface between social and cultural work. She currently works at the Theater Lüneburg, and as a freelance theater pedagogue for the Thalia Theater, where she leads the inclusive theater group Eisenhans. At Theater Lüneburg, she is responsible for the youth clubs, the accompanying program for the Jungen Bühne, and dramaturgical introductions. With the music theater director Kerstin Steeb, she has recently created the opera film *Der Wald*, based on an opera about right-wing mindsets in Germany by the British composer Ethel Smyth.

HABIT@

DR. YASMINE ABBAS is architecture and design faculty at the Pennsylvania State University. She is investigating the making of environments for living across contemporary conditions of expanded physical, digital, and mental mobilities. She has worked in multicultural environments employing design thinking methods to generate pan-urban intelligence and drive urban innovation. She co-founded the Agbogbloshie Makerspace Platform (AMP), winner of the Rockefeller Foundation's Centennial Innovation Challenge 2013, the 2017 SEED award for Public Interest Design, and Le Monde Urban Innovation Award—Citizen Engagement, Le Monde Cities (2020).

DK OSSEO-ASARE is principal of transatlantic architecture studio Low Design Office (LowDO), is an Architectural League of New York 2021 Emerging Voices award-winner, and assistant professor of architecture and engineering design at Pennsylvania State University where he directs the Humanitarian Materials Lab. He co-founded the pan-African open maker tech initiative Agbogbloshie Makerspace Platform (AMP) and led urban design for the Anam City and Koumbi City new town projects in Nigeria and Ghana. He is a TED Global Fellow and received his MArch. from Harvard GSD. His research explores material assemblies optimised for massively scalable radical resilience.

HABITAT THEATRE: HOW TO TRANSFORM A TERRITORY INTO A STAGE—A MANUAL

INITIATIVE FOR APPLIED MELANCHOLY (BARBARA BOSS, DAMIÀN DLABOHA, MAXIMILIAN GRÜNEWALD, MIRA HIRTZ, AND BÉLA ROTHENBÜHLER) have found each other through mutual projects and their shared aim to develop a theatre of the anthropocene in their fight against the crises of humankind with the means of performative arts.

INDIGENOUS LANGUAGE OF TAŞLICA: A CASE OF INTER SPECIES COMMUNICATION

EYLÜL ŞENSES graduated from the Architecture Department of Middle East Technical University (METU), Ankara, Turkey, and she participated in a one-year exchange program at Universidad Politécnica de Madrid (UPM), Spain. After taking part in various projects with the design collective called Plankton Project, she worked as a program coordinator in TAK Kartal, a creative hub empowering collective decision-making processes on an urban scale. She worked as operations and public programme associate at the 4th Istanbul Design Biennial realized by the Istanbul Foundation for Culture and Arts (IKSV). She received a master's degree from the architecture and urban studies program, Kadir Has University (KHAS). She took part in research and exhibition projects within SALT and KHAS. Recently she has worked as a public programme associate at the 5th Istanbul Design Biennial and has been part of The Young Curators Group

established within the biennial. She is one of the founding members of the Urban Studies Cooperative (Urban.koop), a collective network of urbanists, artists, and creatives who are willing to co-develop urban policies, programs, and projects for the local communities.

PLANETARY PERSONHOOD—A UNIVERSAL DECLARATION OF MARTIAN RIGHTS

NONHUMAN NONSENSE is a research-driven design and art studio creating near-future fabulations and experiments somewhere between utopia and dystopia. They seek to transmute our relationship to the non-human, by embracing the contradictory and the paradoxical—telling stories that open the public imaginary to futures that currently seem impossible.

Nonhuman Nonsense work in the embryonic stages of system transformation, in the realm of social dreaming and world-making processes. Aiming to redirect focus to the underlying ethical and political issues, to challenge the power structures that enable and aggravate the current destruction of the (non)human world—allowing other entities to exist. Founded by Leo Fidjeland and Linnea Våglund, it is based between Berlin and Stockholm.

RIPPLE, RIPPLE, RIPPLING

JINGRU (CYAN) CHENG is a transdisciplinary design researcher, whose path meanders through architecture, anthropology and visual art. Cyan's practice does not dwell on a defined subject matter, but rather as a form of personal enquiry, and indeed, struggles. Driven by an urge to unsettle the domination of all those constituted as others, the wide-ranging themes include, non-canonical histories and socio-spatial models, diverse ways of cultural knowing and being, aesthetic agency, and modes of co-existence and affinity between human and non-human. Her work received commendations by the RIBA President's Awards for Research from the Royal Institute of British Architects, in 2018 and 2020, respectively, and has been exhibited at Critical Zones: Observatories for Earthly Politics (ZKM, 2020-21), Seoul Biennale of Architecture and Urbanism (2019), and Venice Architecture Biennale (2018), among others. Cyan co-leads an architectural design studio, ADS7, at the Royal College of Art, exploring politics of the atmosphere. She holds a PhD by Design from the Architectural Association (AA) in London, and was the co-director of AA Wuhan Visiting School (2015-17). Cyan is currently working on a short film with Chen Zhan, *Orchid, Wasp and I*, a dystopian story seeking to unsettle the anthropocentric practices that exacerbate the climate crisis.

CHEN ZHAN is an architect, anthropologist and independent filmmaker. Chen's film practice focuses on the socio-political struggles of the marginalised through the lens of the everyday. Her short documentary, *Ahmad*, tells the story of a Lebanese asylum seeker who rebuilds his life through cooking and food-sharing. The film debuted at the London International Documentary Festival (2019). Her anthropological research develops a critical analysis of future-making at the intersection between design, material culture and consumerism. In architecture, Chen was dedicated to the realisation of Maggie's Cancer Care Centre in Leeds. Chen is currently working on a short film with Jingru (Cyan) Cheng, *Orchid, Wasp and I*, a dystopian story seeking to unsettle the anthropocentric practices that exacerbate the climate crisis.

THE ROOTED SEA: HALOPHYTIC FUTURES

SONIA MEHRA CHAWLA is a multi-disciplinary artist and researcher based in New Delhi, India. Chawla works at the intersection of art, science and technology, exploring themes of ecology, sustainability and conservation. Sonia's practice is inextricably linked to an ethic, even a politics of multi-species co-existence and co-habitation. Her research is a political act, in which she collaborates with climate-change scientists, ecologists, microbiologists, as well as fishermen, farmers and indigenous people who speak from the deep reserves of their traditional wisdom.

Chawla is a fellow and awardee of the Charles Wallace India Trust of the British Council. She is a fellow of the International Art+ Science International residency program instituted by Wellcome Trust UK/DBT India Alliance & Khoj, India. Furthermore, Chawla is a fellow of Akademie Schloss Solitude, Stuttgart, for Social Sciences. Her forthcoming project in Scotland, has been supported by a research fellowship from Marine Scotland and ASCUS Art & Science. Chawla's work has been exhibited at, among others, the Yinchuan Biennale 2016, China; Essl Museum, Austria; Tate Modern, London; Albertina Museum, Vienna; ET4U Contemporary Visual Art Projects, Denmark; Yinchuan Museum of Contemporary Art, China; CSMVS Museum, Mumbai; Today Art Museum, Beijing.

MIRIAM WALSH (ASCUS ART & SCIENCE) ASCUS Art & Science is a non-profit organization based in Edinburgh, Scotland, committed to bridging the gap between art, design and the sciences. ASCUS aims to provide a joint platform for artists, designers and scientists to work together on a diverse array of projects, including science communication, science, art and design collaborative projects, and trans-disciplinary research, serving as an established hub between like-minded organizations both nationally and internationally. ASCUS brings this work to public audiences through its exhibitions and its digital program of workshops, events, lab training and DIY resources.

RUM_A: MULTISPECIES URBAN REFUGE IN CLUSTER

CLARA ACIOLI Born and based in Rio de Janeiro, Clara Acioli is an artist, researcher and designer who graduated from the School of Design of the Federal University of Rio de Janeiro (UFRJ). She works at the intersection of the arts, design, biology and contemporary critical studies in search for new understandings of the world we live in. Since 2017, Acioli has been part of and collaborates with NANO lab – Nucleus of Arts and New Organisms, an interdisciplinary laboratory in the School of Fine Arts at UFRJ that articulates art with science and technology. She has been researching organic materials such as biodegradable composites and bioplastics to be used both in artistic and design projects.

SERVER FARM

JAMES BRIDLE is a writer and artist working across technologies and disciplines. Their artworks have been commissioned by galleries and institutions and exhibited worldwide and on the internet. Their writing on literature, culture and networks has appeared in magazines and newspapers including *Wired*, the *Atlantic*, the *New Statesman*, the *Guardian*, and the *Observer*. *New Dark Age*, their book about technology, knowledge, and the end of the future, was published by Verso (UK & US) in 2018, and they wrote and presented *New Ways of Seeing* for BBC Radio 4 in 2019. Their work can be found at http://jamesbridle.com

SUPERLOCAL—0 MILES PRODUCTION

ANDREA DE CHIRICO was born in Rome and is based in Turin (IT). He holds an MA in Social Design from Design Academy Eindhoven and a BA in Industrial Design from ISIA in Rome. His work focuses on the intersection between conventional, traditional and modern making. He designs tools, systems and objects with social and environmental awareness, always linked with a rigorous analysis of the context. His practice is open and accessible, creating a platform to connect with different groups internationally, remodelling everyday products for different contexts.

Appointed as researcher at Free University of Bolzano from 2016 to 2019 and Designer in Residence 2016 for the Design Museum in London, Andrea's work has been exhibited in the Design Museum in London, the Triennale Design Museum, and Z33 House for Contemporary Art among others. De Chirico lectures in various universities and institutions such as University of Bolzano, NABA, University of West England, New Designers in London and Design Connections by the British Council.

TOXICITY DISTRIBUTED—POST-EXTRACTIVISM ECONOMIES

AHORA (LINDA SCHILLING CUELLAR AND CLAUDIO ASTUDILLO BARRA) is a research and design practice lead by architects

Linda Schilling Cuellar and Claudio Astudillo Barra, based in Santiago, Chile. Formed in 2020, it looks at extraction economies, with particular attention to the ones that take place in Chile, and asks what will happen after it's all gone. To realize possible futures led by local communities, AHORA defends that we must understand the transformed landscapes inherited by the current economic value-ways through the lens of what was and what could be moving towards a post-extractivism scenario.

By looking at the documents that enclose most of the knowledge about the territories and the Environmental Impact Assessments, AHORA takes on new mediums of representation to visualize and discuss the impacts of extractions with local organizations and academia. Working in close collaboration with designers, biologists, and engineers, AHORA draws the story of a place through its human and non-human inhabitants' relationships to challenge and propose new ways of being together.

THE TROPICAL TURN—MANEUVERS FOR A PLANETARY EMBODIMENT

JUAN PABLO GARCÍA SOSSA (JPGS) (*Bogotá) is a designer, researcher and artist fascinated by the clash between emerging technologies and grass-root popular culture in tropical territories. His practice explores the development of cultures, visions, realities and worlds through the remix and reappropriation of technologies from a *Tropikós* perspective (Tropics as Region and Mindset). JPGS has been part of diverse research institutions and design studios and currently is a design research member at SAVVY Contemporary The Laboratory of Form-Ideas' Design Department in Berlin and Co-Director of Estación Terrena, a space for arts, research and technologies in Bogotá. JPGS is a 2020 Rapid Response for a Better Digital Future Fellow at EYEBEAM.

DRIVING THE HUMAN EXPERTS

KIM ALBRECHT visualizes cultural, technological, and scientific forms of knowledge. His diagrams unfold and question the structures of representation and explore the aesthetics of technology and society. Kim is a principal researcher at metaLAB (at) Harvard, director of metaLAB (at) FU Berlin, and holds a Ph. D. from the University of Potsdam in media theory. As a design researcher, Kim Albrecht explores the boundaries of visual knowledge in the post-digital age. Working and living in Berlin, Kim exhibited, among others, at Harvard Art Museums, MIT List Visual Arts Center, Four Domes Pavilion Wrocław, Ars Electronica Center, Cooper Hewitt, Cube design museum, ZKM Center for Art and Media Karlsruhe, Kaestner Gesellschaft, The Wrong Biennial, Istanbul Contemporary Art Museum, and Kunsthaus Graz.

BRIGITTE BAPTISTE is a Colombian biologist graduated from the Pontificia Universidad Javeriana,with a Master's degree in Tropical Conservation and Development from the University of Florida. She is Doctor Honoris Causa in Environmental Management from Unipaz University and was recently awarded with an Honoris Causa degree in Law from the University of Regina.

She was the director of the Alexander Von Humboldt Biological Resources Research Institute for nearly 10 years and currently serves as the President of the Ean University, a higher education Institution focused on sustainable entrepreneurship. She is considered an expert on environmental and biodiversity issues and is an important leader in gender diversity, being recognized for its participation at international congresses related to these topics. It has also been a reference in the achievement of important bridges between politics, academia and science and was chosen as one of the 25 world experts of the Intergovernmental Platform for Biodiversity and Ecosystem Services (IPBES) between 2016 and 2019.

TULGA BEYERLE has been director of the Museum für Kunst und Gewerbe Hamburg (MK&G) since 1 December 2018. In keeping with the goal of museums of applied and decorative arts everywhere to provide inspiration for the best in design both in the present and future, Beyerle strives to position MK&G as a place of myriad possibilities and a platform for discourse and negotiation at the highest level and yet without excluding any members of society.

The esteemed design expert was director of the Kunstgewerbemuseum Dresden, Schloss Pillnitz, from 2014 to 2018 and concurrently a member of the management board of the Staatliche Kunstsammlungen Dresden, one of Germany's leading museum networks. Previously she was Co-director of Vienna Design Week, which she co-founded in 2006. She also worked successfully as an independent curator throughout Europe.

Beyerle comes to the field of design based on practical experience: after completing her journeyman's qualification in carpentry, she studied industrial design in Vienna and taught design history and theory at the University of Applied Arts there for seven years. She is a member of the programme council of the Kulturstiftung der Länder, the Bundeskunsthalle Bonn, the advisory board of mudac, the Museum of Contemporary Design and Applied Arts in Lausanne, the jury of the 16th Design Parade Hyères 2022 and the jury of the Austrian contribution to the 18th International Architecture Exhibition, La Biennale di Venezia 2023, among others.

TATIANA BILBAO, architect, born in 1972, began her eponymous studio in 2004. Prior to founding her architecture studio, was an Advisor in the Ministry of Development and Housing of the Government of the Federal District of Mexico City. Bilbao holds a recurrent visiting teaching position at Yale University School of Architecture and has taught at Harvard University GSD, Columbia University GSAPP, Rice University, AA in London Summer School, University of Andrés Bello in Chile, and Peter Behrens School of Arts at Dusseldorf in Germany. Bilbao's studio has work across typologies and in different parts of the world, for which she has been recognized with several distinctions, among those: the Kunstpreis Berlin in 2012, the Global Award for Sustainable Architecture Prize by the LOCUS Foundation in 2014, the Marcus Prize Award 2019, Tau Sigma Delta Gold Medal of the ACSA 2020, Honorary Fellow of the Royal Architectural Institute of Canada (RAIC) 2021, and the Richard Neutra Award in 2022.

JOSEPH HALLIGAN is a founding member of Assemble, a multi-disciplinary collective, which formed in 2010. Focusing on work in the arts, Joe has designed and delivered a number projects including much of the collective's work in Liverpool, for which they were awarded the Turner Prize in 2015. Joe has lectured and taught internationally at a variety of universities including Yale, Cambridge and the ETH in Zurich. Joseph was visiting professor at the EPFL in Lausanne from 2020-21. Joe has recently completed the design and delivery of a new permanent gallery at the Wellcome Collection in London and is currently working with the Luma foundation in Arles on a new workspace for the experimental think tank, production workshop and learning network, Atelier Luma.

ALEXANDER HICKS was born 1983 in Houston, Texas, and is an expert when it comes to chilis, starting his chili eating career before he even turned one. At 14 years old he started cooking with chilis, and shortly after that he started growing this plant. Finding many interesting new varieties from all over the world he has grown over 2000 different varieties over the years. Recently, he introduced his chili passion to an array of people by presenting interesting facts in many outlets, such as social media and in different TV shows. Hicks organic grown chili plants received awards at major garden shows, and his presentations in schools show young people the different aspects about this plant that has a cultural impact all over the world.

   With experience in renewable energy and agriculture, he is now exploring energy efficient growing environments to produce crops. One project is a rooftop Greenhouse with a cradle 2 cradle concept that will be able to produce fresh chilis year-round, with a minimum of external energy. Margit Rosen.

ELISE MISAO HUNCHUCK (b. tkaronto/Toronto) is a landscape researcher, editor, educator and curator trained in landscape architecture, philosophy, and geography (University of Toronto, CA). Based in Berlin and Milan, her research uses cartographic, photographic, and text-based practices to document political ecologies, exploring material landscapes and relationships between resources, infrastructures, natural processes, human and other-than-human existences. She is a Visiting Lecturer at the Royal College of Art School of Architecture, a Senior Researcher and Lecturer at The Bartlett School of Architecture, London, and a member of the editorial board of Scapegoat. She is also the editor and a curator for transmediale.

SUSANNE KADNER Convinced that reaching our climate targets requires a fundamentally different way of using resources, Susanne Kadner initiated the Circular Economy Initiative Germany at acatech – National Academy of Science and Engineering. She leads the Head Office of the state and industry-funded initiative, which aims at defining the transition towards a resource-efficient and digitally-enabled Circular Economy with stakeholders from Politics, Science, Industry and Civil Society. Before that, Kadner worked for ten years at the Potsdam Institute for Climate Impact Research, where she was Head of Science and Deputy Head of the Intergovernmental Panel on Climate Change (IPCC). In this function, she co-authored and managed among other things the fifth *Assessment Report*, which provided the scientific basis for the United Nations Framework Convention on Climate Change Paris Agreement. Before starting her career on the science-policy interface, she studied Oceanography at the University of Southampton and received a PhD in Analytical Chemistry and Marine Microbiology from the University of East Anglia.

KABELO MALATSIE is a curator and organiser living in Bern. She recently became director of Kunsthalle Bern (April 2022). Her ongoing curatorial research project explores the exhibitionary mode as unlikely starting points that place incongruous practices together, to instigate other ways of making and reading the world we inhabit. As an organiser she is preoccupied with the notion of autonomy and the underground. She was director of Visual Arts Network of South Africa (2018-2019) and an associate in the curatorial team at Stevenson gallery in Cape Town and Johannesburg (2011 – 2016). She co-curated the exhibition Deliberation on Discursive Justice for the Yokohama Triennale (Japan 2020), participated In the Open or in Stealth for Barcelona's MACBA (Spain 2018), and curated solo exhibitions across various institutions in South Africa for artists such as Nicholas Hlobo, Moshekwa Langa and Sabelo Mlangeni. Malatsie holds a Master's degree in Art History from the University of Witwatersrand.

VERA MEYER runs the Chair of Molecular and Applied Microbiology at TU Berlin since 2011. The focus is on researching and optimising fungal cell factories, with the aim of making more effective use of fungal metabolic potentials for the production of medicines, platform chemicals, enzymes and biomaterials in the sense of a sustainable bioeconomy and circular economy. Together with her team, she pursues a holistic approach and develops and combines methods from systems biology and synthetic biology. Vera Meyer is the spokesperson for the European think tank EUROFUNG, a board member of DECHEMA and a member of acatech. Her inter- and transdisciplinary research projects combine natural and engineering sciences with art, design and architecture and create bio-based scenarios for possible living and housing worlds of the future. Vera Meyer is also active as a visual artist under the pseudonym V. meer and uses the means of art to make society more aware of the potential of mushrooms for a sustainable future.

HEMAL NAIK is a postdoctoral researcher at the Max Planck Institute of Animal Behavior. Hemal's research focuses on developing software to study animal behavior using technologies like computer vision, augmented and virtual reality. Along with scientific projects, Hemal is deeply interested in sharing scientific findings with the community through public talks and collaborative art projects.

   He is working on several art projects that focus on wildlife and conservation with independent artists (Akademie Schloss Solitude) and institutions such as Merz Akademie.

CORINE PELLUCHON, Philosopher, professor at Gustave Eiffel University (in Paris Region) and currently Fellow at The New Institute in Hamburg, Germany. Specialist in political philosophy and applied ethics (bioethics, philosophy of the environment and animal ethics). Author of fifteen books, most of which have been translated into other languages, she received the Günther Anders Prize for Critical Thinking in February 2020 for her whole work. She has been heard about 30 times by the French Parliament, the Senate or by political parties for questions related to the end of life, to the support of people with disabilities, to the animal cause and to the ecological transition. For this theoretical and practical work, she was named Knight of the Legion of Honor in July 2021. Last books : *Les Lumières à l'âge du vivant*, Seuil, 2021 ; *Paul Ricoeur, philosophe de la reconstruction. Soin, attestation, justice*, PUF, 2022. Forthcoming in January 2023 : *L'Espérance ou la traversée de l'impossible*.

DR. SUZANNE PIERRE is soil microbial ecologist and biogeochemist, a writer, and transformer of social systems. She is the founder and the lead investigator of the Critical Ecology Lab, a nonprofit organization creating novel processes and spaces for communities of people with scientific and generational knowledge to destabilize oppressive systems and fight back against escalating social and planetary disaster. She received an interdisciplinary B.A. in Environmental Studies from

New York University, a Ph.D. in Ecology and Evolutionary Biology from Cornell University, and was a University of California President's Postdoctoral Fellow at UC Berkeley. Her technical expertise is in applying molecular and stable isotope approaches to characterizing the biophysical mechanisms controlling nutrient and carbon cycling in plant and microbial systems experiencing climate change. Pierre is a transdisciplinary scientist developing the new field of critical ecology, the study of basic ecological processes through the analytical lens of decoloniality and social liberation theory. Her goal is to explain the phenomena of global ecological change as responses to systems of global colonialism and capitalism. Pierre speaks and writes about the intersections identity, liberation, and ecology in publications such as MOLD, Loam, and a forthcoming nonfiction book. She also collaborates with artists and curators to convey these topics through art and exhibitions internationally. She is a 2022 recipient of the National Geographic Wayfinder Award and is a National Geographic Explorer.

MANUEL RIVERA studied sociology, philosophy and Latin American Studies at the Freie Universität Berlin and at the National University of Buenos Aires. After receiving his diploma (master degree) with a thesis on environmental awareness, he served as a project officer for the German Council for Sustainable Development (RNE), Berlin, and, temporarily, for the European Network of Environmental Advisory Councils (EEAC), Brussels, until 2007. The following years he worked as an actor at several German municipal theatres, before returning to sustainability issues by joining IASS in March 2011. In 2015, he obtained his PhD in Social Sciences from the University of Stuttgart, with a study about *Theatre as a Political Public Sphere*.

   At the IASS, he has been working on issues as different as urban studies, Latin American alternatives to development, the German energy transition, or the idea of Nature in the Anthropocene. He co-lead the Economics & Culture program from May 2015 to December 2016, inter alia conducting a study about attitudes toward economic growth in the German Bundestag. Currently, he leads the project *Narratives and Images of Sustainability*, with the focus on a critical analysis of current academic and political sustainability discourses.

ANNE-CATHERINE ROBERT-HAUGLUSTAINE is the General Director of the Air and Space Museum, Paris-Le Bourget since 2017. She is also Adjunct Professor at Université Paris 1 Panthéon-Sorbonne, History UFR, Heritage and Museums Master, and Member of the Academy of Technology. Anne-Catherine is a Research Associate at the CHS, Centre d'Histoire Sociale du XXe Siècle (20th Century Social History Centre), Paris 1 Panthéon-Sorbonne. Her professional career includes positions as General Director of ICOM, International Council of

Museums, Paris; and General Director of MuseDoma, Paris. She was also Director of the Exhibitions and Publications Department and member of the Executive Management Team of the Musée des Arts et Métiers (in charge of partnerships and sponsorships); and Editor-in-chief of the Revue du Musée des arts et métiers, among other positions. Anne-Catherine received several international awards, and authored more than twenty publications in prominent journals.

MARGIT ROSEN studied art history, political science, philosophy and media arts at the Ludwig Maximilians University Munich, the Karlsruhe University of Arts and Design (HfG), and the University of Paris I (Panthéon-Sorbonne). She has been research associate and curator at the ZKM | Center for Art and Media Karlsruhe since 1999. Together with Christian Schön, she also curated the lothringer13/halle, the Municipal Art Gallery, Munich in 2002–2003. In 2016 she was appointed Head of Collections, Archives & Research at ZKM.

Margit Rosen taught at HfG | University of art And Design Karlsruhe, at CAFA Beijing and is a faculty member of the Master's program MediaArtHistories at the Danube University Krems. In 2011 and 2013, she was a visiting professor at the Art Academy Münster. She publishes on 20th and 21st century art, art and politics and the history of the electronic arts.

JAIME SEVILLA is an explorer of the weirdness of reality. His work spans communication with alien artificial minds, building tools for precognition and helping humanity flourish.

YURI TUMA is a Brazilian multidisciplinary artist focusing on the investigation of contemporary narratives related to diverse ecologies through sound art, installation, and performance as a way to address and reevaluate the human/animal binomial imposed by science, politics, and culture. In line with his artistic concerns, in 2020 he co-founded the Institute for Postnatural Studies, a center for artistic experimentation from which to explore and problematize postnature as a framework for contemporary creation. More actively, besides project management, curating, and academic programming, Tuma coordinates the Institute's publishing project, Cthulhu Books, to become a showcase for the political potential of imagining new worlds and possible futures for the planet through academic and artistic research. In addition to participating in residencies and coordinating workshops around interspecies thinking and practices, he collaborates in educational and mediation programs with Spanish institutions such as the Museo Nacional Centro de Arte Reina Sofía, La Casa Encendida, Matadero, and INLAND, among others.

BIAO XIANG 项飙 is Director of Max Planck Institute for Social Anthropology in Germany since 2020, and Professor of Social Anthropology at the University of Oxford before that. Xiang's research addresses various types of migration – internal and international, unskilled and highly skilled, emigration and return migration, and the places and people left behind – in China, India and other parts of Asia. Xiang is the winner of the 2008 Anthony Leeds Prize for his book *Global Bodyshopping* and the 2012 William L. Holland Prize for his article *Predatory Princes*. His 2000 Chinese book 跨越边界的社区 (published in English as *Transcending Boundaries*, 2005) was reprinted in 2018 as a contemporary classic, and 自己作为方法 (*Self as Method*, co-authored with Wu Qi) was ranked the Most Impactful Book 2020. His work has been translated into Japanese, French, Korean, Spanish, German and Italian.

DRIVING THE HUMAN PROJECT PARTNERS

JAN BOELEN is a curator of design, architecture, and contemporary art. He is artistic director of Atelier Luma, an experimental laboratory for design in Arles, France. Boelen studied Product Design at the Media & Design Academy in Genk and is the founder and former artistic director of Z33 – House for contemporary art in Hasselt, Belgium. He was curator of the 4th Istanbul Design Biennial in Istanbul (2018) and initiated Manifesta 9 in Belgium (2012). Over the years he has been fashioning projects and exhibitions that encourage the visitor to look at everyday objects in a novel manner. Boelen recently edited *Social Matter, Social Design: For Good or Bad, all Design in Social* (Valiz, 2020), and his writing addresses the implications of design in everyday life, and how artistic practices shape the discipline.

SARAH DONDERER is a curator focusing on the intersections of art, science and technology. After studying art history and sociology in Munich, she worked as a coordinator and curatorial assistant at Kunstverein München and completed her academic traineeship at Deichtorhallen Hamburg. She has been involved in various exhibitions and art projects among others at the design museum Die Neue Sammlung in the Pinaktothek der Moderne in Munich and the Deutsches Hygiene-Museum Dresden. Since 2020 she has been holding the position of a curator at the ZKM | Center for Art and Media Karlsruhe and has co-curated and co-coordinated the digital opening festival of the scientific and artistic collaboration project Driving the Human.

SANDRA FENDL is a scientific advisor at acatech, the German Academy of Science an Engineering, where she *translates* and communicates complex science to the public. She is an author for the acatech *HORIZONS series*, which addresses cutting-edge technology fields in a manner that is scientifically robust yet still clear and easy to understand. Furthermore, she co-coordinates the science-art collaboration project Driving the Human. Before her work at acatech, she studied biology in Regensburg and Munich and received her PhD from the Max Planck Institute of Neurobiology where she contributed to the understanding of the fruit fly's brain. Besides her scientific work, she was engaged in the Max Planck PhDNet as a podcast host discussing diversity and inclusion in academia.

INA GRABOSCH lives, works and studies in Karlsruhe and Freiburg. She has worked as Assistant to the Directors for the Vitra Design Museum and as an industrial clerk for the company Vitra. With her studies in product design at the Karlsruhe University of Arts and Design (HfG) she now follows her passion for a change towards more sustainability in industry. Alongside she works as a research assistant in the Bio Design Lab at the HfG Karlsruhe and as a product designer for the toy company Plasticant mobilo.

JULIA IHLS is an interdisciplinary researcher and designer at the intersections of (natural-)philosophy, media theory and scenography. After studying art/media studies (M.A.) in Konstanz and Cork, and scenography/media art (Dipl.) in Karlsruhe, she worked as a concept designer and writer, among others for the ZKM Karlsruhe. Since April 2021, she is the head of the Bio Design Lab at the HfG Karlsruhe, where – besides teaching and curating – she researches on new (bio-)materials and convivialism.

FREO MAJER is the founder and artistic director of Forecast, an international mentorship program that transcends disciplines and geographical locations to connect cultural practitioners with renowned mentors.

Trained as an opera director, Majer looks back at a career as a director and producer in European theaters, opera houses, and at festivals, including at Mainz State Theater, Lucerne Theater, Bremen Theater, and the international festival "Theater der Welt." Driven by his own experience, and recognizing a gap in the type of support available to cultural workers, he changed paths and founded Forecast in 2015.

Together with curators and festival directors from various European cities, he initiated the interdisciplinary research project *Housing the Human* (2017-2019). In 2020, Majer began a three-year collaboration with the ZKM and HfG in Karlsruhe and the National Academy of Science and Engineering acatech, developing prototypes on the eco-social research program *Driving the Human*.

ANTHEA OESTREICHER is an interdisciplinary designer and researcher working on the threshold between science and art. With a diploma in visual communication from Darmstadt and working as an Art Director, she is a narrator, combining content and form and craft practice.

She is interested in the concepts around interspecies dependencies, symbiotic design and co-laboration, the role of food, and systems change in the face of ecological crisis.

DARIA PARKHOMENKO is the founding director of LABORATORIA Art&Science Foundation (from 2008), the first exhibition and research centre in Russia focused on constructing platforms of interdisciplinary interaction between contemporary art, science, and society. She is the author of the Know-How Methodology of integrating artists and scientists into each other's fields. She has curated over 30 international art&science exhibitions, and more than 20 interdisciplinary conferences and symposia on the topics of AI, Quantum Physics, Climate Change, Big Data, Biochemistry and other. Her curatorial projects were held in Russia and abroad: in Tretyakov Gallery, Moscow, Garage, Moscow, MMOMA, Moscow, Polytechnic Museum, Moscow, Itaú Cultural, Sao-Paulo, Brazil, Riga, Latvia. She is also the author of the course Methodologies and Practices of Science-Art. Daria served as a jury member for: Prix Ars Electronica, Austria; Crespo Foundation for 'ArtNature/ NatureArt' residency, Germany; Innovation award in the field of contemporary art, Russia. She studied sociology, art history and cultural management at Lomonosov Moscow State University and Moscow School of Social and Economic Sciences. Currently, she is residing in Germany and works at ZKM.

MARTINA SCHRAUDNER is head of the Fraunhofer Center for Responsible Research and Innovation and of the department Gender and Diversity in Technology and Product Development at the Technical University of Berlin. From 2018-2021, she was on the board of directors of acatech - German Academy of Science and Engineering e. V. She deals with methods, instruments and processes that make diversity, understood as different perspectives, accessible and usable in research and development. Schraudner is active in expert groups for Structural Change of the European Union and national and international selection committees for application-oriented research and innovation projects. She is a member of the Council of the University of Paderborn, of the Board of Trustees of the European Academy for Women in Politics and Economics (EAF) and the Board of the Competence Centre Technology-Diversity-Equal Opportunities e. V.

PHILIPP ZIEGLER is a curator in the field of art and technology. He is currently the head of the Curatorial Department at ZKM | Center for Art and Media Karlsruhe, Germany, and has been responsible for numerous exhibitions there since 2012. He curated or co-curated several international projects such as the ifa (Institute for foreign Relations) exhibition *Future Perfect. Contemporary Art from Germany* which has toured internationally since 2013. In 2018 he was one of the curators of the 6th Guangzhou Triennial at the Guangdong Museum of Art, Guangzhou, China. Ziegler has written articles and essays in various magazines and catalogues and was recently the co-editor of the publication *Digital Imaginaries. African Positions Beyond Binaries*. He studied art history and history in Stuttgart, Germany and Milan, Italy.

MODERATORS AND ACTIVATORS

SONG TAE CHONG PHD is a New York City and Berlin based educator and curator. Currently a Trustee of the Martin Parr Foundation, Song focuses on praxis based curatorial work and theoretical practice. As the former Director of Milk Gallery in Chelsea, Song mounted over 40 exhibitions and numerous special projects. She is part time faculty at NYU where she specializes in postcolonial visual culture and history and theory of photography. She also teaches in the MFA Program at Parsons in NYC and was a visiting lecturer at Fordham University. Her research interests include epistemologies of memory, photographic theory, architecture and landscape photography, decolonizing the archive, and 20th century documentary photography. Her practice includes curation, zine and book publishing, artist advisement, research and exhibition design.

DANIEL CREMER appears as performance artist, writer and somatic explorer. The experiential spaces he creates are focused on intimate encounters between bodies, words, ideas and gestures. Addressing his audiences directly, Daniel is using cheeky humor, altered states of consciousness and a criticial reflection of the status quo in order to investigate shared moments of alertness and social imagination.

Working freelance in this field since 2007, his most recent work has been produced at theaters like the Maxim Gorki Theater Berlin, Mousonturm Frankfurt (Main) and Nationaltheater Mannheim. He toured internationally and was invited to renowned festivals like Radikal Jung in Munich (2020) and the Stückemarkt at Berliner Theatertreffen. In 2015 he received the Preis der Autoren for the invention of immersive performative simulations in a made-up language called *Fremdsprache* under label TALKING STRAIGHT. He co-founded the eponymous theatre group which he was part of until 2017.

ARIANA DONGUS is a media scholar, journalist and teacher based in Berlin and Karlsruhe. In exploring the intersection of biometrics, colonial pasts, new forms of work, and machine intelligence, she contributes to a critique of today's digital economies.

MATYLDA KRZYKOWSKI plans, design, writes and talks about physical and digital space. Her transdisciplinary work focuses on developing cultural and commercial formats that range from exhibitions, installations and exhibits to choreography, talks and video, to name a few.

Krzykowski writes *Things Might*, a column about the built environment, for *Arts of the Working Class* Magazine. She is one half of Foreign Legion, curatorial and spatial initiate for systemic change. Recently she wrote a concept for a process focused museum for Omer Arbel titled *The Ongoing Museum*, an essay titled *Opening the Digital Interior* for the journal of The Centre of Philosophical Technologies and co-curated and developed the scenography for the exhibition *Total Space* at Museum für Gestaltung Zürich. She scripted and moderated AIRTIME, Internet TV Show about contemporary (Swiss) Design, as responds to a request for an online exhibition. Currently Matylda Krzykowski is the curator of Civic, newly established exhibition and discourse platform at Academy of Art and Design in Basel and co-curator of Institution Building at Civa Brussels.

KAY MESEBERG was born in Bad Belzig in East Germany studied political sciences at the University of Potsdam. Parallel to his career in television, he has been involved since the late nineties in conceiving and implementing numerous award-winning online projects and building platforms. He moved to ARTE in 2013, where he developed the platform ARTE Future and later joined the editorial board of the magazine SQUARE IDEE. Following the success of Polar Sea 360°, he continued exploring content from a 360° video and virtual reality perspective. Kay is since 2018 Head of Mission Innovation and works on the TV of after tomorrow which includes subjects such as data/AI, immersive media, eco-responsibility.

Kay received numerous distinctions, including three Grimme Online Awards, Deutscher Reporter- preis, two times Deutscher Wirtschaftsfilmpreis, LEAD Award, French-German Journalism Award. He is also Ambassador of Innovation at the IMZ in Vienna, cofounded by UNESCO, and member of the Board of Directors of the ICC association ACCRO in Strasbourg. He held masterclasses, keynotes, lectures, participated on panel discussions at top international universities such as Yale, among others.

In 2019, he published with Regina Kaplan Rakowski: *Immersive Media and their Future*, a chapter in the Yearbook of Educational Technology and Media, Springer.

ANTON RAHLWES is the editor-in-chief of form magazine together with Nina Sieverding since 2020. Trained as a designer at FH Potsdam, he writes, produces and designs with a focus on social issues specially in the tension between critical practice and speculative theory. At his alma mater, he taught in the context of gender design - a subject close that is close to his heart. He is co-founder of the Berlin-based furniture label OUT - Objekte unserer Tage. For the internationally active label he was responsible for the visual appearance of the brand, various designs, and trade fair appearances at the IMM Cologne. He is currently devoting himself to aesthetic theory and its interconnections with a current concept of design.

VERA SACCHETTI is a Basel-based design critic and curator. She serves in a variety of curatorial, research and editorial roles, most recently as program coordinator for the multidisciplinary research initiative *Driving the Human* (2020-2023) and curator of the initial edition of architecture festival *Archipelago: Architectures for the Multiverse* (2021). She is co-curator of TEOK Basel and one half of the curatorial initiative Foreign Legion. Sacchetti was associate curator of the 4th Istanbul Design Biennial, A School of Schools, curatorial advisor for the BIO 50 Biennial of Design in Ljubljana, Slovenia, and, as part of editorial consultancy Superscript, headed the "Towards a New Avant-Garde" event series at the 2014 Venice Architecture Biennale. She has recently edited *Design as a Tool for Transition: The Atelier Luma Approach*; and *Design As Learning: A School of Schools Reader*. Her writing has appeared in *Disegno*, *Metropolis*, and *The Avery Review*, among others. Sacchetti teaches at ETH Zurich and HEAD Geneva, and in 2020 joined the Federal Design Commission of Switzerland.

NINA SIEVERDING Since 2020, Nina Sieverding is running *form* Magazine together with her co-editor-in-chief, Anton Rahlwes. She studied design in Braunschweig, Bremen and Valencia and interned at Bauhaus Dessau Foundation and in the graphic department of *Zeit Campus* magazine. As a journalist, copywriter and graphic designer she has worked, among others, for Typo Berlin and the Berliner Festspiels. She has received awards from ADC Germany and Deutscher Designer Club (DDC).

ANTJE STAHL works as a staff writer for the Swiss publication Republik and as a lecturer at the Institute for the History and Theory of Architecture, ETH Zürich. In her texts and teaching, she takes a feminist and eco critical approach towards the field of art and architecture, which was awarded with "Michael-Althen-Prize for criticism", among others. She studied art history and philosophy in Berlin, Paris and New York and worked as the head editor for Architecture at Neue Zürcher Zeitung.

CHLOE STEAD is a Berlin-based writer and editor specialising in contemporary art. Her writing has appeared in publications such as *Artnet*, *frieze*, *Mousse* and *Spike Art Magazine*. Stead also regularly contributes to artist monographs and has taken part in or moderated talks at Damien & the Love Guru, Brussels, Vienna Contemporary, Hamburger Bahnhof, Berlin, Kunstverein Hamburger Banhof, Hamburg, and Migros

Museum, Zurich. She studied fine art at Goldsmiths University of London and HFBK University of Fine Arts Hamburg.

JAMES TAYLOR-FOSTER is a writer and cultural critic trained in architecture. He is the curator of contemporary architecture and design at ArkDes, the Swedish Centre for Architecture and Design. In 2016 he co-curated the Nordic Pavilion at the 15th Biennale Architettura di Venezia and in 2018 participated in the central exhibition at the 16th. He has developed a number of curatorial projects in Stockholm including, most recently, the first museum exhibition to explore the culture and creative field of ASMR. He was formerly editor-at-large for ArchDaily.

MUSICIANS

MARINA HERLOP sheds the classical trappings of her accomplished previous albums Nanook andBabasha to emerge in vibrant, polymorphous form on her hypnotizing new album Pripyat, out May 20, 2022 via PAN. With Pripyat the Catalonian, conservatory trained composer, vocalist, and pianist channels her environment in truly posthuman form; Herlop performs alien vocal acrobatics, drawing inspiration from Carnatic music of Southern India, while planting a diversity of sonic seeds which blossom brilliantly in her sumptuous garden of chimeric compositions, produced for the first time exclusively electronically. Herlop blew the audience away with her ensemble's Rewire debut this April and will be performing at Primavera Barcelona and LA, CTM, Mutek, Dekmantel and Le Guess Who? amongst other notable upcoming events worldwide in 2022, with more exciting news soon to be shared.

LOW KHEY is an unidentified human machine. The music of the artificial anthropoid is juggling between epic choirs, cutting-edge trap and pre-apocalyptic soundscapes. A mutation of sonic expressions across deadly clever integrations of trap, drill, post club and soundtrack elements. The result is rich and more complex yet very precise and readable owing to Low Khey's most destructive weapon: the lethal ability in sound design.

With its last EP *Ten Effective Ways To Achieve Immortality*, Low Khey team up with the Berlin-based producer and singer Catnapp and also the French producer Enae. Those collaborations seal the deal with humanity. Perched on a faraway planet, Low Khey's artificial intelligence reached its final form and looks at Earth with benevolence. Through a puzzling cyber noir storytelling, LK teach us how to overtake our inevitable programmed death. The machine learning process is complete, it's now time for Human learning. The whole project has hidden references to artificial intelligence and problems that human are facing regarding the technology. The world in which Low Khey lives is dominated by machines, and mankind is having a rough time to say the least, as revealed is first EP *Never Trust A Cyborg*.

LOCAL INITIATIVES (FESTIVAL BERLIN 2022)

FLOATING KIDSUNI The Floating University Berlin in the Kreuzberg retention basin is a place for experiments between art and ecology, where action in the context of the climate crisis is practically explored. The Children's University programme invites young people to act, research and reflect on the city, art and space. Young people, artists and scientists come together in different settings to explore, talk about and play with different possibilities in the rainwater basin. The participation at the Driving the Human event is with Ute Lindenbeck, Lena Düspohl and Jade Dreyfuss.

Ute Lindenbeck coordinates and directs, with Sabine Zahn and Anja Fiedler, the Floating Kidsuni, apart from working as a freelance stage and costume designer since 2003 and developing theatre projects on current issues in urban society. Lena Düspohl creates encounters in the context of performative art and theatre education and has developed various projects in public spaces. Jade Dreyfuss works collaboratively in the fields of cultural education, artistic mediation and documentation, theater staging and exhibition production, in the alternative scene. She is an active member of the Floating University association where she develops workshops for children on learning through art and non-human life.

KULTURLABOR TRIAL&ERROR E.V. is a non profit organization and intercultural collective with an open projectroom for neighborhood activities. They have been working for 12 years with topics such as environmental awareness, re-and upcycling, zero-waste, community & solidarity structures, education, circular economy, with a special focus on gift economy, sustainable and solidarity life concepts, in the context of a neighborhood.

KUNST-STOFFE – ZENTRALSTELLE FÜR WIEDERVERWENDBARE MATERIALIEN E.V. The Berlin-based organisation Kunst-Stoffe promotes an artistic, aesthetic and sociological exploration of reuse and second hand culture. It maintains a large collection of used, discarded and surplus materials and makes them available as a sustainable resource. Further, it provides equipped studio space and offers educational training in creative reuse and sustainable strategies.

ORT-SCHAFFT-MATERIAL organizes workshops intending to use the available materials of the surrounding landscape. Each workshop deals with a different material, so to speak with a different facet of the city of Berlin. A further aim of Ort-Schafft-Material is the networking between participants, experts, and the public and a very interesting place, the "Haus der Statistik" (House of Statistics). This is located near Alexanderplatz and offers a pool of different resources that can be found and used.

RESTE DER RESTE is a "Do-it-yourself-and-together" group from Berlin, experimenting with tree fungi and what you can make out of them. Working with mycelial cultures has brought them together from art, design and natural science in the House of Materialization (Haus der Materialisierung). For the past year, they have been working under the title Remains of What Remains (Reste der Reste) to use fungi to grow new materials and art objects from wood waste.

SOYDIVISION is a contemporary art collective of Indonesians living in Berlin that works at the intersection of art and activism. Soydivision curates performances, organizes workshops, culinary art activities, film screenings, and discussion panels. Their focus is to create socially engaged art through social practice with cathartic experiences. Re-questioning, or therapeutic healing, are recurring themes of Soydivision's artistic output or activities. Their diasporic perspective underlies an alternative approach to contemporary issues through art and encourages new forms of dialogue and engagement.

DRIVING THE HUMAN PROJECT

DRIVING THE HUMAN PARTNERS
Jan Boelen (Karlsruhe University of Arts and Design),
Freo Majer (Forecast), Martina Schraudner (acatech),
Peter Weibel (ZKM | Center for Art and Media)

**FEDERAL MINISTRY FOR THE ENVIRONMENT,
NATURE CONSERVATION AND NUCLEAR SAFETY**
Sandra Köster, Vera Günther, Martina Grigull

PROJECT COORDINATOR
Nikola Joetze

PROGRAM COORDINATOR
Vera Sacchetti

COMMUNICATIONS AND PRESS
Inês Revés, Kathrin Luz, Camille N'Dri

ASSISTANTS
Greta Kallsen, Luisa Cossu

THANKS TO
Agata Lorkowska (Project Manager Skills e.V.)
Hili Perlson (Managing Editor Forecast)

DRIVING THE HUMAN OPENING FESTIVAL

The Driving the Human Opening Festival was organized
and hosted by ZKM | Center for Art and Media Karlsruhe
and Karlsruhe University of Arts and Design

CONCEPT AND IDEA
Jan Boelen and Peter Weibel with Sarah Donderer
and Teresa Retzer

MAIN MODERATION
Barbara Kiolbassa, Julien McHardy

PANEL MODERATION
Ariana Dongus, Sabine Faller, Anett Holzheid,
Michael Kaethler, Lena Reitschuster, Vera Sacchetti

COORDINATION
Sarah Donderer, Laura Morcillo (Karlsruhe University of
Arts and Design Filmcrew), Teresa Retzer, Vera Sacchetti,
Philipp Ziegler

PROJECT ASSISTANCE
Annina Guntli, Laura C. Schmidt

TECHNICAL LEAD AND DIRECTION
Moritz Büchner

CAMERA & EDITING
Johannes Bauer, Benjamin Breitkopf, Moritz Büchner,
Mustafa Emin Büyükcoskun, Pauline Cemeris,
Jule Heinzmann, Alejandra Miranda Janus,
Andy Koch, Xenia Leidig, Peter Müller, Olga Öhler,
Sophie Reißfelder, Quirin Thalhammer,
Victor van Wetten, Christina Zartmann

DRIVING THE HUMAN VISUAL IDENTITY
Studio Yukiko, Berlin

GRAPHIC DESIGN
Felix Plachtzik

ZOOM COORDINATION
Clara Runge

COMMUNICATION & EDITING
Lena Becker, Luisa Cossu, Sarah Donderer, Alexandra
Hermann, Juliane Hohlbaum, Sabine Jäger, Nikola Joetze,
Greta Kallsen, Jessica Menger, Beate Münzenmaier,
Teresa Retzer, Inês Revés, Vera Sacchetti, Laura C. Schmidt,
Lena Schneider, Dominika Szope, Johannes Wiesel

PHOTOGRAPHY
Uli Deck, Felix Grünschloss

MUSIC
Yannick Schütte

MAKE-UP ARTIST
Sotirios Noutsos

SPECIAL THANKS TO
Nikola Joetze, Anna Maganuco, Freo Majer, Daria Mille,
Martina Schraudner, Jan Speckenbach, Desiree Weiler

TEAM

ARTISTIC DIRECTOR
Freo Majer
HEAD OF PROJECTS AND TEAM
Agata Lorkowska
PROJECT COORDINATOR
Nikola Joetze
PROGRAM COORDINATOR
Vera Sacchetti
COMMUNICATION AND PRESS
Inês Revés
GERMAN PRESS RELATIONS
Kathrin Luz
PRODUCTION ASSISTANT
Greta Kallsen
PROJECT ASSISTANT
Rabea Kaczor
WORKING STUDENT (SOCIAL MEDIA)
Camille N'Dri
TRAINEE
Jennifer Leja
INTERN
Kim Kampe
DRIVING THE HUMAN VISUAL IDENTITY AND WEBSITE
Studio Yukiko
THANKS TO
Nina Lange, Patrick Liwitzki, Hili Perlson
RADIALSYSTEM ARTISTIC DIRECTOR
Matthias Mohr

We thank the production and communication department, technical team, and all staff at radialsystem.

FESTIVAL

EXPERTS
Susanne Kadner, Elise Misao Hunchuck, Joe Halligan,
Vera Meyer, Manuel Rivera, Anne-Catherine Robert-
Hauglustaine, Margit Rosen, Jaime Sevilla, Biao Xiang
MODERATION
Julia Ihls, Matylda Krzykowski, Kay Meseberg (ARTE),
Anton Rahlwes (*form* magazine), Vera Sacchetti, James
Taylor-Foster
SPATIAL DESIGN
ConstructLab
STAGE MANAGER
Helga Angarano, Florian Greß, Klara Kopperschmidt,
Hana Peterson
ARTIST SUPPORT
Leonie Kreipe
VIDEO DOCUMENTATION
Stephan Talneau, Christina Voigt
PHOTOGRAPHY
Camille Blake

COPYEDITING
Kimberly Bradley
TECHNICAL SUPPORT & CAMERA
AMBION GmbH
EXHIBITION SUPPORT
kujawa raumdesign
HAIR & MAKE UP
Sue Eden

COOPERATION

Driving the Human was initiated by Forecast, and further
developed in continuous conversations between Freo Majer
with Jan Boelen (HfG/Atelier LUMA), Martina Schraudner
(acatech/CERRI), and the curatorial team of ZKM.

ACATECH
Sandra Fendl, Iris Michalik, Martina Schraudner, Regina
Straub, Annette Wiedemann
KARLSRUHE UNIVERSITY OF ARTS AND DESIGN (HFG)
Marion Augustin, Jan Boelen, Monika Theilmann
Ina Grabosch, Julia Ihls, Anthea Oestreicher (HfG Bio
Design Lab)
ZKM | CENTER FOR ART AND MEDIA KARLSRUHE
Lena Becker, Sarah Donderer, Hannah Jung, Peter Weibel,
Philipp Ziegler

TEAM FORECAST

ARTISTIC DIRECTOR
Freo Majer
HEAD OF PROJECTS AND TEAM
Agata Lorkowska

TEAM DRIVING THE HUMAN

PROJECT COORDINATOR
Nikola Joetze
PROGRAM COORDINATOR
Vera Sacchetti
COMMUNICATION AND PRESS
Inês Revés
GERMAN PRESS RELATIONS
Kathrin Luz
PRODUCTION ASSISTANT
Sarah Lipszyc
PROJECT ASSISTANT
Rabea Kaczor
ASSISTANT TO THE ARTISTIC DIRECTOR
Melissa Marx
WORKING STUDENT (SOCIAL MEDIA)
Aisha Altenhofen
TRAINEE
Christina Braun
INTERN
Justus Lietzke
DRIVING THE HUMAN VISUAL IDENTITY AND WEBSITE
Studio Yukiko
SILENT GREEN ARTISTIC DIRECTOR
Bettina Ellerkamp and Jörg Heitmann
WE THANK
Louise Hoffmeister, Richard König, and Linda Winkler, the production and communication department, technical team, and all staff at silent green.

SEVEN PROTOTYPES

Akwasi Bediako Afrane, Anne-Sofie Belling, Bea Delgado Corrales, Lena Geerts Danau, Mang Dian, Hyeseon Jeong, Romy Kaiser, Paula Nerlich, Eliana Otta, Andra Pop-Jurj, Xiaoyu (Iris) Qu曲晓宇, Vincent Rumahloine, Seongmin Yuk
EXPERTS
Kim Albrecht, Brigitte Baptiste, Tatiana Bilbao, Washington Fajardo, Jan-Micha Gamer, Alexander Hicks, Kabelo Malatsie, Hemal Naik, Corine Pelluchon, Suzanne Pierre, Margit Rosen, Yuri Tuma
MODERATORS AND ACTIVATORS
Song Tae Chong, Daniel Cremer, Ariana Dongus, Anton Rahlwes, Vera Sacchetti, Nina Sieverding, Antje Stahl, Chloe Stead
LINA PLATFORM FELLOWS
Tevi Allan Mensah, Jonathan Steiger, Eileen Stornebrink, Willie Vogel

CONCERT
Marina Herlop, Low Khey
LOCAL INITIATIVES
Floating Kidsuni, Kulturlabor Trial&Error e.V., Kunst-Stoffe – Zentralstelle für wiederverwendbare Materialien e.V., Ort-Schafft-Material, Soydivision, Reste der Reste
SPATIAL DESIGN
Studio Judith Seng and Constructlab (Alexander Römer)
STAGE MANAGER
Ndona Kasukamako, Esther Madubuko, Hana Petersen
HOSPITALITY
Sophie Charleson
ARTIST SUPPORT
Marc Abadie, Vedat Dayan
VIDEO DOCUMENTATION
Stephan Talneau
PHOTOGRAPHY
Camille Blake
TECHNICAL COORDINATION
Production Office Ingenieurbüro für Entertainment
TECHNICAL SERVICE PROVIDER
AMBION GmbH Lighting
DESIGN
Henning Schletter
COPYEDITING
Joanna Durier, BarbaraHauß, Julia Thorson
EXHIBITION SUPPORT
kujawa raumdesign
FESTIVAL SUPPORT TEAM
Clara Böckers, Maximilian Hornisch, Kim Kampe, Lara Mühlinghaus, Donna Schons, Valerie Stötzer, Sergen Yener
SUPPORTED BY
PRIMOZA, Die Seedball-Manufaktur, FVG Folien-Vertriebs GmbH
THANKS TO
Kristin Hjellegjerde Gallery, MARS | Küche & Bar, Georgia Goody-Miceli, Patrick Liwitzki, Hili Perlson

Driving the Human was initiated by Forecast, and further developed in continuous conversations between Freo Majer with Jan Boelen (Atelier LUMA), Martina Schraudner (Fraunhofer Center for Responsible Research and Innovation (CeRRI)), and the curatorial team of ZKM.

ACATECH
Sandra Fendl, Doerthe Winter-Berke, Hannah Lecheler
KARLSRUHE UNIVERSITY OF ARTS AND DESIGN (HFG) / BIO DESIGN LAB
Julia Ihls, Anthea Oestreicher, Hajo Eickbusch, Jehad Othman
ZKM | CENTER FOR ART AND MEDIA KARLSRUHE
Peter Weibel, Sarah Donderer, Daria Parkhomenko, Philipp Ziegler
ZKM – SCIENTIST IN RESIDENCE PROGRAM
Kim Albrecht, Maya Indira Ganesh, Xandra van der Eyck, Iris Long

DRIVING THE HUMAN: 7 PROTOTYPES FOR ECO-SOCIAL RENEWAL

Driving the Human is supported by the Federal Ministry for the Environment, Nature Conservation, Nuclear Safety and Consumer Protection. The cooperation was initiated by the international mentoring program Forecast and coordinated by the four institutions: acatech – National Academy of Science and Engineering, Forecast, the Karlsruhe University of Arts and Design, and ZKM | Center for Art and Media Karlsruhe.

TEAM FORECAST

ARTISTIC DIRECTOR
Freo Majer
HEAD OF PROJECTS AND TEAM
Agata Lorkowska

TEAM DRIVING THE HUMAN

PROJECT COORDINATOR
Nikola Joetze
PROGRAM COORDINATOR
Vera Sacchetti
COMMUNICATION AND PRESS
Inês Revés
PRODUCTION AND PROJECT ASSISTANT
Sarah Lipszyc and Rabea Kaczor
TRAINEE
Christina Braun
WORKING STUDENT (SOCIAL MEDIA)
Aisha Altenhofen
FORMER DRIVING THE HUMAN TEAM MEMBERS
Luisa Cossu, Greta Kallsen, Kim Kampe, Jennifer Leja, Justus Lietzke, Camille N'Dri
FEDERAL MINISTRY FOR THE ENVIRONMENT, NATURE CONSERVATION, NUCLEAR SAFETY, AND CONSUMER PROTECTION (BMUV)
Martina Grigull, Uwe Nestle
SPECIAL THANKS
Jan Boelen, Marion Augustin, Anke Brummer-Kohler, Lisa Ertel, Martin Fokken, Ina Grabosch, Vera Günther, Jörg Heitmann, Derviş Hızarcı, Sandra Köster, Christiane Linsel, Patrick Liwitzki, Lisa Lomberg, Kathrin Luz, Melissa Marx, Dirk Meyer, Matthias Mohr, Laura Morcillo, André Nourbakhsch, Anne-Sophie Oberkrome, Jehad Othman, Hili Perlson, Michel Picke, Anton Rahlwes, Margit Rosen, Martina Schraudner, Martin Schwarz, Nina Sieverding, Jule Sievert, Eva Stelzer, Regina Straub, Monika Theilmann, Annette Wiedemann, Johannes Wiesel, Linda Winkler

SPECIAL THANKS TO OUR SUPPORTERS
Acción Cultural Española (AC/E), Federal Ministry for the Environment, Nature Conservation, Nuclear Safety and Consumer Protection (BMUV), Future Architecture Platform (FAP), Goethe Institut, Institut für Auslandsbeziehungen (ifa), Learning, Interacting and Networking in Architecture (LINA), Mondriaan Fund, Österreichisches Kulturforum

DRIVING THE HUMAN - 21 CONCEPTS

DISSUASION ENGINE
Chris Salter, Erik Adigard, Alexandre Quessy
DO AIS DREAM OF CLIMATE CHAOS — SYMBIOTIC AI
Xiaoyu Iris Qu (曲晓宇)
DOWN TO THE ECONOMY
Vienne Chan, Katja Meier
∀I : TOWARDS EARTHLY TECHNOSYMBIOGENESIS
Matthew C. Wilson
HABIT@
Yasmine Abbas, DK Osseo-Asare
HABITAT THEATRE
Barbara Boss, Damiàn Dlaboha, Maximilian Grünewald, Mira Hirtz, Béla Rothenbühler
HUMAN-BACTERIA INTERFACES—AN EXPLORATION OF THE PRESENT AND FUTURE OF HUMAN-MICROBIAL ECOSYSTEMS
Anne-Sofie Belling, Bea Delgado Coralles, Romy Kaiser, Paula Nerlich
INDIGENOUS LANGUAGE OF TAŞLICA—A CASE OF INTERSPECIES COMMUNICATION
Eylül Şenses
MONSTERS AND GHOSTS OF THE FAR NORTH
alternaa (Andra Pop-Jurj, Lena Geerts Danau)
PLANETARY PERSONHOOD—A UNIVERSAL DECLARATION OF MARTIAN RIGHTS
Nonhuman Nonsense (Leo Fidjeland, Linnea Våglund)
RIPPLE, RIPPLE, RIPPLING
Jingru (Cyan) Cheng, Chen Zhan
RUM_A: MULTISPECIES URBAN REFUGE IN CLUSTER
Clara Acioli
SEDEKAH BENIH
Vincent Rumahloine, Mang Dian
SERVER FARM
James Bridle
SUPERLOCAL—0 MILES PRODUCTION
Andrea de Chirico
THE BACKPACK OF WINGS: MODERN MYTHOLOGY
Hyeseon Jeong, Seongmin Yuk
THE ROOTED SEA: HALOPHYTIC FUTURES
Sonia Mehra Chawla, Miriam Walsh (ASCUS Art & Science) in collaboration with Ray Interactive
THE TROPICAL TURN—MANEUVERS FOR A PLANETARY EMBODIMENT
Juan Pablo García Sossa

TOXICITY DISTRIBUTED—POST-EXTRACTION LOCAL ECONOMIES
AHORA (Linda Schilling, Claudio Cuellar Astudillo Barra)
TRONS'R'US
Akwasi Bediako Afrane
VIRTUAL SANCTUARY FOR FERTILIZING MOURNING
Eliana Otta

DRIVING THE HUMAN - 7 PROTOTYPES

Do AIs Dream of Climate Chaos—Symbiotic AI: Xiaoyu
(Iris) Qu 曲晓宇
Human-Bacteria Interfaces: Anne-Sofie Belling, Bea
Delgado Coralles, Romy Kaiser, Paula Nerlich
Monsters and Ghosts of the Far North: alternaa (Andra
Pop-Jurj, Lena Geerts Danau)
Sedekah Benih: Vincent Rumahloine, Mang Dian
The Backpack of Wings—Modern Mythology: Hyeseon
Jeong, Seongmin Yuk
TRONS'R'US: Akwasi Bediako Afrane
Virtual Sanctuary for Fertilizing Mourning: Eliana Otta

DRIVING THE HUMAN EXPERTS

Frédérique Aït-Touati, Kim Albrecht, Brigitte Baptiste,
Albert-László Barabási, Michel Bauwens, Tulga Beyerle,
Tatiana Bilbao, Jan Boelen, Melanie Bonajo, Stefan Böschen,
Joanna Bourke, Claudia Chwalisz, Alba G. Corral, Sasha
Costanza-Chock, Daniel Cremer, Sarah Donderer, Ariana
Dongus, Xandra van der Eijk, Lisa Ertel, Washington Fajardo,
Sabine Faller, Sandra Fendl, Jan Fermon, Christian Frei,
Jan-Micha Gamer, Maya Indira Ganesh, Peter Giovannini,
Ina Grabosch, Joe Halligan, Arne Hegemann, Alexander
Hicks, Anett Holzheid, Elise Misao Hunchuck, Julia Ihls,
Maximilian Ilse, Eric Joris, Susanne Kadner, Michael Kaethler,
Raphael Kim, Barbara Zoé Kiolbassa, Bogna Konior, Matylda
Krzykowski, Kim André Lange, Marc Lee, Iris Long, Sarat
Maharaj, Freo Majer, Kabelo Malatsie, Julien McHardy,
Kay Meseberg, Vera Meyer, Daria Mille, Alexandre Monnin,
Hemal Naik, Jeremy Narby, Simone C Niquille, Anne-Sophie
Oberkrome, Hans Ulrich Obrist, Anthea Oestreicher, Julian
Oliver, Daria Parkhomenko, Corine Pelluchon, Suzanne
Pierre, Alexandra Pirici, Guillaume Pitron, Gemma Planell
(TUTU), Volker Rachold, Anton Rahlwes, Lena Reitschuster,
Teresa Retzer, Manuel Rivera, Anne-Catherine Robert-
Hauglustaine, Margit Rosen, Martina Schraudner, Jaime
Sevilla, Jeremy Shaw, Nina Sieverding, Jonas Staal, Antje
Stahl, Chloe Stead, Jenna Sutela, Vivien Tauchmann, Song
Tae Chong, James Taylor-Foster, John Thackara, Yuri Tuma,
Julijonas Urbonas, Nomeda & Gediminas Urbonas, Barbara
Di Ventura, Peter Weibel (1944-2023), Cary Wolfe, Richard
D. Wolff, Biao Xiang, Feifei Zhou, Philipp Ziegler

COLLABORATING INITIATIVES

Floating Kidsuni, Ort-Schafft-Material, Kulturlabor
Trial&Error e.V., Kunst-Stoffe – Zentralstelle für wiederverwendbare Materialien e.V., Soydivision, Reste der Reste

DRIVING THE HUMAN PROJECT PARTNERS

Driving the Human has been initiated by Forecast, and
further developed in continuous conversations between
Freo Majer with Jan Boelen (HfG Karlsruhe), Martina
Schraudner (Fraunhofer IAO, Center for Responsible
Research and Innovation (CeRRI)), and the curatorial
team of ZKM.
FORECAST
Freo Majer, Agata Lorkowska
ACATECH
Sandra Fendl, Doerthe Winter-Berke, Hannah Lecheler
HFG KARLSRUHE UNIVERSITY OF ARTS AND DESIGN /
BIO DESIGN LAB
Jan Boelen, Julia Ihls, Anthea Oestreicher, Hajo Eickbusch
ZKM | CENTER FOR ART AND MEDIA KARLSRUHE
Peter Weibel(†), Sarah Donderer, Philipp Ziegler, Hannah
Jung, Nina Liechti, Teresa Retzer
Scientists in Residence: Kim Albrecht, Maya Indira
Ganesh, Xandra van der Eyck, Iris Long

DRIVING THE HUMAN PUBLICATION

EDITED BY
Vera Sacchetti, Edward Wang
EDITORIAL COORDINATION
Nikola Joetze
EDITORIAL ASSISTANCE
Aisha Altenhofen, Christina Braun, Sarah Lipszyc,
Inés Revés
CONTRIBUTORS
Kim Albrecht, Brigitte Baptiste, Tulga Beyerle, Tatiana
Bilbao, Jan Boelen, Sarah Donderer, Ariana Dongus,
Washington Fajardo, Sandra Fendl, Maya Indira Ganesh,
Julia Ihls, Freo Majer, Kabelo Malatsie, Anthea Oestreicher,
Daria Parkhomenko, Corine Pelluchon, Suzanne Pierre,
Margit Rosen, Vera Sacchetti, Martina Schraudner, Antje
Stahl, Chloe Stead, Yuri Tuma

CONTRIBUTING PROJECTS AND PARTICIPANTS
DISSUASION ENGINE
Chris Salter, Erik Adigard, Alexandre Quessy
DO AIS DREAM OF CLIMATE CHAOS—SYMBIOTIC AI
Xiaoyu Iris Qu (曲晓宇)
DOWN TO THE ECONOMY
Vienne Chan, Katja Meier
Ɐl : TOWARDS EARTHLY TECHNOSYMBIOGENESIS
Matthew C. Wilson

HABIT@
Yasmine Abbas, DK Osseo-Asare
HABITAT THEATRE
Barbara Boss, Damiàn Dlaboha, Maximilian Grünewald,
Mira Hirtz, Béla Rothenbühler
**HUMAN-BACTERIA INTERFACES—AN EXPLORATION OF THE
PRESENT AND FUTURE OF HUMAN-MICROBIAL ECOSYSTEMS**
Anne-Sofie Belling, Bea Delgado Coralles, Romy Kaiser,
Paula Nerlich
**INDIGENOUS LANGUAGE OF TAŞLICA—A CASE OF INTERSPECIES
COMMUNICATION**
Eylül Şenses
MONSTERS AND GHOSTS OF THE FAR NORTH
alternaa (Andra Pop-Jurj, Lena Geerts Danau)
**PLANETARY PERSONHOOD—A UNIVERSAL DECLARATION OF
MARTIAN RIGHTS**
Nonhuman Nonsense (Leo Fidjeland, Linnea Våglund)
RIPPLE, RIPPLE, RIPPLING
Jingru (Cyan) Cheng, Chen Zhan
RUM_A: MULTISPECIES URBAN REFUGE IN CLUSTER
Clara Acioli
SEDEKAH BENIH
Vincent Rumahloine, Mang Dian
SERVER FARM
James Bridle
SUPERLOCAL—0 MILES PRODUCTION
Andrea de Chirico
THE BACKPACK OF WINGS: MODERN MYTHOLOGY
Hyeseon Jeong, Seongmin Yuk
THE ROOTED SEA: HALOPHYTIC FUTURES
Sonia Mehra Chawla, Miriam Walsh (ASCUS Art & Science)
in collaboration with Ray Interactive
**THE TROPICAL TURN—MANEUVERS FOR A PLANETARY
EMBODIMENT**
Juan Pablo García Sossa
TOXICITY DISTRIBUTED—POST-EXTRACTION LOCAL ECONOMIES
AHORA (Linda Schilling, Claudio Cuellar Astudillo Barra)
TRONS'R'US
Akwasi Bediako Afrane
VIRTUAL SANCTUARY FOR FERTILIZING MOURNING
Eliana Otta

**DRIVING THE HUMAN VISUAL IDENTITY /
COVER ILLUSTRATION**
Studio Yukiko

MOUSSE HEAD OF PUBLICATIONS
Ilaria Bombelli
PUBLISHING EDITOR
Agnese Cantelmi
GRAPHIC DESIGN
Mousse

PUBLISHED AND DISTRIBUTED BY
Mousse Publishing
Contrappunto S.r.l.
via Decembrio 28, 20137 Milan–Italy

AVAILABLE THROUGH
Mousse Publishing, Milan
moussemagazine.it
DAP | Distributed Art Publishers, New York
artbook.com
Le presses du réel, Dijon
lespressesdureel.com
Antenne Books, London
antennebooks.com
Motto Books, Berlin
mottodistribution.com

FIRST EDITION 2023

PRINTED IN ITALY BY Intergrafica Verona

ISBN 978-88-6749-587-0

27 € / 30 $

CREDITS
All photographs unless otherwise indicated
© Camille Blake

All concept, prototype, and project images unless
otherwise indicated
© Project authors

© 2023 Mousse Publishing, Driving the Human,
and the authors of the text

drivingthehuman.com
@drivingthehuman
#drivingthehuman
#ecosocialrenewal

Supported by:

Federal Ministry
for the Environment, Nature Conservation,
Nuclear Safety and Consumer Protection

based on a decision of
the German Bundestag